The KENNEDYS and the WINDSORS

The KENNEDYS and the WINDSORS

The Story of Two Dynasties,

One Born, One Made

Caroline Hallemann

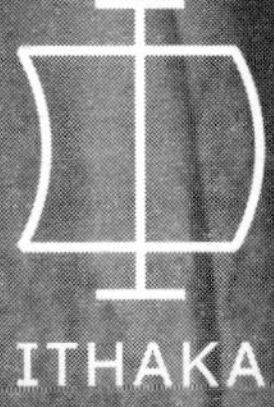

First published in the US by Putnam,
An imprint of Penguin Random House LLC
First published in the UK in 2026 by Ithaka Press
An imprint of Bonnier Books UK
5th Floor, HYLO, 105 Bunhill Row,
London, EC1Y 8LZ

A CIP catalogue record for this book is available from the British Library.

Hardback ISBN: 978-1-80418-536-0
Trade Paperback ISBN: 978-1-80617-164-4

Also available as an ebook and an audiobook

1 3 5 7 9 10 8 6 4 2

Design and Typeset by William Ruoto
Title page photo courtesy of Bettmann/Getty Images
Printed and bound in Great Britain by CPI (UK) Ltd, Croydon CR0 4YY

At Bonnier Books UK, we are committed to publishing sustainably.
Find out more here: bonnierbooks.co.uk/sustainability

Every reasonable effort has been made to trace copyright holders of
material reproduced in this book, but if any have been inadvertently
overlooked the publishers would be glad to hear from them.

The authorised representative in the EEA is Bonnier Books UK (Ireland) Limited.
Registered office address:
Block B, The Crescent Building
Northwood, Santry Dublin 9, D09 C6X8
Ireland
compliance@bonnierbooks.ie
www.bonnierbooks.co.uk

For my family. I love you so much.

CONTENTS

CHAPTER 18

CHAPTER 19

CHAPTER 20

CONCLUSION

"Two Households, Both Alike in Dignity"

SHAKESPEARE KNEW. SO DID LOUISA MAY ALCOTT, JOHN STEINbeck, and E. M. Forster. And frankly, so does Kris Jenner. There's just something about family drama that keeps us coming back for more. And a story that lasts for generations, with a whole cast of vibrant characters: leaders and villains, fashion icons, womanizers and humanitarians? That's particularly intriguing.

Over the past one hundred years, few families have so thoroughly occupied the public discourse as the Windsors and the Kennedys—the British royal family and the closest thing America has to one. They offer a juxtaposition of modern dynasties: While one's success stood on centuries of ceremony and ritual, a position they believed was God-given, the other's was carved out of ambition. The Windsors had status; the Kennedys had to claw their way to attain it. Over time, to their admirers, both dynasties came to represent high aspirations and lofty ideals, the very best of their countries' cultures. For the Windsors, that was duty, consistency, loyalty, heritage, and the quintessentially British "Keep Calm and Carry On" mentality. And for the Kennedys—particularly Jacqueline and John F. Kennedy—

that was American exceptionalism, youth, progress, prosperity, and vitality.

Theirs are parallel narratives of power, wealth, privilege, and service . . . but also stark tragedy. These families have been romanticized, and that parasocial connection (whether between subject and monarch or between the voting class and a political machine) has its benefits. It can inspire a nation and bring people together, particularly during times of war or national misfortune. That sense—real or imagined—that the country or even the world is in a sort of reciprocal relationship with these families is what allows a dynasty to endure.

But there's a downside as well. Once they've been elevated to such heights, these families' images must be maintained, or else the glamour of the fairy tale will be dispelled. There is an expectation that the public and the press will be allowed to share in their private joys and struggles with equal access. And when that unspoken covenant is broken, there's hell to pay. Both the Windsors and Kennedys are all too familiar with the gilded cage of fame, the unrelenting glare of media attention, and what it means to share your personal grief with a deeply invested world.

While the Windsors have the Kennedys beat on longevity in the public eye, the experiences of these families are core to the DNA of the countries they have come to represent. For the royals, that's hundreds of years at the center of politics and society. But for the Kennedys, it's a tragic starring role in one of the most significant moments in twentieth-century American life, the fallout of which continues to influence policy and culture today. All this history weighs heavily on the modern Kennedys and the Windsors. For them, the past is present, as the younger generations serve as stewards of these enormous legacies. The ultimate nepo babies, they reap the benefits of connections and status—but that comes at a price. And in a world where dynasties are on the decline, increasingly viewed as a vestige of another age—and to their detractors, as relics with little purpose in the current cultural and political landscapes—what does it mean to be part of these storied clans?

What has never been fully explored before is how closely the Kennedy and Windsor stories are intertwined. At key points throughout the twentieth and twenty-first centuries, these two families of mythic reputation served as witnesses to each other's histories. The Kennedy origin story chronicles how the descendants of Irish Catholic immigrants with rich political connections but little entrée into WASPy New England society came to host dinner parties for British royalty. And how, as matriarch Rose Kennedy put it, their time in London in the years before World War II "probably put Jack on the first rung of the ladder to the presidency."

Jacqueline Bouvier was there at Queen Elizabeth's coronation. Sure, she was among the people in the streets reporting on the revelry, while Elizabeth was being crowned inside Westminster Abbey, but they were both in London, two women on the brink of exceptional lives. And when President Kennedy died, it was Prince Philip who helped keep young John Jr. occupied while Jackie played hostess at the White House one last time.

In the 1990s, Diana and JFK Jr. had tea in the penthouse of New York City's Carlyle hotel, a meeting kept secret from the press to tamp down tabloid fantasies of a transatlantic romance between two of the most famous people in the world. More recently, Princes William and Harry have each forged their own bonds with different branches of the Kennedy family.

The fascination with the royals and the Kennedys stems from nostalgia, but it continues to be fed by spectacle, spurred on by feuds that dominate the news cycle. Sibling rivalries are all too relatable, and whether they are dubbed "royal rifts" or "end of Camelot" squabbles (referencing the King Arthur–inspired nickname for the idealized Kennedy legacy myth), the public clashes make for excellent newspaper headlines.

And so the question remains: Do these fights have the power not only to break apart families but also to tarnish institutions—be they the monarchy or the fabled Kennedy brand—beyond recognition in the long term? It's too soon to tell, but regardless of what's to come in the next chapter of these families' stories, people simply cannot look away.

One thing is certain: By tracing a calendar of moments when they spent time together—moments that coincide with some of the most meaningful events in recent world history—the truest, deepest, most nuanced story of the Kennedys and the Windsors over the last hundred years becomes clear. Even into the twenty-first century, these two first families continue to circle each other, a living reminder of the enduring, if changed, power they hold.

CHAPTER 1

The Kennedys at Court

JOSEPH P. KENNEDY WAS AN UNUSUAL CHOICE FOR AMBASSADOR to the Court of St. James's in 1937. An Irish Catholic Bostonian, he and his family had always been on the outskirts of WASPy New England society.

Joe's wife, Rose Fitzgerald Kennedy, once described Boston as being made up of two separate communities. One of them was Protestant and English, essentially constituting the descendants of the original colonists—"proper Bostonians," or Boston Brahmin as they were sometimes called. "With the advantages of inherited wealth and status and close-knit interfamily ties, they controlled the banks, insurance companies, the big law firms, the big shipping and mercantile enterprises, and almost all the usual routes to success, and thus were a self-perpetuating aristocracy," Rose explained in her memoir, *Times to Remember*. It was a "closed" society.

The other predominant group in Boston was the Irish Catholics, many of whom were the descendants of those who had fled Ireland during the Great Hunger of the mid-1800s. "Between the two groups feelings were, at best, suspicious, and in general amounted to a state of chronic, mutual antagonism," Rose wrote, explaining that this discord had "stemmed from the ancient unhappy relationship between

England and Ireland," and had been sustained across not only geography but also generations. Irish Catholic Bostonians often gained clout through politics. At least, that's how it worked for Rose's family. She was the daughter of John Francis "Honey Fitz" Fitzgerald, a colorful "pixielike" man, who rose to prominence as Boston's mayor and, later, used his influence in the local Democratic Party to give his grandson (his namesake, John Fitzgerald Kennedy) a leg up. The Kennedys were already at the center of Boston's Irish community by the early twentieth century. But with Joe's appointment as ambassador, they found themselves navigating the complexities of the English upper class. It was not always easy.

Then, as now, many of the cushiest ambassadorships were given to campaign supporters. Joe's was one such appointment; the position was granted as a thank-you of sorts for his support of President Franklin D. Roosevelt's 1936 reelection campaign, despite his complete lack of relevant diplomatic experience. After attending Harvard University, Joe had built his fortune first as a banker and then as a producer in Hollywood.

While many have alleged that Joe made millions transporting and selling alcohol during the Prohibition era, a rumor that began during his lifetime, there's no credible evidence of that sort of illicit behavior. But as historian Daniel Okrent put it in his book *Last Call: The Rise and Fall of Prohibition*, "One cannot prove a negative." And the allegations are rooted in a kernel of truth. As the amendment to repeal Prohibition was gaining popularity in the fall of 1933, Joe traveled to England with James Roosevelt, the son of FDR. While in the UK, they met with the managing directors of the conglomerate Distillers Company, securing the rights to become the sole American importer of Dewar's and Haig & Haig whiskey and Gordon's gin. Joe had already procured a medicinal liquor permit, as well as warehouse space for the alcohol, and so they prudently imported the goods in November, preparing for the day when imbibing alcohol was once again legal in the US. They were ready for the raucous celebrations on December 6, 1933. However, as this story was repeated, the legality of Joe's actions was left out, and so, as Okrent put it, "from such acorns, nourished by a lifetime's accumulation of rumors, enemies, and vast sums of money, arose the widely accepted story of Joseph P. Kennedy, bootlegger."

With another term secured for FDR, Joe had his eye on another post entirely—that of secretary of the treasury—but that simply wasn't an option. "Father was not going to remove Henry Morgenthau from office. Father did not tell Joe in so many words, but in time it became clear to him," James Roosevelt wrote in his memoirs, noting that while the treasury secretary post was off the table, his father did want to give Joe something in return for his loyalty.

"We've got to do something for old Joe, but I don't know what," FDR told his son. "He wants what he can't have, but there must be something we can give him he'll be happy with."

There was one other job Joe would be willing to consider. "I'd like to be ambassador to England," he told James one evening. If status for his family was what he was seeking, he would have been hard-pressed to pick a better position. The list of ambassadors up to that point included many successful politicians, including five future presidents (John Adams, James Monroe, John Quincy Adams, Martin Van Buren, and James Buchanan) as well as numerous notable businessmen.

"He wanted to build as high a platform as possible from which his children could be launched. He wanted them to start out with every possible advantage, advantages that he himself hadn't had," Jack Kennedy's longtime close friend Kirk LeMoyne "Lem" Billings would later say. "I don't think there's any question about it, the post of the American Ambassador to the Court of St. James's couldn't do anything but help build prestige for the Kennedy family."

When James Roosevelt relayed Joe's ambition to his father, FDR allegedly "laughed so hard he almost toppled from his wheelchair." Yet, Joe Kennedy had a way of getting what he wanted. And in this case, Roosevelt was easily convinced. After all, sending Joe across the ocean made it far more difficult for him to interfere in politics at home. Plus, Roosevelt knew that Joe had deep pockets and would be willing to entertain on his own dime. Kennedy biographer Susan Ronald also suggests that the idea of Joe as ambassador "appealed to Roosevelt's mischievous sense of humor, picturing an Irish Catholic in the bastion of Anglicanism." And so, on February 18, 1938, Joe Kennedy was sworn in as the US ambassador to Great Britain by Supreme Court Justice Stanley Reed, as President Roosevelt looked on. A few days later, on February 23, he boarded the SS *Manhattan* and set forth across the Atlantic.

FROM THE MOMENT A KENNEDY STEPPED FOOT IN LONDON, THE British press was fascinated by the family. Reporters captured Joe's arrival in Plymouth, and they were there as he first saw his new residence in London, a six-story Beaux-Arts–style property just off Hyde Park. He had several American creature comforts sent over to immediately make the fifty-two-room mansion feel more like home: candy from a specific store on Cape Cod, Maxwell House coffee, toiletries including Nivea and Jergens lotions, Cheracol cough syrup, and dozens of cans of New England clam chowder. The cellar was stocked with champagne for hosting, and he had arranged to borrow works of art from William Randolph Hearst's castle in Wales to adorn the walls. He also took note of how close 14 Prince's Gate was to "Rotten Row," a specific area in the park where the upper class were often seen horse riding.

After much conversation about whether or not Joe would wear the customary knee breeches at court (he eventually opted for long trousers, bucking British tradition in something of a faux pas), he became a "full fledged" ambassador by presenting his letter of credence to King George VI on March 8, 1938. "The coaches, with their scarlet-coated drivers and footmen, came for us at the Embassy a little after eleven," Joe wrote in his diary. "The show at Buckingham Palace was set up to expectations, and I chatted informally with the King for five minutes. I found him charming in every way."

A few days later, Rose arrived with her second-eldest daughter, Kathleen "Kick" (born 1920), as well as the four younger Kennedy children: Patricia "Pat" (born 1924), Robert "Bobby" (born 1925), Jean (born 1928), and Edward "Teddy" (born 1932). At that point, the two eldest sons, Joseph "Joe" P. Kennedy Jr. (born 1915) and John "Jack" F. Kennedy (born 1917) were in college, and Eunice (born 1921) was finishing the school term at the Convent of the Sacred Heart in Noroton, Connecticut. Eunice and Rosemary (born 1918) traveled over separately. But the entire brood immediately made an impression on the British public.

Deborah Cavendish, Duchess of Devonshire (aka Debo, one of the iconic Mitford sisters, who would go on to become Kick's sister-in-law by marriage), would later write, "Nothing like the Kennedy family had been seen before in the rarefied atmosphere of London diplomatic circles. For the next seventeen months they enlivened the scene." As *Life* magazine put it, Great Britain got "eleven Ambassadors for the price of one." The press covered their every move as if they were celebrities.

They had arrived in London at the start of the social season of parties, balls, and court functions, and the family found themselves with a full and lively calendar. It was not by accident. Word had been "passed around (before [Joe's] arrival) to be nice," Winston

Churchill's son Randolph explained to journalist C. L. Sulzberger. "Consequentially the Establishment went to work. [The Kennedys were] invited to house parties, dinners, golf and shooting by dukes and earls"—the full upper-crust British experience.

"Those first months passed in a whirl of introductions and social and official events," Rose recalled. A few days after she arrived, Rose, as the wife of an ambassador, was received by Queen Elizabeth at Buckingham Palace. Queen Elizabeth, later known as the Queen Mother, was eager to welcome the new ambassador's family to the country. Immediately, Rose felt "at ease" with the royal, describing her smile as "happy" and her manner as "friendly." They sat together on a small sofa near a fireplace, as Elizabeth asked her questions about her children, their schools, and the family's initial impressions of England. The conversation flowed easily, no doubt aided by the fact that then Princess Elizabeth and Princess Margaret were about the same age as Bobby and Jean. These were just two mothers talking about their babies.

Soon after that initial conversation, the Kennedys were invited to Windsor Castle for a weekend visit alongside Prime Minister Neville Chamberlain and his wife, Anne—a strategic move by UK officials. For as much as Joe viewed this embassy position as an opportunity to improve his family's standing, the royals and the government had their own agendas. The British establishment was keen to impress Joe (and by extension, the Roosevelt administration); on March 12, 1938, Germany had invaded Austria, marking the first act of the Nazi regime's territorial expansion. With a potential war on the horizon, American support was essential to the British government, and the British royal family would be key to winning that favor.

"It was a period during which I would guess *any* ambassador would have been popular in London, because they obviously needed our help during this period and knew they were going to need it more," Lem later summarized in an oral history for the John F. Kennedy Presidential Library and Museum. "Mr. Kennedy, although being probably the first American of Irish descent who had been Ambassador to the Court of St. James's, was exceedingly popular in the beginning and he became a very close and fast friend, for instance, of the King [George VI] and Queen [Elizabeth]. He was a great admirer of Queen Elizabeth (the present Queen Mother) and thought she was one of the most capable, charming women whom he'd ever met. I heard him say this time and time again."

Joe and Rose arrived at Windsor Castle by car on April 9 and were met by a man in a gray suit who swiftly escorted them to where they would be staying. "Rose, this is a helluva long way from East Boston," Joe Kennedy said to his wife as they explored their bedrooms in one of the towers with a "lovely view of the park." Rose's room was outfitted with an enormous bed upholstered in red damask and set up so high a step stool was needed to get into it.

During dinner that night, Joe sat next to the Queen. They spoke of the American press and relations between the two countries. "She impressed me as a most charming person with a fine head," he wrote in his diary. His wife was equally captivated. "She has a very pleasing voice, a beautiful English complexion, great dignity and charm; is simple in manner, stands very erect and holds herself well and is every inch a Queen," she wrote in her diary. "We talked, among other things, about the difficulty of sleeping in London, and the Queen was very much amused that I put wax in my ears," Rose wrote of the evening spent chatting in the drawing room.

That night, Rose lay awake in that bed thinking, "I must be dreaming that I, Rose Kennedy, a simple young matron from Boston, am really here at Windsor Castle, the guest of the Queen and two little princesses."

The next few days were filled with walks in the gardens and tours of the castle. Joe made a point to speak with one of the King's secretaries, mentioning that they might take a tour of the United States—perhaps the seed of the royals' historic 1939 trip to New York and Washington, DC, the first time a reigning British monarch had ever visited the United States. "I insisted they would help Great Britain immensely," Joe said.

After Palm Sunday Mass in town, Rose and Joe met up with the Windsors once again for lunch. This time, Princess Elizabeth sat between Ambassador Kennedy and Prime Minister Chamberlain. "I suppose this was a pattern of regular procedure—associating with older people even when she was very young," Rose observed in her diary. Joe spoke with the young princess about her love of geography, swimming, horseback riding, and movies, particularly *Snow White and the Seven Dwarfs*. (Perhaps this remained top of mind as he gave her a color drawing from the film signed by Walt Disney for her thirteenth birthday.)

Rose later ranked this as one of the top weekends of her life. Her daughter Kick had a similar response to a weekend in the countryside with the English aristocracy, describing a weekend at Cliveden, the home of Lord and Lady Astor, as "the best thing that ever happened to [her]."

In the months following the meeting in Windsor, the royals' and the Kennedys' paths continued to cross at various events. In May, Rose and her two eldest daughters, Rosemary and Kick, were presented at court in what Rose described as "one of the most utterly simple and intensely complicated events imaginable." Rosemary, then age nineteen, had been born with intellectual disabilities, though the Kennedys were keen to include her in as many family activities as possible. It was within Joe's right as ambassador to arrange presentations for high-profile Americans, but one of his first acts in his position had been to greatly reduce the number of women who were given the honor. "Mr. Kennedy, who had planned this step from the time he decided to come to London, did not actually make the decision until he had discussed the matter with court officials and even with the King and Queen," reported *The New York Times*. Exceptions were made for his own family, of course; Joe was never one to miss an opportunity to push his offspring up a rung on the social ladder.

Finding the right dresses for not only Kick and Rosemary but also Rose was of utmost importance. "The girls and I had decided in advance that we should be in white, or else a very light pastel shade of ivory, because this would look best with the white plumes, which every woman presented wore in her hair," Rose remembered, referencing the trio of ostrich feathers adorning each debutant. As a married woman, Rose wore a tiara, one borrowed from a new friend, Lady Bessborough, noting in her memoir that she felt "a little like Cinderella." The presentation, she wrote, was "a gigantic theatrical. The Palace illuminated; the Guards resplendent; the Beefeaters in costume with maces, lining the Grand Stairway; passing through anteroom after anteroom attended by footmen in full livery; at last the ballroom and a sight of the royal dais."

That night, the family made quite the impression, especially Kick, who even prior to that evening had already been named the "Debutante of 1938." Hardly an English rose, Kick was different from her peers, more vibrant and curious, charmingly American, all part of her appeal. In her diary, she details how the long train that trailed behind her dress wasn't fastened properly, and how fast the actual presentation felt. "Walked by very quickly," she wrote. Her sister Rosemary unfortunately stumbled at a key moment in the ceremony but was able to recover. In her memoir, Rose put the evening in the context of England hurtling toward war: "While all the pomp and circumstance and romantic storybook traditions that I have described were continuing with hardly a ripple to blemish them, events were, in fact, building toward the general disaster (and for us, very personal disasters) of the Second World War."

Joe continued to advocate that the United States and the United Kingdom should stay out of the war, a position that was becoming more and more untenable (and unpopular) as tensions in mainland Europe heightened throughout 1938. But that didn't seem to affect his daughter Kick's social calendar, which was filled with parties and dinners and events with Britain's upper echelon of young aristocrats. "Vital, intelligent and outgoing, Kick was able to talk to anyone with ease and her shining niceness somehow ruled out any jealousy," recalled the Duchess of Devonshire. "Suitors appeared instantly but I noticed from the start that none of the girls was annoyed by her success and I never heard a catty remark made behind her back." Kick attended Wimbledon and Royal Ascot and watched the royal procession, on which her father commented, "Well, if that's not just like Hollywood!" When Kick's brother Jack arrived in London for the summer, she introduced him to her new social set, even throwing a party for him at Prince's Gate. Among the group were connections that would become invaluable in his presidency, including David Ormsby-Gore, the future Lord Harlech, who would become the UK ambassador to the US during the Kennedy administration. Gore's future wife Sylvia "Sissie" Thomas was Kick's close friend.

In July 1938, Kick, her parents, and her brothers Joe and Jack were invited to attend a garden party at Buckingham Palace. It was a beautiful day, but Kick was less than impressed with the festivities, describing the event as a "very hot and very dull procedure." But she was on the lookout for one particular young man whom she had recently met: Billy Hartington. Or more formally, William Cavendish, Marquess of Hartington, the eldest son of the 10th Duke of Devonshire and a member of one of England's oldest and most prestigious—and decidedly Protestant—families.

Throughout that fall, Rose's diary entries offer a juxtaposition of social events and preparations for war in England. On September 27, for example, she wrote of attending the launch of the RMS *Queen Elizabeth*. "Queen came without King as the times are so uncertain," Rose wrote. "She was dressed in gray with a small smart hat and looked much thinner than in the spring. Little Princess Margaret Rose saw me in the group, smiled, told her sister, Princess Elizabeth, who immediately told the Queen, who looked over and bowed." The following day Rose referenced needing to make plans for her children "because war is imminent." On September 29, she wrote of the Munich Agreement, "Everyone expects Prime Minister's visit to be crowned with success, though preparations for war are still being carried out. Trenches are being dug and gas masks fitted."

There were celebrations when Chamberlain returned, but the peace wouldn't last. "In the end it was an illusion," Rose wrote in her memoir. "But everyone clung to it until the Nazis broke their pledge six months later and took over the rest of Czechoslovakia."

While young Jack Kennedy didn't live in London with his family, he did visit in the spring of 1939, as Europe stood on the brink of war. Yet, he wrote that he was "having a great time." Notably, in March, he was thrilled to meet the King at a court levee. "It takes place in the morning and you wear tails. The King stands and you go up and bow," he described in a letter to Lem. After meeting Queen Mary, he went to "tea with the Princess Elizabeth with whom I made a great deal of time," he boasted. "Thursday night—am going to Court in my new silk breeches, which are cut to my crotch tightly, and in which I look mighty attractive."

"Everyone thinks war inevitable before the year is out. I personally don't," Jack wrote to Lem, "though dad does."

In May 1939, Joe and Rose hosted a banquet in honor of the King and Queen, a send-off ahead of the royals' tour of Canada and the US. Rose meticulously planned the evening, calling in flowers and making sure the meal and decor were perfect but not pretentious. The guests watched multiple films, including *Goodbye, Mr. Chips*, a new drama about a beloved boarding-school teacher. "It was quite sad, and after it was finished, it was plain to see that the Queen had had a little weep, as had most people."

Like her sisters had a year prior, Eunice made her debut at Buckingham Palace, in another white dress, carrying a fan gifted to her by Queen Mary. "As I entered the Palace more excitement and joy seized me then [sic] ever before in my life," she wrote in a rather dramatic recollection of the event. Eunice had the honor of being the first debutante at court that July. She was presented by her mother as well as Lady Halifax, the wife of the foreign secretary. "During the few moments of waiting, I was breathlessly excited; then a strong rich voice called MISS KENNEDY and I started to walk alone toward Their Majesties," she wrote. Once in front of them, she made her curtsy first to the Queen and again to the King. "I realized that in this moment I was the center of interest of this King and Queen and all the pompous ceremony that England holds so sacred." After her formal presentation, Eunice made her way back to her original place to watch the rest of the ceremony. "Endlessly, the people came; tirelessly the Monarchs stood, for this was the life of England," she recalled.

But the Kennedys' time in the country wasn't meant to last. Less than two months after Eunice's debut, Joe Jr., Jack, Kick, and Rose were present in Parliament to hear Chamberlain's speech at the outbreak of World War II. Chamberlain had committed to Poland's independence from Germany. After Hitler invaded the country on September 1, 1939, Britain issued an ultimatum demanding that Germany withdraw its troops. When the demand was ignored and the deadline for a retreat had passed, it became clear that the policy of appeasement had failed. "This country is at war with Germany," Chamberlain said. "Everything I have worked for, everything that I have hoped for, everything that I have believed in during my public life, has crashed into ruins."

On the way home, as air-raid sirens wailed, the Kennedys ran into the basement of Molyneux, the British designer Rose had trusted to craft her dress for court. "What an ironic way for a woman to begin her war experiences," she later thought. "It was time to get our children back home."

While most of the Kennedys quickly returned stateside, Joe and Rosemary stayed behind. She was doing well at her school, so Joe and Rose decided it was best for her to remain where she was. (The school was in Hertfordshire, thirty miles from London and presumably safe from any pending bombings.) Joe shifted his home base away from 14 Prince's Gate to a house in the country.

History does not look kindly on Joe Kennedy's time as ambassador. His vocal preference for appeasement—advocating for negotiation with Hitler to try to avoid conflict—waned in popularity over the course of his post. And as one might imagine, opposition to his policies grew more intense once the UK officially declared war on Germany.

In early September, he had tea with King George, who was taken aback by Joe's perspective. "He looked at the War very much from the financial & material viewpoint," the King said of the ambassador in his private diary. "He wondered why we did not let Hitler have S.E. Europe, as it was no good to us from a monetary standpoint. He did not seem to realise that this country was a part of Europe, that it was essential for us to act as policeman, & to uphold the rights of small nations."

During the conversation, the King wrote, Joe prophesied that "'Britain will be thrashed' and there will be nothing left of civilization to save after the war."

The next day, the King wrote to the ambassador: "On thinking over what you said, I would like to make clear to you one or two matters which are in my mind. When referring to the fact that England would be broke at the end of this war, & that in this statement you also inferred that your country, the United States of America, would be likewise broke, is it not possible for you to put this fact before the American Press." As biographer Susan Ronald explained, "The King's words 'not possible' meant 'don't.'" The King continued, "You were speaking about the loss of prestige of the British Empire under the changed conditions in which we live since the last war. England, my country, owing to its geographical position in the World, is part of Europe. She has been expected to act, & has had to act, as the policeman, and has always been the upholder of the rights of smaller nations."

But despite the King's warning, the ambassador couldn't keep his opinions out of the press forever. In November 1940, Joe told a reporter for *The Boston Globe*, "Democracy is finished in England." He continued, "If we get into war it will be [finished] in this country too . . . Everything we hold dear would be gone." You can only imagine how his lack of faith in the British war effort went over with those citizens who were holding strong even as the Germans bombed their cities in the Blitz—or in America after the US entered the war in December 1941 after Pearl Harbor. He later claimed the quote had been off the record, but the damage was done; his political career was over, and he was branded a defeatist. It was a reputation that not only Joe would have to contend with, but also Jack, who was cognizant of the need to distance himself from his father's views in order to have any chance politically.

Though his time in the UK was brief, it had a lasting impact on Jack, in ways that could be seen throughout his administration all those years later. Rose, too, left an impression on a young Princess Elizabeth, one that would last decades. The Kennedy matriarch had paid attention to the young royal at a time when no one else had. The specifics of their encounter have been lost to history, but when a relative of Princess Elizabeth's died, she and Princess Margaret were tucked away while their parents received dignitaries. "Only Rose Kennedy came into the room and chatted with them," former Canadian Prime Minister Brian Mulroney wrote in his memoir. "They were ignored by the other guests—and she remembered it some forty years later!"

Rose also kept in touch with the Queen Mother over the years, particularly during difficult times. "So deeply shocked & grieved to learn of this great tragedy," Elizabeth wrote to Rose via telegram following her son Bobby's death in 1968. "I send you my truly heartfelt sympathy, & the assurance of my thoughts & prayers in this moment of sorrow."

But perhaps the Kennedys' strongest ties to England and to its aristocracy remained Kick. Kick returned home to the US with the rest of her family, but she couldn't stay away from the dashing Billy Hartington for long. After working at the *Washington Times-Herald*, Kick returned to England in 1943 with the Red Cross and began a serious relationship with Billy, much to her mother's disappointment. In April 1944, Billy wrote to Rose, confirming that despite the two families' religious differences, he loved her daughter and wanted to be with her. "I could not believe, either, that God could really intend two loving people, both of whom wanted to do the right thing, and both of whom were Christians, to miss the opportunity of being happy, and perhaps even useful, together because of the religious squabbles of His human servants several hundred years ago," he wrote.

Shortly before the wedding, Billy's father received a letter from King George: "I am very glad that you have gone into the matter of her religion so carefully, and that she has promised that the children shall be brought up as Protestants and that she herself may come over to the church later . . . I am sure the girl takes after her mother and not her father, as his behaviour here as ambassador in the early days of the war was anything but helpful."

Billy and Kick married in a civil ceremony in May 1944, and her older brother Joe was the only family member in attendance. The bride wore a pale pink dress, which she paired with a blue and pink hat with ostrich feathers. "There were very great difficulties in the way of marriage between Kick and Billy, and I think I must make them clear," Rose wrote in her memoir. Namely, religion and Kick's Irish heritage. Kick had been brought up in the Catholic Church, and even if she wasn't particularly religious, her mother was. On the other hand, Billy's ancestors had long been involved in the English rule over Ireland. To put it simply, neither side of the family was happy with this match. But despite that, Rose wrote that the Kennedys "were very fond of Billy" and his family was "equally fond of Kick. This would have been 'a marriage made in Heaven' except for the special and ironic circumstances of religious loyalties."

Three months after Kick's wedding day, her brother Joe, who was serving in the US Navy, was killed during a secret military mission in England. One month later, her husband Billy was killed by a sniper while serving in the British Army's Coldstream Guards regiment in Belgium. They had been married for only four months. After the war, Kick became romantically involved with the 8th Earl Fitzwilliam, a married man in the process of divorcing his wife. Once again, Kick's mother did not approve. In May 1948, Kick and

Lord Fitzwilliam were killed in a plane crash near Privas, France. Her remains were taken to Paris, where, per *The New York Times*, "her father received condolences" from Princess Elizabeth. Kick was then buried in St. Peter's churchyard, Edensor. Her headstone reads "Joy she gave. Joy she has found."

Tragedy, in life and love, was only beginning for both the Kennedys and the Windsors.

Two Unlikely Leaders

It wasn't supposed to be Jack Kennedy.

His older brother, Joe, had been groomed for the American presidency since birth. When Joe was born, his grandfather, the storied Boston mayor John "Honey Fitz" Fitzgerald, reportedly told the media, "This child is the future president of the nation."

So Joe's young adult life had followed a prescribed path for political success. He attended the prestigious Choate boarding school in Connecticut and the London School of Economics, before matriculating into Harvard. He graduated with honors in 1938. In 1940, he took his initial steps into politics, serving as a Massachusetts delegate to the Democratic National Convention. One fellow attendee wrote to Joe Sr. about the "excellent impression" his son had made. "I am sure he can have a political future if he wants one," read the letter.

Joe began studies at Harvard Law School, but keenly aware of the positive effect military service can have on a political career, he signed up for the Navy before he could graduate. His decision was also impacted by lingering concerns over his father's well-known stance on the war. He explained his decision in a letter to Joe Sr.: "With your stand on the war . . . people will wonder what the devil I am doing back at school with everyone else working for the national defense." In May 1942, he earned his pilot wings. Joe began by flying patrols in the Caribbean before he was sent to England in 1943.

By the summer of 1944, Joe had completed more than enough combat missions to fulfill his tour of duty and return home, but instead he volunteered for one last secret operation: Aphrodite. Some historians believe that he volunteered in pursuit of the same kind of military glory his younger brother, Jack, had already received. While Joe was flying planes in England, Jack was deployed to the Pacific, where he commanded a patrol torpedo boat (PT-109). When his boat was struck by a Japanese destroyer off the coast of the Solomon Islands, Jack was essential in rescuing the surviving members of his crew. For his heroism, Jack received the Navy and Marine Corps Medal. His injuries also qualified him for a Purple Heart.

"In their long brotherly, friendly rivalry, I expect this was the first time Jack had won such an 'advantage' by such a clear margin," Rose Kennedy wrote in her memoir. "And I daresay it . . . must have rankled Joe Jr."

"It may be felt, perhaps, that Joe should not have pushed his luck so far and should have accepted his leave and come home," Jack later wrote of his brother. "But two facts must be borne in mind. First, at the time of his death, he had completed probably more combat missions in heavy bombers than any other pilot of his rank in the Navy and therefore was preeminently qualified, and secondly, as he told a friend early in August, he considered the odds at least fifty-fifty, and Joe never asked for any better odds than that."

The plan was for Joe and a copilot, Lieutenant Wilford J. Willy, to take a plane filled with explosives into the air and, as described by a fellow officer, "to stay with it until two 'mother' planes had achieved complete radio control over the drone. They were then to bail out over England; the 'drone,' under the control of the mother planes, was to proceed on the mission which was to culminate in a crash-dive on the target, a V-2 rocket launching site in Normandy."

"I am going to do something different for the next three weeks," Joe wrote to his parents of the plan. "It is secret and I am not allowed to say what it is, but it isn't dangerous so don't worry."

But on August 12 at 6:20 p.m., shortly after taking off, the plane exploded. Neither pilot survived, and their remains were never recovered. Four days after Joe's death, *The Washington Post* ran a story that read in part, "One of the greatest evils of war is the loss of those young men who might normally [have] been expected to become the leaders of their generation."

There was no question that Joe Jr.'s dream would now become his brother Jack's. Joe was dead, but the Kennedy ambition persisted in the family's oldest living son. "Now the burden falls to me," Jack told a friend. "Just as I went into politics because Joe died, if anything happened to me tomorrow, my brother Bobby would run for my seat in the Senate. And if Bobby died Teddy would take over for him," he once said, almost prophesying what would happen in their family. Indeed, after Jack's assassination in 1963, Bobby Kennedy would go on to run for the presidency in 1968, only to be shot and killed during his campaign. Teddy then took up the mantle. He never made it to the White House, but became the "Lion of the Senate," an elder statesman, and the keeper of the family name in politics. For this generation of Kennedys, political ambition persisted.

JFK's father took credit for pushing his second son into the spotlight after the death of his first.

"I got Jack into politics. I was the one. I told him Joe was dead and that it was therefore his responsibility to run for Congress," Joe Kennedy said in 1957. "He didn't want to do it. He felt he didn't have the ability and he still feels that way. But I told him he had to do it."

That isn't quite how Jack saw it. "We all liked politics," Jack said, "but Joe seemed a natural to run for office. Obviously, you can't have a whole mess of Kennedys asking for votes. So when Joe was denied his chance, I wanted to run and was glad I could." In his mind, there was only room for one Kennedy in politics. And even if Jack had never meant to be that Kennedy, he was now.

JUST AS JACK KENNEDY WASN'T INITIALLY DESTINED TO BECOME president, young Princess Elizabeth was not born to be queen. Of course, it wasn't impossible. After all, at birth she was third in line to the throne. But as the daughter of the *second* son of King George V, it was highly unlikely that young Elizabeth would ever reign, because her father was never expected to be king.

All that changed over the course of several chaotic months in 1936.

On January 20 of that year, Elizabeth's grandfather King George V died and his firstborn son, Edward VIII (David as he was known to close friends and family), ascended to the throne. But Edward VIII never had a coronation; instead, he chose to abdicate in December of that year in order to marry Wallis Simpson, an American divorcée who, at the time, would not have been an acceptable queen. This made Edward VIII the first British monarch to voluntarily give up the throne, prompting a constitutional crisis.

"I have found it impossible to carry on the heavy burden of responsibility and to discharge the duties of King, as I would wish to do, without the help and support of the woman I love," Edward VIII said in a final radio broadcast, relinquishing his position. "And now we all have a new King. I wish him and you his people happiness and prosperity with all my heart. God bless you all. God save the King!" He was given the title of Duke of Windsor, and in June 1937 he and

Wallis married in France, where they lived in relative exile for the rest of their lives.

His decision rerouted royal history, putting his brother, the newly named King George VI, on the throne and a young Princess Elizabeth on the path to becoming queen. George VI was reluctant and unprepared, but he threw himself into his duty, rebuilding the reputation of the monarchy after a monumental scandal and reestablishing his position as one of steadfast consistency as his country barreled toward the eve of war. But the stress took a toll on the King and his health suffered. He died at age fifty-six of a coronary thrombosis in 1952, and immediately, twenty-five-year-old Elizabeth became queen.

The abdication cast a long shadow on the royal family. It is why even in her old age, Elizabeth never chose to give up her duties in favor of her son. At twenty-one, she had pledged to the United Kingdom and the Commonwealth nations, "My whole life whether it be long or short will be devoted to your service." And she kept that promise, becoming the longest-reigning monarch in British history.

Neither Queen Elizabeth nor President Kennedy were supposed to lead, and yet they became two of the most significant cultural figures of the last hundred years in the Western world. Both Jack and Elizabeth were bound by familial obligation, but of two very different varieties.

For Elizabeth, it was her duty to assume the position of heir apparent to the throne and then eventually queen. Her father had helped stabilize not only the monarchy but also the country following the abdication and then through World War II. Elizabeth took very seriously the role of providing consistency to her people. But for Jack, his political rise was the culmination of his father's unyielding ambition.

CHAPTER 3

A Royal Debut

According to legend, "rain never falls" on graduation day at Farmington—that's what most alums call Miss Porter's, the tony all-girls' boarding school in Farmington, Connecticut. It's a ceremony rich in symbolism: The senior girls, wearing all white, carry a garland of daisies, the school's signature flower, and sing songs recognizing the transition of power.

In 1947, Jacqueline Bouvier was one of those girls in white dresses. After the requisite singing and services at the First Church, she dined on chicken salad and strawberry tarts, visited with family, and paged through a book of poems by Edna St. Vincent Millay, which she had won as a prize for excellence in literature, on the campus lawn.

"It happened gradually over the three years I spent at boarding school trying to imitate girls who had callers every Saturday," Jackie would later write in a 1951 self-portrait essay for *Vogue* magazine's Prix de Paris contest, reflecting on her Farmington years.

"I passed the finish line when I learned to smoke, from the balcony of the Normandie theater in New York from a girl who pressed a Longfellow upon me then led me from the theater when the usher told her that other people could not hear the film with so much coughing going on. Growing up was not so hard."

In her school days, Jackie was a bit of an outsider. She was well liked but not well known by her classmates. "By nature, she was a loner," Jackie's close friend Nancy "Tucky" Tuckerman, who went on to serve as the White House social secretary during the Kennedy administration, recalled many years later. "After evening study hall, for instance, Jackie seldom joined in, happily staying in her room, reading, writing poetry or drawing." Reading, like riding, had always been a way for her to escape into another world, especially when her life at home was difficult.

That complicated home life further set Jackie apart from her peers. Not only was she Catholic in a predominately Protestant community, but her parents were also divorced. In the 1940s, the concept of divorce itself was controversial, especially among Catholics like the Bouviers, but Jackie's parents' breakup was so nasty that it became tabloid fodder. On January 26, 1940, the *New York Daily Mirror* published an exposé on Janet and Jack Bouvier's dysfunctional relationship with the headline "Society Broker Sued for Divorce." The story, which was reprinted in publications across the country, included details of Jackie's father's affairs—reportedly supplied by Janet's lawyers—alongside photos of the women. Her mother would go on to marry Hugh D. Auchincloss, an old-money stockbroker (who, too, had been previously divorced) who promised the stability her wild and charismatic first husband lacked.

Naturally curious, Jackie flourished in school and was able to establish her identity apart from that of her family. She excelled in the classroom—but didn't want to be seen as a know-it-all—and she was playful, drawing less-than-flattering comics of her teachers, instigating pranks, stealing cookies, and sneaking cigarettes. In her senior yearbook, after proclaiming that her favorite song was "Lime House Blues" and that she could always be found "laughing with

Tucky," she revealed that her greatest ambition was "not to be a housewife."

In the years following World War II, the role of women in the US was shifting, and for young ladies in the upper echelons of American society, that meant expectations and opportunities were changing, too, in regard to higher education and also working outside the home. Jackie's cousin Edith Beale—who would later come to know fame as "Little Edie" in the 1975 documentary film *Grey Gardens*—graduated from Farmington twelve years ahead of the future First Lady, and her outlook on postsecondary education was quite different from Jackie's.

"If you were a 'Farmington' girl, you were trained not only in the classics and all kinds of literature, language, and so forth, but it was also a training for life," Beale once reflected. "You were bred with deportment and elocution—how to move, how to speak, how to behave. The girls were good, they behaved, but were not particularly encouraged to pursue a college education. But what woman was back then?"

In the early decades of the twentieth century, Miss Porter's had a well-established reputation as a finishing school, with instruction in manners, diction, and curtsying in addition to academic courses. Students were primarily girls from prominent families, who were preparing for marriage and would never have the need to work outside the home if they didn't want to. But by the 1940s, its trustees hired new heads of school who emphasized academics at Farmington, specifically college preparation. Jackie was a product of this era of the school and had earned a place in the freshman class of Vassar in the fall 1947 semester.

But while being a dutiful wife was no longer the sole aspiration for girls in the monied classes, that doesn't mean they did away with the time-honored dating ritual of the debutante season.

When Jacqueline Bouvier made her official entrance into society in the summer after her high school graduation, it was hardly the formal court presentation the Kennedy women had taken part in before the war in London. But despite the lack of royal pomp and circumstance, Jackie's "coming out" tea dance still made the local papers.

The party was hosted at Hammersmith Farm, the Victorian mansion in Newport, Rhode Island, owned by Jackie's stepfather, Hugh. The event celebrated both eighteen-year-old Jackie and her five-month-old half brother James "Jamie" Lee Auchincloss, who had been christened earlier in the day. As *The Newport Mercury and Weekly News* put it, "Miss Bouvier's coming out party took the form [of] a reception and dance from 5 to 7 P.M.," with local favorite piano player Clifford Hall providing the music for roughly three hundred attendees.

While Jackie was certainly the center of attention that evening, her mother, Janet, couldn't help showing off her baby; she literally placed him on display alongside the food on the buffet table. As guests filled their plates, they walked right past Jamie, who was dozing in a silver punch bowl—one that had previously been used to hold eggnog. "No, I cannot explain it," Jamie would tell Kennedy biographer J. Randy Taraborrelli. "I, of course, was a cute baby, but Jackie was the focus of attention in her coming-out gown."

Jackie herself would later remember the event as simply "nice." She was showered with flowers throughout the day, and as her authorized biographer Mary Van Rensselaer Thayer described, felt the fete was "the way all coming-out parties should be—teas instead of expensive dances."

A few weeks later, though, Jackie shared the spotlight again at a coming-out dance at the Clambake Club of Newport, an old-school members-only institution known for—as one might guess—its impressive clambakes. Both she and fellow debutante Rose Grosvenor were the honorees at the evening of dinner and dancing.

Jackie was nervous before the party, posing for portraits in an elegant tulle off-the-shoulder gown with a bouffant skirt, which showed off not only her fresh summer tan and her nipped-in waist but also her excellent posture, hard-earned from years of riding horses.

Jackie's dark curls were loose, hitting right at her collarbone, and in her gloved hands she carried a small bouquet of bouvardia and sweetheart roses. (In contrast, Jackie's sister Lee, then just fourteen, made quite the impression by arriving at the dance in a flashy pink satin gown with rhinestones, which she herself would later describe as "a cheap strapless number." Despite it being Jackie's party, Lee eagerly sought the spotlight, making an impression on the eligible men in attendance, in perhaps an early example of the sisters' rivalry. That said, Jackie reportedly didn't seem to mind all that much.)

Both Jackie and Rose stood alongside their mothers as they greeted attendees in a receiving line. Upwards of three hundred people attended the party, with the younger set dancing to the music of Meyer Davis's orchestra until the early hours of the morning in a ballroom covered in flowers from the Auchincloss and Grosvenor gardens. As guests wandered out on the terrace, lit by blue lights on the warm mid-August night, they were treated to a stunning ocean view.

While the invite list was hardly lacking, the number of Jackie's close friends in attendance was small. Her fellow debutantes were quick to describe the future First Lady as fashionable, if a bit shy and standoffish. But few of her contemporaries knew the real Jackie. Over her years at Miss Porter's, she had learned to craft a careful facade—and to keep her circle of confidants close.

Her coming-out was early in the season; a full slate of parties continued into the fall after she started her freshman year at Vassar. And in January 1948, Jackie was named Debutante of the Year of the 1947 season by Igor Cassini, the brother of fashion designer Oleg Cassini, who was writing as a gossip columnist under the name Cholly Knickerbocker. "Queen Deb of the Year is Jacqueline Bouvier, a regal debutante who has classic features and the daintiness of Dresden porcelain," Igor wrote, noting that she had "poise" and was "soft-spoken and intelligent, everything the leading debutante should be."

Later he shared: "I felt something very special in her, an understated elegance. Although shy and extremely private, she stood out in a crowd. She had that certain something, I don't know precisely what word to use to describe this quality: beauty, charm, charisma, style, any or all of the above. Whatever it happened to be, she had it."

THE SUMMER AFTER JACKIE WAS NAMED SOCIETY ROYALTY, SHE met King George VI and Queen Elizabeth, the future Queen Mother. During her break from Vassar, Jackie took her first trip to Europe and "fell irrevocably in love" with the continent as she toured England, France, Switzerland, and Italy. For six jam-packed weeks, she traveled alongside her friends Julia Bissell and Helen "Bow" Bowdoin, Bow's sister Judy, and their "heavenly"—and permissive—chaperone, Miss Helen Shearman, who had been a Latin teacher at Holton-Arms, Jackie's grammar school in DC.

Before they set sail on the *Queen Mary*, Jackie wanted to be prepared for the trip in every way possible, reading guidebooks and histories and practicing her language skills. But once they were on the boat, she wasn't opposed to having a little fun. As the quintet crossed the Atlantic, Jackie was known to indulge in a martini or two.

They arrived in Southampton on July 14. From there, they took a train to London, and a few days later they were strolling into a garden party on the grounds of Buckingham Palace. Each of the girls

clutched a small card, which read: "THEIR MAJESTIES' AFTER-
NOON PARTY BUCKINGHAM PALACE, Thursday, 22nd July, 1948.
This Card, which cannot be replaced, must be given up at the en-
trance."

Tickets to the party came courtesy of Bow's stepfather, Edward
H. Foley, who was serving as an undersecretary of the treasury in
the Truman administration. He had made a few calls to ensure that
the girls were among the one hundred or so Americans invited to
what was described by *The New York Times* as the "most festive garden party since the war's end." Fortunately, their mothers had insisted they pack "the requisite dressy afternoon gowns" as well as
wide-brimmed straw hats and two pairs of elbow-length white gloves
each, should one go missing, so they were well prepared for such an
occasion.

While events have been thrown on the Buckingham Palace
grounds by many monarchs throughout history, garden parties were
codified as a regular royal event in the 1860s. They were initially established as an organized way for the increasingly reclusive Queen
Victoria to socialize after the tragic death of her beloved husband,
Prince Albert, at age forty-two. In the summer of 1868, Victoria
hosted the first-ever garden party at Buckingham Palace. "The afternoon splendid, & not too hot," she wrote in her journal, calling the
event "very puzzling & bewildering."

But under the reign of King George VI, the festivities evolved.
Post–World War II, the guest lists still often included aristocrats but
also became more inclusive, as servicemen and commoners were invited to spend time sipping tea with members of the royal family.
George VI's daughter, Queen Elizabeth II, and her son Charles have
continued to make these events more democratic, with modern-day
garden party guests that include people "from all walks of life, all of
whom have made a positive impact in their community." (On certain

occasions there has been a more notable thread to tie attendees together. For example, in 1997, the Queen hosted a party to mark fifty years since her wedding to Prince Philip; all guests at that garden party were couples also celebrating their fiftieth wedding anniversary. It's a keen public relations strategy for the royals to foster goodwill with the people. But in 1948, three years after the end of the war in Europe, the parties were also a moment of joy in a country still recovering from the devastation.)

As Jackie and her traveling companions wandered the palace grounds, they were among the more than six thousand guests gathered at the royal residence to mingle not only with King George, looking quite dapper in his naval uniform, and his wife, Queen Elizabeth, in a delphinium blue gown, but also the Shah of Iran, Winston Churchill, the royals' close relative Lord Louis Mountbatten, American publisher and businessman Colonel Robert R. McCormick, and US Ambassador Lewis W. Douglas.

While some accounts of fete praise the weather—*The New York Times* noted that guests "shared hospitality and sunshine in a setting showing scant signs of anti-aircraft shrapnel that fell there only a few years ago"—others paint a rather different picture.

Jackie's authorized biographer described the event as a "mob scene," as guests crowded under the refreshment tent during a storm. Despite the rain, the event was more than worth it for Jackie, who proclaimed that meeting the King and Queen was "the most exciting moment of [her] life." "Although not a monarchist, Jackie respected the grandeur if not the pomp of royalty," her stepbrother Hugh D. "Yusha" Auchincloss III recalled. And while a garden party receiving line wasn't a formal presentation in a ball gown with a bouquet, like the young Kennedy women experienced, King George and Queen Elizabeth, the future Queen Mother, smiled at Jackie and her friends as she greeted them.

Jackie and her friends actually went through the line twice. "They had spotted Winston Churchill and moved right in on him," wrote Thayer. "Mr. Churchill was gracious and shook their hands."

After starting the trip on such a high, the young women filled the rest of their time in England with sightseeing and visiting with family friends. But the country was still in transition, rebuilding from the terrors of the war. They couldn't escape reminders of the Blitz. "We could all see that they hadn't built the city back again, but were trying," Jackie's companion Bow would later reflect. "It was very emotional, to see great buildings like St. Paul's Cathedral half-destroyed and just standing there. I think it was England that left the greatest impression on us because clearly they had not recovered." Soon they were on their way to France.

Jackie was always a Francophile at heart, perhaps given her father's ancestry. During the war, too, she was especially impressed by the resolve of French President Charles de Gaulle, even naming her pet poodle after him. "I wonder if she ever told the General, when she met him as President, that she had done so, and the reason why—because he was straight and proud with a prominent nose, and a fighter," Jackie's stepbrother Yusha mused. "I am positive he would have been complimented. Had she had a pet pug with a loud bark, I am sure she would have named him Winston."

But while Jackie would study at the Sorbonne during college, and return to the city many times, her postgraduate career as a writer and photographer at the *Washington Times-Herald* in DC would bring her back to London.

CHAPTER 4

Inquiring Camera Girl

DESPITE OVERCAST SKIES AND THE PROMISE OF RAIN, MORE THAN five hundred thousand people turned up to welcome Princess Elizabeth and Prince Philip to Washington, DC, on October 31, 1951. Among the crowds of onlookers lining the streets, hoping to catch a glimpse of the glamorous heir to the British throne and her handsome husband, was a young Jacqueline Bouvier.

Jackie had only recently started working at the *Washington Times-Herald*. Arthur Krock, the Washington bureau chief of *The New York Times* and a friend of Jackie's stepfather's, had put in a good word for her with the *Times-Herald*'s executive editor, Frank Waldrop. (Krock had a habit of helping young women pursue journalism; a decade earlier, he had recommended Kick Kennedy for a research position at the same publication.) Initially, Jackie was hired to perform general secretarial tasks: fetching coffee, answering phones, and serving as a receptionist. But she quickly won over Frank, and by week three, he had made her his personal assistant.

Elizabeth and Philip's stopover marked the first major royal visit to America since King George VI and Queen Elizabeth's prewar trip in 1939. Given the significance of the tour, Frank sent Jackie down to witness the couple's arrival in the capital. Jackie wasn't on assignment as a reporter, but she saw it as an opportunity to prove her mettle.

The future Queen was in the US for a mere forty-eight hours, in the middle of a longer trip to Canada. She stepped off the plane at Washington National Airport (now named for Ronald Reagan) in an ensemble paying homage to the Great White North; her military-inspired coat was a vibrant red, in a nod to the Canadian flag, with a maple leaf–shaped brooch pinned to the lapel. Following the official welcome ceremony, President Truman and Princess Elizabeth reviewed the guard of honor before departing for Blair House, where the royals would stay during their brief time in the capital.

After zooming through the streets in an open-top car alongside the President, Elizabeth's first day in DC culminated in a reception for the press at the Statler Hotel. More than nine hundred representatives from local media gathered in the presidential room for a meet-and-greet with the royals. The princess, who appeared tired after the rigorous tour, made introductions, received gifts, and gave a short address referencing her father's recent illness. Just a month prior, King George had undergone surgery to remove his left lung following the discovery of a malignant growth. While the extent of the King's cancer diagnosis was not publicly shared, Princess Elizabeth's private secretary Martin Charteris kept the paperwork required for the princess's ascension "under his bed throughout the trip" should it become necessary, but also, superstitiously, "to guard against the possibility of his death." The King would die a few months later, on February 6, 1952.

"I want you all to know how deeply my family, and our whole country, was moved by the sympathy and I might say affection shown to my father, the King, by the people and press of the United States during his recent illness," Elizabeth said to the room full of reporters. "In those anxious days, I think we felt something of the real friendship and unity of purpose, which binds and I'm sure will always bind our two nations together."

Once again among the crowd was Jackie; she had snuck into the reception, perhaps by flashing her badge from the *Times-Herald*. Betty Beale, who was a friend of Jackie's mother's and also served as a society writer for Washington's *Evening Star*, later recalled, "I know everyone in town and I've known Jackie since she was a teenager and I saw that right in the middle of all the *invited* press was Jackie. She didn't belong there. She wasn't press. She was a secretary! That's Jackie! Pushes to get what she wants, ignores the rules when they don't suit her . . . Oh, she was that girl!"

Once Elizabeth finished the requisite shaking of hands, Jackie raced to craft her observations into an article before returning to the office. But when she presented Frank with the story of the crowds and their enthusiasm for the young princess, he told her they couldn't run it. "She was shocked," he later told biographer Carl Sferrazza Anthony. "I snapped, 'You're not a reporter!'"

That said, Frank was so impressed with Jackie's brazen (if unassigned) attempt at journalism that he offered her the opportunity to try out for the paper's Inquiring Photografer column. Published six days a week, the regular feature asked a half dozen or so people the same question and printed their responses paired with their photographs.

While the column was popular with readers, it wasn't a highly sought-after assignment at the paper. Still, Jackie took the audition seriously. Finding her own angle on the franchise, she asked six of the paper's photographers: "Is Princess Elizabeth as pretty as her picture?" (Their answers ranged from "I think she is much better looking than her average picture" to "If she wasn't a princess no one would turn around twice to look at her.")

Frank saw Jackie's potential and gave her a shot to continue writing the column. Eventually, Inquiring Photografer was renamed Inquiring Camera Girl, with Jackie at the helm.

Armed with a Graflex camera and unyielding inquisitiveness, she spent roughly the next year and a half asking Washingtonians about current events and modern life. Some of her person-on-the-street columns proved to be more prescient than others, like when she posed the question, "What would you talk about if you had a date with Marilyn Monroe?" When Vice President Richard Nixon and Senator John Kennedy appeared in the same column in April 1953, she asked them both, "What's it like observing the [Senate] pages at close range?"

But even though she had a young Princess Elizabeth to thank for her burgeoning career as a writer, Jackie initially didn't want to travel to the UK to cover the new queen's coronation. When her friend Aileen Bowdoin (sister of Bow and Judy) telephoned Jackie late one night to invite her to London for the June 2 event, the future First Lady had no interest in going either for work or as a vacation.

Her reaction was unusual. Jackie was enamored with Europe and, for that matter, somewhat fascinated by royalty—interests that were only fueled by her previous trips across the Atlantic. But she had just recently started dating Jack Kennedy, the handsome junior senator from Massachusetts, and had to be convinced that a long international trip—even one reporting on something as exciting as the crowning of a new Queen—would be worth the time apart from her new beau.

JACK AND JACKIE FIRST MET AT A DINNER PARTY HOSTED BY MUtual friends in June 1951, but it wasn't until a second gathering at the same house the following summer that he started to court her in earnest. "He began taking her out all the time. Instead of taking out a lot of different girls, he concentrated on Jackie," Jack's friend Lem Billings recalled. "There was no question in my mind, finally, that he was more interested in Jackie than he had been in any other girl," Lem said referring to May 1953, before hedging only slightly: "However, he was always interested in girls, so I wasn't actually that sure."

Jackie's mother, Janet Auchincloss, refused to take no for an answer regarding the coronation trip and assured her daughter that the distance would only help to kindle any serious feelings Jack might have for her.

"If you're so much in love with Jack Kennedy that you don't want to leave him, I should think he would be much more likely to find out how he felt about you if you were seeing exciting people and doing exciting things instead of sitting here waiting for the telephone to ring," she recalled telling her daughter many years later. Janet also thought a change of scenery would be good for her eldest daughter, who had been in a bit of a funk. Jackie's younger sister, Lee, had recently married Michael Canfield, an American diplomat who was also rumored to be a secret member of the royal family. (Canfield, so the story went, was an illegitimate son of Prince George, Duke of Kent—also known as Princess Elizabeth's uncle.) For Jackie, serving as maid of honor while her younger sister beat her down the aisle only fanned the flames of their lifelong rivalry.

"I should think the *Times-Herald* would be happy to send you and another reporter to write up the Coronation," Janet said. "And if they don't want to, I'd like to give you the trip because I think it would be a great experience for you."

Eventually, Jackie relented and saw the visit for the career opportunity it was. She approached her editors to work out assignments: a few features about the coronation in addition to her regularly scheduled Inquiring Camera Girl column. Though, it should be noted, accounts differ as to who actually paid for the trip. Some historians assert that even with the assignments, Janet still covered the bill, while Aileen recalled that the paper *did* reimburse at least a portion of expenses, and that Jackie "saved every receipt."

And so on May 22, as champagne corks popped and band music filled the promenade deck, Jackie and Aileen bid goodbye to the people waving their handkerchiefs on the pier and set sail on the SS *United States*. Kennedy biographers largely skip over Jackie's trip to the coronation, mentioning it only in passing or omitting it altogether. But the future First Lady's writings during that time offer a rare look into her unvarnished perspective on fame and notoriety before she herself was thrust onto the world stage.

While the focus of Jackie's trip was, of course, the crowning of a new monarch of the United Kingdom and all the enthusiasm surrounding it, she used the voyage itself—the "coronation crossing," as she dubbed it—as fodder for her *Times-Herald* assignments. She chronicled the leisurely nature of life on the boat: days that didn't start in earnest until 11 a.m. and were filled with playing deck games, watching movies, indulging in cocktail hours, and dancing in the ballroom. Ever the observer, she documented the "tingling excitement" and sartorial choices of her fellow travelers, and she kept her ear open for gossip about the other passengers.

She pored over the first-class manifest—"like all great literature, the passenger list makes better reading the second time," she wrote in an early column—calling out legendary hostess Mrs. Robert Bacon, jeweler Louis Arpels of Van Cleef & Arpels, author F. Hugh Herbert, CBS commentator Walter Cronkite (whom she spotted doing "a mean Mexican hat dance") and his wife, and several ambassadors. Also on board (and of particular interest to Jackie) were the Duke and Duchess of Windsor—formerly known as King Edward VIII and Wallis Simpson.

"Passengers stare at the Duke, aware that if he had not abdicated, they would not be sailing to the coronation of his niece," Jackie pointed out, noting how he could be found strolling the deck in a sports jacket and gray flannel trousers, happy to give autographs to any children who might ask. The duchess was more discreet, appearing in public only at dinner, when she and her husband dined alongside James Donahue, heir to the Woolworth retail fortune, and his mother, Jessie.

The Windsors were joined by their three dogs: the duchess's pugs, Dizzy and Trooper, and the duke's cairn, Thomas, which were a key focus in Jackie's report on the pet accommodations of the SS *United States*. In a piece titled "Dog's Life Not So Bad on Ship to Coronation," she detailed how the Duke's valet would fetch the dogs from the ship's kennel every morning and bring them to the couple's stateroom. Strictly speaking, that wasn't allowed, but money talks. As the ship's kennel master Al Euvrard explained to Jackie, "If you're a really big stockholder, you can take them down." While the pugs were well behaved and stylish, wearing blue collars with silver medallions, Thomas, on the other hand, was a menace. "You can't do nothing with that Thomas when the Duke's around," the kennel master said. "He'll sink his teeth in you if you try to get near him."

The Windsors (and their dogs) got off early at Le Havre on their way to Paris. They weren't invited to the coronation; instead, the former King watched the ceremony on television at a party hosted by an American in Paris, Mrs. Margaret Thompson Biddle, alongside one hundred or so other guests. "It was a very impressive ceremony," he was quoted as saying.

When Jackie and Aileen had boarded the SS *United States*, the two young women weren't entirely sure where they were going to stay in London. But by the time they landed in Southampton on May 27, holding tight to their passports, their families had arranged accommodations in a Mayfair flat of the Queen's lady-in-waiting Lady Abel

Smith (who was living at the palace that week), seats for the coronation procession, invitations to the US embassy, and dinners with fellow American travelers.

After disembarking, they made their way to London via the dedicated train for boat passengers. As Jackie looked out the window, she saw that nearly every home they passed had a picture of the Queen in the window. It was a preview of the overwhelming excitement they could expect in London.

"Wait 'til you see the old place—everything's so bright and pretty," the porter at Waterloo Station said to Jackie and Aileen upon their arrival in the capital city. "We haven't had it like this in years."

Indeed, as Jackie took in the vibrant bunting and lavish decorations, she quickly began documenting the city's transformation for the paper. The hordes of tourists—and in particular, Americans—also didn't escape her notice. On the ship, she had overheard her fellow passengers talking about "how the English rent their flats for a fortune and then head to the seaside" and how "London is so jammed, the double-decker buses can't get through the streets."

Jackie confirmed that the traffic was "unbelievably congested." "Everyone's out in his car taking a peek at the decorations," one cabbie said. "I was telling my missus we should have something like this every year."

In Jackie's conversations with locals, the American fascination with the coronation (and the royal family, more broadly) was a source of curiosity. "Are you people in America as interested in the coronation as our papers say you are?" asked Mr. Woodham, the nightwatchman at her flat. "It seems strange to us that people so far away take notice of our queen." He later brought Jackie and Aileen an enormous American flag to hang in their front window; it had been a gift from an American naval officer who stayed in the building during World War II.

For her features, Jackie interviewed everyone from luggage porters to a close friend of Prince Philip's to one of the Queen's ladies-in-waiting, documenting their reactions to this historic event. (The unnamed lady-in-waiting shared that the group had to arrive at Westminster Abbey by 6:30 a.m., but the hairdressers were expected at the palace by 3 a.m. "We wear tiaras, you know, and that takes a bit of arranging," she said.)

But in general, Jackie followed the crowd, writing about theater performances (including one frequented by Princess Margaret) and watching a young Prince Charles and Princess Anne take in the Changing of the Guard at Buckingham Palace. The beautiful black horses of the Canadian Mounties camped in the park outside the palace were of particular interest to Jackie, who loved all things equestrian. So was the "secret" mark on the crown of St. Edward, placed there to ensure that the Archbishop of Canterbury oriented it correctly on the Queen's head.

Everywhere Jackie went in the city, the feeling of exuberance was palpable. It was as if the people of London were embracing the coronation as a moment of optimism and collective joy in a society trying to rebuild after World War II. Not only was the new queen a symbol of vitality, but the coronation marked the beginning of a new era for the UK, a new Elizabethan age. Plus, for the first time in history, all the pomp and circumstance would be televised, modernizing the monarchy and allowing everyday people to have access to the ceremony—and to the royals—in a way they never had before: in their own homes.

In Jackie's spare moments, she stopped by the storied Dorchester Hotel. During the war, the well-fortified building sheltered General Dwight D. Eisenhower as he plotted the Normandy invasion. Now, in peacetime, a new facade from theater production designer Oliver Messel featured "pale blue balconets with purple and gold draperies," and it served as a home base for many visitors taking in the week's festivities. While in the lobby, Jackie heard two women discussing having lunch at Claridge's. "That's where all the [deposed] monarchs are staying," one said. She later sketched the scene for an illustration to accompany her article.

ONE EVENING, SHE WENT DANCING AT THE 400 CLUB, A SMALL private nightclub in Mayfair. With "accordion-pleated red velvet" lining the walls, the club looked "like the inside of a jewel box," with a "postage-stamp sized dance floor." The size made it exclusive, and the guest list reflected that; Jackie spent time in the company of marquesses, earls, and even the Maharaja of Jaipur that night.

She also found herself paging through the British society magazine *Tatler* for tips on how best to take in the coronation parade—get a pedicure, bring sunglasses, and wear a small hat—and she scoured local bookstores, picking up volumes on history and legislation. She amassed a stack so heavy that she had to pay more than one hundred dollars in fees for her overweight baggage on the way home. It took some prodding from Aileen, but Jackie eventually confessed that these books were gifts for Jack.

Despite the distance, the two stayed in touch while Jackie was in Europe. Jack sent her at least one telegram about her work, which read in part, "Articles excellent—but you are missed." And Jack's friend Lem recalled the senator's "many transatlantic calls" while Jackie was on the trip. Aileen confirmed as much to biographer Carl Sferrazza Anthony. "She had a number of urgent calls coming in from him. He was afraid she had changed her mind [about their future together]." And indeed, she did have doubts, Aileen recalled. Not about Jack as a person or a husband, but about the life she would have with him. "She was worried about being taken over by politics and another family, because she always wanted to be herself," Aileen said. "I think that losing her own personality was what she was most worried about."

IN TYPICAL ENGLISH FASHION, ON THE DAY OF THE CORONATION, June 2, 1953, rain poured. Jackie's future sister-in-law Patricia Kennedy, who was also in London for the festivities, later recalled that she had "never been so cold" in her whole life as the day Elizabeth was crowned queen. Jackie felt the chill acutely, as the apartment she and Aileen were staying in had no heat.

But the dreary, unseasonably frigid weather could not dampen the elation of the people—or Jackie's determination to get a good story. Even with all her connections, both personal and professional, she couldn't secure a seat inside Westminster Abbey for the ceremony, so instead, she watched the Queen's grand carriage roll by from a perch outside a Burberry raincoat store. The young Queen looked glamorous as she paraded through the streets in the historic Gold State Coach, led by eight gray gelding horses, but a pleasant face and calm demeanor belied the truth. She would later describe the journey in the bumpy coach as "horrible," and while a stunning bouquet of white flowers sat in her lap (orchids and lilies of the valley from England, stephanotis from Scotland, orchids from Wales, and carnations from Northern Ireland and the Isle of Man), a hot water bottle was discreetly tucked under her seat to keep her warm.

Once the Queen made her way to the church, Jackie waded out into the crowds of Piccadilly Circus, taking her Inquiring Camera Girl column international. She spoke with housewives, laborers, and students about their reactions to the day, but one comment from an American tourist stands out. "I've noticed how the English newspapers play up everything the Queen does," said the man from St. Louis. "I suppose she's the symbol of state to them, but if I were living in a fishbowl like that, I'd jump into the North Sea." Little did Jackie know that soon enough, she would become all too familiar with such a life in the public eye.

After a day out in the drizzle, Jackie and Aileen came back to the apartment and promptly put their feet in the tub to thaw out in the hot water. But they didn't have much time to rest and recover; that night, they went to Perle Mesta's extravagant ball at Londonderry House. The legendary hostess, who was fresh off a stint as the US ambassador to Luxembourg, had rented the 1853 mansion on Park Lane as the venue for what she would later describe as "the most lavish party" she had ever given.

What started as a small affair grew to an intimate dinner of 150 or so, followed by a larger supper dance with a guest list pushing seven hundred. Tickets were a hot commodity. There were several parties that evening, as London sought to celebrate both the country's new queen and an over-the-top postwar frivolity, but Perle's was a particularly coveted invite for Americans.

"One hears a lot on the promenade deck," Jackie wrote in a story for the *Times-Herald*, quoting one of her fellow passengers as saying, "I have hotel rooms and seats for the coronation, but I still haven't been asked to Perle Mesta's party."

Neither had Jackie, for that matter. But when she landed in London, she went about securing her own invitation to the event. "A striking young girl, hatless, swinging her camera, chattering enthusiastically to her companion, rapped on the door of my apartment in Grosvenor Square," Perle recalled several years later. Perle's sister opened the door, but the diplomat was quick to join the conversation. Jackie then explained that both she and Aileen were the daughters of Perle's old friends.

"I'm here on assignment," Jackie said with an air of confidence, explaining her column for the *Times-Herald*. At the time, Perle couldn't have predicted that Jackie would go on to marry Jack Kennedy, or that she would become First Lady. "I did not know, of course, that this was her last story, for an attractive young Senator from Massachusetts had been squiring her around and was even now sending her cables from Washington," she wrote. "Although my crystal ball wasn't working too well that day, one thing I *did* know: Young girls like parties." And so she extended invitations to Jackie and Aileen.

Even with its large reception rooms and impressive gilded ballroom—which were outfitted with rococo chandeliers, antique furniture, and frescoed ceilings painted with birds—the townhome "practically bulged" that evening to accommodate the crowd.

Hollywood stars including Lauren Bacall (whom Jackie described as "the belle of the ball" in a "tight white lace dress") and Humphrey Bogart mingled with society doyennes like Mrs. Cornelius Vanderbilt Whitney and Elizabeth Arden, as well as media mogul William Randolph Hearst Jr. Meanwhile, politicians mixed with royalty from Norway, the Netherlands, and Luxembourg. Jackie and Aileen took it all in. The men were dressed in military uniforms complete with medals on their chests or full-dress suits with tails, while women wore vibrant gowns and striking jewelry.

"The guests circulated between the huge ballroom and the large library, where champagne and cocktails were served, and then to the dining room downstairs where supper was served all night. What a sight it was to see all the distinguished and handsome people, the colorful gowns and sparkling tiaras!" Perle recalled in her memoir. Agents from Scotland Yard were even called in to keep an eye on all the jewels in the room.

While Patricia Kennedy went to a reception at the French embassy following the coronation, she heard tell of Perle Mesta's party, describing it to her mother and father in a letter as "full of everybody who is anybody in this town, with tiaras!"

Jackie was one of those young women whirling around the ballroom to the music of Tim Clayton. As Perle's niece wrote in her memoir, "Young Jacqueline Bouvier, who was covering the coronation, came to the ball and was cut in by many attractive men."

Eventually some of those performers in the crowd couldn't resist adding to the evening's entertainment. Around 1 a.m., Billie Worth, who was then starring in the London company of *Call Me Madam*, a musical inspired by Perle herself, sang a few numbers. She was followed by musical theater actor Charles Bangs, and Lord Foley, who took to the piano.

"While these impromptu performances were going on, many of the guests just sat down in the middle of the dance floor, ball gowns and all," Perle wrote. "They moved quickly out of the way when Prince Jean of Luxembourg led me to the center of the floor and swept me around the room to the strains of 'Hostess with the Mostes' on the Ball.'" (Another song from *Call Me Madam*.)

The music played on until the early hours of the morning. "We started serving scrambled eggs and sausage about three o'clock. When I started down the stairs at five, after dismissing the orchestra, I met Prince Jean of Luxembourg and his bride rushing up the steps," Perle recalled. "'May we have just one more dance?'" they begged. "So I went back and persuaded the orchestra to play a final number."

The guests finally made their way out the door, but a lively chant of "God save our Perle" could be heard above the early-morning rumblings. In a story published on June 9, Jackie described the fete as "the show to see in London last week," declaring it "second only to the Coronation."

After their time in London, Jackie (ever the Francophile) and Aileen stopped over in France for a quick visit before heading home.

As it turns out, Jackie's mother was correct: Absence did indeed make the heart grow fonder for Jack Kennedy. When their plane touched down in Boston and the girls walked into the terminal to wait for their next flight to New York, he was there to greet Jackie, leaning handsomely against a counter. He'd called her mother to find out what flight she was on. "It was the first time that I felt that this was really a serious romance," Jackie's mother recalled. "I had suspected that Jackie cared a lot, although she had never really said so because she is the sort of girl who covers her feelings."

Jackie thought he might pull such a stunt, and, at least according to Aileen, was "ready to kill" actor Zsa Zsa Gabor, who was hogging the restroom on the plane. Jackie had wanted to freshen up before they landed.

While the exact timing of Jack and Jackie's engagement depends on whom you ask, it's clear that time apart from Jackie—and the accounts of her adventures abroad—inspired the senator to make their relationship status official in the public eye. Not long after she returned from London, Jackie made a long-distance telephone call to her aunt Maude, one of her father's younger sisters. "I just want you to know that I'm engaged to Jack Kennedy," she said, warning her to keep things quiet for a little while "because it wouldn't be fair to *The Saturday Evening Post.*"

The *Post* was set to publish a cover story titled "Jack Kennedy—the Senate's Gay Young Bachelor." But perhaps, Jackie had already tipped her hand via her column. The question that ran days after the coronation was "What is your candid opinion of marriage?"

CHAPTER 5

Royal Weddings

Following the announcement of Jack and Jackie's engage-ment, there was a swell of press interest in the young couple. People wanted to know about the woman who had captured the attention of the Senate's most eligible young bachelor—and so an informal photo shoot was organized at the Kennedy home in Hyannis Port on Cape Cod over the Fourth of July weekend, when Jackie would be visiting. Photographers from multiple outlets were there, but the images taken by sports photographer Hy Peskin would serve as a public debut for Jack and Jackie on the national stage.

In July 1953, one of Peskin's pictures, a candid shot of Jack looking confident on his boat, the *Victura*, with his bride-to-be beaming alongside him, appeared on the cover of *Life*, with the headline "Senator Kennedy Goes a-Courting."

Inside the issue, the magazine ran a multipage feature that captures the couple's easygoing beauty and vitality, the tenets of what would become the Kennedy family brand on a national scale. Alongside photos of the couple playing softball and football was an image showcasing the family's history with the aristocracy, including King George VI and the Queen Mother as well as Queen Elizabeth II, subtly suggesting the "American royalty" narrative that continues to this day. "The handsomest young member of the U.S. Senate was acting last week like any young man in love," read the text of the story.

Jackie appears carefree in the photos, but she was very aware that this scene was all for the press. "Now you know how it feels to be on the other side of the camera," joked one photographer. Several years later, following the presidential election of 1960, *The New York Times* referenced "honeymoon pictures of her posed nautically in a sailboat" and suggested that she must be a "great sailing enthusiast." Jackie's response? "They just shoved me into that boat long enough to take the picture."

Already, too, her fashion choices were of interest. The *Boston Globe* reporter in attendance at the photo-call suggested that "Jackie should have been posing for color pictures," calling out how her "deep tan set off strawberry-colored linen shorts, a sleeveless yellow shirt, and bright blue ballet slippers, their toes embroidered with pearls." Curiously, the paper also noted her belt, which featured the words "Bats in Your Belfry" alongside tiny paintings of golden bats flying about.

Jackie didn't want a big wedding. In fact, she explicitly told *The Boston Globe* that she was "planning a small wedding," later clarifying in an interview alongside her fiancé, "very small—just family, we think." But "very small" didn't work for Joe Kennedy. Much like for the royals, for the Kennedys, a family wedding is a PR moment, and Joe wasn't about to let this one pass him by. His son's bride-to-be was Catholic, intelligent, and good-looking, and she offered the Kennedys an entrée into WASPy society by way of her stepfather, Hugh Auchincloss. As much as she was Jack's future wife, she was also a political asset, and Joe wanted to show off the match. "Joe Kennedy not only condoned the marriage, he ordained it," Lem said.

From day one, it was clear that Jackie was marrying into a family and that the family came first, superseding the individual desires of its members. So despite her preference for an intimate celebration, guests completely filled St. Mary's Church in Newport, Rhode Island, which had a capacity of seven hundred. And while it was not (quite) as high profile an affair as the British coronation just over three months earlier, public interest in the September 12, 1953, wedding of John Fitzgerald Kennedy and Jacqueline Lee Bouvier was intense. "Jackie didn't want to have reporters at the wedding," recalled Rose Kennedy. "Her mother was so sensitive to having publicity of any kind. She thought it was demeaning and vulgar. Mr. Kennedy said in our case there'll have to be reporters at the wedding because he is a public figure." Thousands of onlookers, some of whom had traveled via a chartered bus to catch a glimpse of the newlyweds, waited outside the church in anticipation. Per *The New York Times*, the crowd was so eager, it became unruly and "broke through police lines and nearly crushed the bride." As Jackie's stepbrother Yusha Auchincloss recalled, "The crowds were unbelievable . . . One photographer had this long telephoto-type lens and pushed it right into her face, almost right onto her. This is as she was coming into the church, to go down the aisle and be married! I had to push the lens back into his camera."

A larger group of guests, a list of approximately 1,200 that included diplomats, politicians, and members of the upper echelons of high society, was invited to the reception on the terrace of Jackie's stepfather's three-hundred-acre oceanfront estate Hammersmith Farm, the same site as her coming-out party. Jackie's mother was a formidable presence in the planning process, but she was no match for Joe regarding the guest list, complaining to a friend, "The wedding will be just awful—quite dreadful. There will be one hundred Irish politicians!" It took the newlyweds nearly two hours to shake everyone's hand in the receiving line.

While she gave interviews about wedding planning, even resigning from her position at the *Washington Times-Herald* during her engagement, Jackie was far from in control of her nuptials. Her father-in-law-to-be ordered the cake, a tiered vanilla buttercream confection with raspberry filling. He's also rumored to have chosen her engagement ring, a Van Cleef & Arpels *toi et moi* design featuring a diamond and an emerald set side by side. (She later worked with the jeweler to update the look to fit her taste.) He even helped organize their honeymoon, a two-week stay at a pink villa overlooking a bay in Acapulco, Mexico.

Archbishop Cushing, who was a friend of the Kennedy family's, performed the marriage ceremony, accompanied by four other priests, including the former president of Notre Dame and the head of the Christopher Society. Before the wedding mass, the couple received a special blessing from Pope Pius XII, no doubt orchestrated by the father of the groom. But perhaps most emblematic of Joe's attempt to control the narrative around the wedding was how he dictated what the bride's dress should look like.

Even before her life in the public eye began, Jackie had set herself apart with her style choices. Inspired by her recent visit to France, she was interested in a simple bridal look, but Joe wanted to curate a more classic aesthetic, one that would suggest the idea of American royalty. He got what he wanted. Jackie wore an ivory silk taffeta gown with a portrait neckline and a full bouffant skirt by Ann Lowe, who had previously made dresses for Jackie's mother, Janet (including her wedding gown for her marriage to Hugh), and was the first Black couturier to own a Madison Avenue salon. Jackie paired the dress with a rose point lace veil, which had originally belonged to her grandmother Margaret Merritt Lee, draped over a small tiara of lace and orange blossoms. There were orange-blossom embellishments on the dress as well, another nod to royalty, as the flower has been associated with royal brides ever since Queen Victoria wore a simple wreath of orange blossoms in her hair for her wedding to Prince Albert in 1840.

Jackie wasn't happy with her dress, reportedly saying it looked like a "lampshade." But to give Joe credit, the gown has stood the test of time, becoming one of the most iconic bridal looks in American history. There is some suggestion that Jackie's feelings about the dress also softened over the years. In 1962, Ann Lowe declared bankruptcy and an anonymous friend paid off her debts to the IRS; many believe that friend to have been Jackie.

Jackie didn't foster any ill will toward her father-in-law for taking control. In the years to come, she grew to love Joe. "[Jackie] told me that at the beginning she identified more with Old Joe," said Doris Kearns Goodwin, a historian with close ties to the Kennedy administration, "that she'd sit with Joe and listen to classical music, and he'd tell her not to worry about touch football and that he'd rather talk to her anyway. He really did love classical music, and he was an interesting fellow, and probably he was much more interesting to talk to at that stage of her life than Rose would have been. He was worldly, he had adventures, he was a flirt. I can see that she would have liked him."

Further, any lingering feelings about dessert or dresses or the guest list were dwarfed by Jackie's disappointment on her wedding day that her beloved father was too hungover to walk her down the aisle. Instead, her stepfather gave her away.

"I never saw my father out of it or drunk until the worst day there could have been in his whole life, at Jackie's wedding," Lee later told Jackie biographer Sarah Bradford. "It was more than understandable but I think that perhaps I was the only one who knew how he felt in *total* enemy territory, *completely* on his own." Janet had made it clear that, while he was welcome at the ceremony, Black Jack Bouvier was not invited to the reception. He was also excluded from the dinner the night before the wedding. "Understandably," Lee said, "he just got completely drunk the night before, unable to give his beloved daughter away the next day." They told the press that he had taken ill.

Despite the hurt she was feeling, Jackie didn't let her emotions show. She performed the role of a perfect bride for the cameras, again proving herself an ideal match for a future president. One guest described the scene as "just like the coronation." It was the culmination of a carefully curated public relations campaign—a successful one at that.

When they tied the knot, it was national news. "The marriage of Washington's best-looking young senator to Washington's prettiest inquiring photographer took place in Newport R.I. this month and their wedding turned out to be the most impressive the old society stronghold had seen in 30 years," read a second story in *Life*, this time showcasing their wedding photos. *The New York Times* ran a wedding photo on its front page, above the fold, with the headline "Notables Attend Senator's Wedding."

Joe Sr.'s plan had worked. Jack and Jackie's nuptials were an opportunity to forge relationships with the press, and to craft a public narrative around the couple, launching them on a national scale.

For centuries, royal marriages have been calculated partnerships: political and economic alliances designed to foster peace and prosperity between nations. Romance, or even the emotions of the bride and groom, often had very little to do with it.

In this way, the union of Princess Elizabeth and Prince Philip was an anomaly—it was a love match. But as with the marriage of politically ambitious John Kennedy and the socially impeccable Jacqueline Bouvier, the royal wedding was a strategic undertaking as well.

Philip and Elizabeth's marriage ceremony had taken place on November 20, 1947—almost six years before Jack and Jackie's Newport nuptials—when the UK was still deep in the throes of post-WWII recovery. A royal wedding offered a moment of levity and joy for a nation trying to rebuild. Throughout the celebration, in a symbol of solidarity with the people, Princess Elizabeth made a point to observe austerity conditions (even if her own deep pocketbook didn't demand it). For example, her cake, while still multitiered, was reduced in size and its ingredients were supplied by other Commonwealth nations.

She also used ration coupons to pay for her dress. The government granted her two hundred extra coupons for the celebration, but admirers of the young royals thought that wasn't enough. Hundreds of people from across the country sent her additional coupons to help, but they were returned with a note of thanks, as they were illegal to share in such a way. The future Queen made the budget work, and even with limitations, her dress was stunning. Designed by Norman Hartnell, the gown was made from ivory silk, duchesse satin, and silver thread; featured a fitted bodice and heart-shaped neckline; and was covered in 10,000 seed pearls. Its fifteen-foot train, inspired by Botticelli's *Primavera*, was covered in flowers: jasmine and roses, as well as foliage—the blooms symbolizing rebirth in Britain after the war.

The royal tradition of a bride leaving her bouquet on the Tomb of the Unknown Warrior took on new meaning just two years after the end of the fighting. Elizabeth's mother had established the ritual in 1923. As she'd entered Westminster Abbey on her wedding day, she had laid her flowers on the tomb in remembrance of her own brother, Fergus, who had died in the Battle of Loos during World War I, and in tribute to all those who had passed away in the conflict, reinforcing the monarchy's close ties to the British military. Elizabeth now proudly carried on the custom almost a quarter century later at her own wedding by sending her flowers back to Westminster Abbey after the ceremony.

While public decorations were minimal, again reflecting the postwar limitations, a sea of well-wishers was there to cheer on newlywed Elizabeth and Philip as they greeted the public on the palace balcony after the ceremony. Every detail was designed both to align the royals with their subjects and to instill a sense of optimism in the country after so many years of challenges. Winston Churchill even hailed the union as "a flash of colour on the hard road we have to travel."

Elizabeth and Philip's wedding wasn't broadcast live on television, but their vows were heard around the world on BBC Radio. Highlights from the day also appeared on television as well as in cinemas around the UK. All these efforts humanized the royals in the eyes of the people.

It was only a hint of the international spectacle that would surround their son's wedding to Diana Spencer more than thirty years later. While Princess Margaret's 1960 wedding was the first to air live on TV, watched by over 20 million people in the UK and 300 million worldwide, those viewing numbers were completely dwarfed by Charles and Diana's. Upwards of 750 million people around the world tuned in on July 29, 1981, as the thirty-two-year-old future King and his twenty-year-old bride said "I do," while 600,000 more lined the streets in London.

It was the first time a prince of Wales had wed in one hundred years—an event proclaimed the "wedding of the century"—and the celebration offered not only a bit of spectacle and festivity to the people of the United Kingdom but also a reminder of the royal family's essential role: that of stability and continuity. And the day was designed with the public in mind. Charles had even argued with his family about the choice of church, thinking about the optics of the ceremony. "Charles said that people could see more and the acoustics were better [at St. Paul's Cathedral]. Great debate in the family about it, it had never happened before," recalled Diana. "'I want it that way,' Charles said." And so that's how it was. With Diana by his side both at St. Paul's and on the Buckingham Palace balcony, Charles was offering the people a preview of what his reign could look like. Of course, things turned out quite differently.

When Charles and Diana's son Prince William wed his university sweetheart Kate Middleton, in April 2011, it introduced the royal family to a new generation. More than 72 million people streamed the ceremony live on YouTube; millions more tuned in to broadcasts shown around the world—the most who had turned their attention to the Windsors since the death of Princess Diana. Only this time, they were watching her eldest child (and the UK's eventual king) find his happiness. Royal-watchers who had grown up on stories of Diana now saw a young, charismatic face representing the monarchy. More than that, William's bride was an English rose, yes, but a middle-class commoner, signaling a shift away from the long-standing tradition that those in the aristocracy must only marry other members of the aristocracy.

And as Kate arrived at Westminster Abbey in a striking Alexander McQueen gown that, per Buckingham Palace, married "tradition and modernity," people were glued to their TV screens but they were following along on social media, too. This was the first major royal wedding of the modern media age.

"This is a first for us," a royal spokesperson said of the royal family's hope that people would follow along with the wedding celebrations on social media. "It's a new and exciting way to add to the enjoyment of the Royal Wedding." Just as Princess Elizabeth sought to relate to postwar Britons with restrictions on decorations and sweets, it was likewise important to Will and Kate (as millennials who had grown up with ever-changing technology) to embrace the internet on their big day.

While there was certainly criticism from some regarding the cost of the wedding to taxpayers, VisitBritain, the tourism board for the UK, estimated that a surge in travel would last multiple years, eventually bringing in two billion pounds in revenue. The global accounting firm PricewaterhouseCoopers estimated that the country immediately saw a 107-million-pound boost by way of hotel stays, restaurant meals, and souvenir shopping.

"I always say that the high watermark of the second Elizabethan age was in that period really from when William and Kate were getting engaged. The upsurge in interest in the royal family was just incredible in my job," recalled longtime royal reporter Richard Palmer, who at the time was the royal correspondent for the *Daily Express*.

If Will and Kate's wedding ushered the royal family into a new feel-good period of public perception, Prince Harry and Meghan Markle's 2018 nuptials pushed the monarchy further into modern times (whether willingly or not). Harry was marrying a mixed-race American divorcée, which would have been unimaginable even eighty or so years prior, when Edward VIII's love for Wallis Simpson, herself an American divorcée, is what prompted the former King's abdication. But Meghan's presence in the royal family was a signal that the stuffy institution could change. And more than that, the ceremony itself offered a blending of cultures through music, fashion, and tradition. The wedding was the antidote to the assertion that the monarchy is out of touch and has been for some time, particularly on issues regarding race. Nods to the Commonwealth, including a tribute hidden within the bride's cathedral-length veil, suggested that Meghan could serve as a bridge to those nations primarily consisting of former members of the British Empire. It's why Harry and Meghan's eventual choice to step back from their senior royal roles was such a blow to those who had seen themselves represented by the royals for the first time, and also to the future of the monarchy itself.

A GLAMOROUS WEDDING ISN'T A GUARANTEE OF A HAPPILY EVER after—far from it for many in these two families. Charles and Diana's relationship, for example, was doomed from the start, despite the Archbishop of Canterbury declaring their nuptials "the stuff of which fairy tales are made." Even as she walked down the aisle of St. Paul's, Diana was looking for her husband's mistress in the crowd. "I knew she was there, of course," she later said. "I spotted Camilla, pale grey, veiled pillbox hat, saw it all, her son Tom standing on a chair. To this day, you know—vivid memory."

Not every member of the House of Windsor or the House of Kennedy is a cheater, but infidelity does seem to be something of an inherited behavior in these two families—or perhaps the male ego is simply impacted by the power and privilege of being part of a dynasty. There's a reason people believed Diana when she revealed that Prince Charles had once told her, "I refuse to be the only Prince of Wales who never had a mistress." His adultery is no secret. He fully admitted having an affair with Camilla Parker Bowles while still married to Princess Diana, and now, Camilla is queen.

In contrast, there's no public proof that Prince Philip was ever unfaithful to Queen Elizabeth, but he had many close friendships with women, prompting speculation, raised eyebrows, and the Prince Consort's reputation as something of a ladies' man. Over the course of his life, there were a number of unsubstantiated rumors by the UK press attempting to link Philip to several alleged paramours, including Penelope "Penny" Knatchbull, who was one of only thirty mourners invited to Prince Philip's private funeral in April 2021, the Queen's cousin Princess Alexandra, the novelist Daphne du Maurier, and even the former French President Valéry Giscard d'Estaing. One rumored mistress, the Duchess of Abercorn, revealed that she and the Prince Consort had a "passionate friendship" but confirmed that she "did not go to bed with him." When pressed further for her thoughts on whether Philip slept with any of his friends, she responded, "I doubt it very much. No, I'm sure not . . . But he's a human being. Who knows? I don't. Unless you are in the room with a lighted candle, who knows?"

Rumors of "the prince and the showgirl" also swirled about Philip and stage actress Pat Kirkwood. While Kirkwood denied that she and Philip were intimate, she was frustrated that Buckingham Palace refused to comment. "A lady is not normally expected to defend her honor. It is the gentleman who should do that," she reportedly told a journalist. "I would have had a happier and easier life if Prince Philip, instead of coming uninvited to my dressing room, had gone home to his pregnant wife on the night in question."

Philip did eventually comment on rumors of infidelity. When a journalist questioned him, he replied, "Have you ever stopped to think that for years, I have never moved anywhere without a policeman accompanying me? So how the hell could I get away with anything like that?"

But Prince William has yet to snap back about quiet, if baseless, speculation that he has been unfaithful to Kate. When a story about Prince William allegedly having an affair with Rose Hanbury, the Marchioness of Cholmondeley, started to pick up steam in March 2024, she denied the allegations outright. Through her lawyers, Hanbury said, "The rumors are completely false," in a statement given to *Business Insider.*

The Kennedys, too, were no strangers to whispers about their private lives, but the rumors were more often based in established fact. Per her memoir, Rose even went so far as to warn Jackie, Bobby's wife Ethel, and later Ted's wife Joan about what life in the political Kennedy family could be like. But it's certainly also tinged with the knowledge that men in that family are prone to scandal. "I made sure to warn them in advance of what they were in for: that they might be hearing and reading all sorts of scandalous gossip and accusations about members of our family, about their husbands, and for that matter about themselves, and eventually even about their children; that they should understand this and be prepared from the beginning, otherwise they might be very unhappy. They took the burden with the blessing," Rose wrote.

Patriarch Joseph Kennedy, for example, had a multiyear-long extramarital relationship with actress Gloria Swanson. Some biographers believe that Robert F. Kennedy was unfaithful in his marriage, as was his brother Ted. Recently, Robert F. Kennedy Jr. was embroiled in an alleged sexting scandal just a few months before he took a role in the Trump administration. It was only the latest in a series of affairs he's been accused of—many of which he's also admitted to.

And of course, as has become legend, Jack is believed to have slept with a number of women during his marriage to Jackie, including actress Marilyn Monroe and White House intern Mimi Alford. It's likely that Jackie knew of his promiscuity from the beginning. In an oral history for the JFK Library, Lem Billings shared that he had spoken to Jackie about Jack's unchaste behavior during their engagement. Lem didn't explicitly spell out his friend's penchant for engaging in casual sex in the official recording, but the implication is clear.

"I'd known Jack a long time, as we've indicated, and I felt I should prepare her a little bit for what I felt were some of the problems that Jack might have in marrying at thirty-five," he said on the tape. "It's always a much bigger step for a man at thirty-five than it is for one at the age of twenty-one." So Lem approached his friend's fiancée at a cocktail party the night of President Eisenhower's first inaugural ball. "I told her that night that I thought she ought to realize that Jack was thirty-five years old, had been around an awful lot all his life, had known many, many girls—this sounds like I'm an awfully disloyal friend, saying these things—that she was going to have to be very understanding at the beginning, that he had never really settled down with one girl before, and that a man of thirty-five is very difficult to live with. She was very understanding about it and accepted everything I said." Later on in the conversation, Lem noted that indeed, "this sort of thing was a problem for Jack when he first got married."

But like his father, Jack understood that image is everything. And in politics, what people believe is often more important than how things really are. Despite being a notorious philanderer, Jack maintained the carefully curated image of a devoted family man, the beginnings of the Kennedy myth that would long outlast him.

CHAPTER 6

Dinner at Buckingham Palace

IT WAS IMPORTANT TO JACK THAT HE BE AT THE BAPTISM. AFTER Jackie's sister Lee divorced her first husband, Michael Canfield, in 1958, she married Polish aristocrat Prince Stanisław, "Stas" Radziwill in 1959. Their first child, Anna Christina, or "Tina" as she was known to family, arrived prematurely in 1960. The Kennedys were all too familiar with difficult pregnancies. By this point, Jackie had suffered one miscarriage and had given birth to a stillborn baby before the arrivals of their two children, Caroline (born 1957) and John (born 1960). So despite nursing an aching back—and a wounded ego following his summit in Vienna with the leader of the Soviet Union, Nikita Khrushchev—President Kennedy rallied to celebrate his new goddaughter in London in June 1961.

"The fact that Tina had survived—she was born three months prematurely—made it an extraordinary event and her christening was an occasion for particular celebration," Lee wrote in her memoir. "Jack, realizing this, made an effort to be there following his frustrating meetings with Khrushchev in Vienna and de Gaulle in Paris."

The private family occasion also served as a reasonable-enough excuse to get Jack to London. He wanted to debrief with British Prime Minister Harold Macmillan about his conversations both with Khrushchev and with the French President Charles de Gaulle, without upsetting the other members of NATO too much. There was concern that the "special relationship" between the US and the UK and, further, the friendship between President Kennedy and Prime Minister MacMillan, took priority for those two countries over the more formal international military alliance. As long as he kept the visit short, Jack thought it wouldn't cause too much of an issue. "The very fact that he would like to stay longer is what would be held against him by those who do not see why we always talk about being partners," read one message from Washington to the UK Foreign Office regarding the scheduling of this trip.

The close relationship between President Kennedy and Prime Minister MacMillan dated from the beginning of the Kennedy administration, despite initial skepticism on the part of the British leader. "I had no particular reason to have any affection for the president," Macmillan told his official biographer, referencing the "contempt" he had for JFK's father, Joe Kennedy. "It was generally thought he was unfriendly and defeatist," Macmillan said, referencing Joe's support of appeasement and of negotiation with Hitler. But Macmillan soon overcame any prejudices, as well as their twenty-three-year age difference, to forge a real bond with the dashing, comparatively young man. As biographer Christopher Sandford put it, "Within twenty-four hours of their first meeting, Kennedy had privately dispensed with the formal address of 'Mr. Prime Minister' in favor of 'Mr. Prime' or 'Harold,' while Macmillan opted to call the president simply 'My Friend.'"

There was a familial association as well—if a somewhat distant one. Macmillan was President Kennedy's late sister Kick's uncle by marriage, as the prime minister's wife, Lady Dorothy Macmillan, was the aunt of Kick's husband, Billy. (Notably, British Ambassador David Ormsby-Gore was related to the Macmillans as well.) Further, Harold Macmillan's mother was American, born in Indianapolis, Indiana. Again, a point of connection. But while there was a personal bond between the two men, it was also a politically necessary one. As the world moved into the nuclear era, the alliance between the US and the UK was essential.

The Kennedy plane finally touched down the evening of June 4 at London Airport (now Heathrow) around 8:30 p.m., an hour delayed because his talks with Khrushchev lasted longer than anticipated. From the tarmac, both political leaders issued statements, in front of a naval honor guard, a nod to Kennedy's own military service.

"You have had a long journey and seen many distinguished personalities," Macmillan said. "I will not disguise from you that I am looking forward to hearing just what happened." Kennedy, on the other hand, emphasized his long-standing ties to the UK in his brief remarks. "I hope I may say that I come not to Great Britain as a stranger. I spent many months here in the days before the Second War," he said. "Two of my sisters had the good judgment to marry citizens of Great Britain. Tomorrow I am about to assume my most sober responsibility, which is to become the godfather of a new English citizen. So I am glad to be here."

After the speeches, the men climbed into an open-top car and set off for central London, while their wives followed close behind in their own vehicle.

Their route was lined with police corralling cheering well-wishers hoping to catch a glimpse of the First Couple, whose glamorous appearance at the Palace of Versailles on June 1 had only increased their international appeal. There were a few protestors opposing Kennedy, but the large crowds, if not as big as those for President Eisenhower the year prior, were primarily supportive of the young US President and his wife as they made their way to the Radziwill family home in Westminster.

Where Jackie and Jack would stay during this trip was much discussed in the months leading up to their arrival. The US embassy was considered, of course, and Queen Elizabeth had invited the First Couple to stay at Buckingham Palace. "The Queen would really be very glad to have the President and Mrs Kennedy as Her guests," reads an April 1961 telegram about the visit. In the end the Kennedys opted to stay with Lee at her "divine house on Buckingham Place," a Georgian brick home a few blocks away from the Queen's royal residence. But while Lee and Stas were eager to host Jack and Jackie, the arrangement wasn't without its complications.

When the Kennedys were in Paris, the Secret Service had extensively searched 4 Buckingham Place and "had turned the house inside out—to the point that the press was able to sneak in under the guise of being moving men, taking photographs of the entire house," recalled Lee. "This was upsetting but in England all the media was fascinated by this unusual end to the President's trip." Indeed, when the Kennedys arrived at the address, they were met by crowds and cameras as the Macmillans said good night. It was the first of many times they encountered such a scene during their visit.

The next morning, in an almost fatherly fashion, Macmillan put his arm around Kennedy's shoulder and offered him a stiff drink as they settled in for a multi-hour discussion at Admiralty House (the temporary residence of the prime minister while 10 Downing Street was being renovated). Macmillan later told the Queen that Kennedy had been "completely overwhelmed by the ruthlessness and barbarity of the Russian premier [who had been] completely impervious to his charm." As Kennedy later told his country via a national broadcast, "It was a very sober two days . . . No spectacular progress was either achieved or pretended," he said, spinning the diplomatic stand-still as a moment for both men to put all their cards on the table, to hear, if not to understand or agree with, each other's perspective.

The Cold War was heating up, and it was becoming clear how far apart the US and the USSR were on nearly every important international issue. "Our most somber talks were on the subject of Germany," he said in his address. (Notably, the Berlin Wall would go up roughly two months after their meeting.) Further, the two men could not come to an agreement on the terms of a treaty to ban nuclear tests, illustrating the simmering Cold War tensions, which had been exacerbated by the Bay of Pigs invasion in April, the failed CIA-organized attempt to overthrow Fidel Castro, which further pushed the country into a public alliance with the Soviet Union.

THE WHIPLASH BETWEEN GOVERNMENT DUTIES AND FAMILY OBLIGATIONS must have been significant for Kennedy, who followed talks with Macmillan with a luncheon ahead of Tina's christening at Westminster Cathedral. The crowd outside the church that day was "unbelievable," recalled Lem. People crushed together for blocks, eager to catch a glimpse of the new American President and his beautiful wife, who had days prior inspired her husband to say: "I am the man who accompanied Jacqueline Kennedy to Paris."

The baptism lasted for only about twenty minutes. Prince Radziwill's sister Countess Potocki served as godmother and held the baby. (As Lee later recalled, the countess "was a lovely woman and we were close, but she was too religious for me.") In a sweet moment, Tina grabbed the baptismal candle as President Kennedy held it. The service was followed by a small party at the Radziwill home, attended by those close friends that JFK particularly wanted to see, including several people he had known when his family had lived in the UK before the war.

"It was a most extraordinary scene, like something out of a novel," described journalist Joseph Alsop, who was an informal adviser and friend of President Kennedy's, "because it was the Radziwill child's christening, and it was really an extraordinary event in itself. It was a frightfully pretty room, lovely afternoon, Prime Minister, the whole damned family, God knows who . . . all the girls in their prettiest clothes."

But against this beautiful backdrop, the President was strained, still processing the difficult conversations he'd had with Khrushchev. "And in the middle of it all, the president, just barely back from Vienna, sort of shoved me into a corner and talked for fifteen minutes in a tense, new Bray about what he had just been through," Alsop continued. "I'd had no idea when I was in Vienna how serious it was, and I had the sense that the thing had come to him as a very great shock which he was just beginning to adjust to. And then he responded to it with extraordinary coolness and resilience. After that, it was when, I think, he really began to be president in the full sense of the word."

The conversations he'd had continued to weigh on his mind, even as later that evening the First Couple was invited to have dinner at Buckingham Palace. Jack had met the Queen previously, when he lived in the UK before the war, and the two had also corresponded in their roles as heads of state. For example, Queen Elizabeth had sent JFK a birthday message on May 29, which read, "I have much pleasure in sending to you Mr President on the anniversary of your birthday my cordial congratulations and good wishes." It was signed "Elizabeth R" meaning it was a personal message from Elizabeth Regina (*regina* being Latin for "queen").

It wasn't a formal state banquet but rather a more intimate visit, which would mark the Queen's first meeting with a sitting US president at the royal residence. Initially, the Radziwills were excluded from the invitation, as Lee and Stas had both previously been divorced—Stas was Lee's second husband; Lee was Stas's third wife. As the head of the Church of England, which frowned upon divorce and remarriage, the Queen saw it as inappropriate to host the couple.

"This caused a little commotion because the Queen does not receive divorced couples," Lem explained. "At first the Radziwills were not invited and it was only due to the President's insistence that they were."

But according to the writer Gore Vidal (who was also Jackie's pseudo-stepbrother, as his mother had previously been married to Hugh Auchincloss), Jack had told the Palace "not to bother about us, we're here unofficially." Eventually, after some back and forth, the Queen relented.

That evening, Jackie wanted to look her best. She was confident and beautiful, and fresh off appearances in France, where she had been praised for her poise and ability. But she was also still finding her feet as First Lady in social situations of this caliber. She wanted everything to be perfect, and no effort was spared. Her gown was made of ice blue silk, a Chez Ninon "freehand interpretation" of a Givenchy number with a nipped waist and an elegant neckline featuring two small bows. As Oleg Cassini put it in his book, *A Thousand Days of Magic*, "The geometric cut was a strong part of the 'Jackie Kennedy look.'"

Her hair was swept off her face, styled by Alexandre of Paris, who had been specifically brought to the UK for the occasion. She and her husband brought a small gift for the royal couple as a token of their gratitude: a portrait of the president in a silver frame from Tiffany, with a handwritten note reading, "To Her Majesty Queen Elizabeth II, with appreciation and highest esteem, John F. Kennedy." It was a modest present, but an appropriate one, given the unofficial nature of the evening.

As the group headed over to the Palace for dinner, the route was again lined with crowds. One paper estimated that five thousand people awaited the arrival of the First Couple outside the gates.

The Queen sparkled in sapphires and diamonds as she and Prince Philip welcomed the Kennedys and the rest of the President's immediate party at the top of the stairs in a small room. The group drank champagne and chatted for about fifteen minutes, posing for photos. In the images from the event, the differences between Jackie's ensemble and that of the British monarch's are striking.

When Queen Elizabeth and Prince Philip visited the White House for a state dinner in their honor in 1957, the British monarch and First Lady Mamie Eisenhower had been dressed quite similarly. Both women wore pastel satin full-skirted ball gowns featuring floral prints and thin shoulder straps, in keeping with what was expected for a formal event. Four years later, Elizabeth's outfit, a voluminous blue tulle crinoline designed by Norman Hartnell, stayed true to that style once again.

While the Queen's dress emphasized her steadfast nature and a consistent appearance, Jackie's sleek and streamlined aesthetic felt modern and elegant—perhaps, as fashion journalist Hamish Bowles suggested, "subliminally reinforcing the Kennedy administration's message of America's forward-thinking dynamism." As *The Washington Post* put it, "The First Lady silently and smilingly stole the show . . . Her popularity rating here is just as high as it was in Paris or Vienna."

Indeed, Jackie's arrival in the UK made her a style icon among the British people.

"London's fashion industry today worked at top pressure to meet a 'just like Jackie' Kennedy sales boom that has swept Britain since

America's First Lady arrived here Sunday. Milliners and dress designers were unashamedly cashing in on the appeal of the little-girl smile and the model-girl figure of the President's wife," reads a report from *The New York Times*. "Milliners in London's fashion center said they were working their staffs day and night to fill orders for jaunty pillbox hats—'just like Jackie's.' Britain's millinery institute said today it has been able to meet the demand largely because the hat is not too difficult to manufacture. Similar optimistic forecasts came from London's clothing manufacturers. They said they were well geared to supply the demand for chic, slim-fitting suits with cropped jackets that Mrs. Kennedy often wears."

Once the doors opened on the reception, the royals ushered in their guests, with Queen Elizabeth taking the President around the room and Prince Philip escorting the First Lady as introductions were made. While Jackie was excited to be there, she couldn't completely hide her disappointment by the selection of attendees. She had hoped to meet Princess Margaret and Princess Marina of Kent, whom the President had met when he lived in London before the war, but neither of the two women was in attendance that evening.

"No Margaret, no Marina, no one except every Commonwealth minister of agriculture they could find," Jackie reportedly told Gore. (Notably, a few places at the table had been allotted for requests of the prime minister. "The Queen very kindly invited those of my leading colleagues whom I [could] not have at luncheon," Macmillan wrote in his diary, referring to Home Secretary Rab Butler and Edward Heath who was serving as Lord Privy Seal.)

Princess Margaret "nodded thoughtfully" when Gore later told her of the drama surrounding the evening's guest list. "That could've been true," she reportedly said. "I know I rang my sister, furious at not being invited, and she said, 'Ah, I thought since you were pregnant you wouldn't want to bother!' Too maddening!" (That November, the Kennedys would send their "heartiest congratulations" to the princess and her husband, Lord Snowdon, on the birth of their son, David. "May your son have a long life of health and happiness," read the message.)

Jackie allegedly shared more about the evening with Gore, noting that while Prince Philip was "nice but nervous," the Queen was rather reserved, polite, but quiet, and "pretty heavy-going." Years later, when Gore repeated this account to Margaret, she retorted, "But that's what she's *there for.*" Of Elizabeth and Philip as a couple, the First Lady reportedly said, "One felt absolutely no relationship between them."

"The queen was human only once," Jackie allegedly told Gore. When the First Lady described her struggles in the spotlight on their recent state visit to Canada and the pressures of being in the spotlight twenty-four hours a day, "the queen looked rather conspiratorial and said, 'One gets crafty after a while and learns how to save oneself.'"

While the company was apparently less than to be desired, the food was indulgent, with multiple courses—fish and lamb and salad—but the thing that stood out the most to Lee were the plastic placemats depicting scenes of London, which she described as "strangely quaint."

Throughout dinner, Jack was distracted. His back was continuing to hurt him (he dealt with chronic pain throughout his presidency, likely stemming from an old football injury that was exacerbated during his military service), and his thoughts were still occupied by the Cold War. British Ambassador David Ormsby-Gore even described him as "depressed about Vienna." Jack later summarized the summit meeting to *New York Times* columnist James Reston as "the roughest thing in my life."

David later told a reporter for *Look* magazine about the dinner, who summarized his account: "As the meal progressed, Harlech recalls, it became apparent that he was preoccupied. He was wondering how to paint a true picture for the American people of what had happened. The report he gave was pretty gloomy. This first direct encounter with Khrushchev had been so contrary to what he expected."

"He was very concerned about preparing for his television broadcast as soon as he got back," recalled David in a separate interview. "He thought it right that the American people should be told immediately what the real position was between the Soviet Union and the United States."

But despite his mind being elsewhere, the President made it through the dinner, politely conversing with the Queen to his left and the Countess of Home to his right.

Once the soufflé of Grand Marnier was served, the Queen led her guests through the Picture Galleries. "That was almost an amusing experience," recalled Angier "Angie" Biddle Duke, the chief of protocol for the Kennedy administration, who was present that evening. The paintings "are hung without regard to school, nationality, era, date or anything. They are just hung—rather haphazardly. It's quite a jigsaw puzzle to figure out what school, what painter, what period, and although very interesting, frankly, I think it's quite a hodgepodge." The Queen described the works to the group in detail. "I was quite impressed by the queen's knowledge of art," Lee would later write, noting that she "had a great deal to say about the history of each painting." Lee and Prince Philip hung back from the group. "You're just like me—you have to walk three steps behind," he said to her.

As they toured the works of the masters, the Queen seemed to focus primarily on the paintings of animals, sharing the history of each work. But when she paused to admire a Van Dyck, she said simply, "That's a good horse." Jackie, at once in awe of this art and somewhat unimpressed by the drafty, aging building, agreed with the somewhat odd statement. You could almost imagine the wheels turning in her mind, of how she would restore the White House, so that it wouldn't disappoint visitors the way the palace had disappointed her.

Accounts of the evening differ significantly. Jackie had dinner with photographer and legendary gossip Cecil Beaton shortly after the Buckingham Palace party. As he recalled in his diaries, Jackie "said they were all tremendously kind and nice, but she was not impressed by the flowers, or the furnishings of the apartments at Buckingham Palace, or by the Queen's dark-blue tulle dress and shoulder straps, or her flat hairstyle."

But the prime minister described the dinner as "very pleasant," as did Angie. "It was a delightful evening," he said, "very pleasant, very charming, very attractive evening! I think everybody enjoyed it very much." For his part, American ambassador to the UK, David K. E. Bruce, wrote in his diary, "The Queen and the Duke of Edinburgh put on a good show in the beautiful reception rooms" of Buckingham Palace.

For a dinner that left such an impression on history, it didn't last very long. The Kennedys were at Buckingham Palace from only 8 to 10:45 p.m. While the President immediately flew home, Jackie stayed with Lee for a few more days.

Whether or not the Kennedys found the evening as "pleasant" as Prime Minister Macmillan had, the President later used the dinner as a symbol of the important relationship between the US and the UK. "Our day in London, capped by a meeting with Queen Elizabeth and Prince Philip, was a strong reminder at the end of a long journey that the West remains united in its determination to hold to its standards," he said in his address to the nation. Shortly after his departure from the UK, Jack also wrote to the Queen, thanking her once again for dinner. "May I also at the same time say how grateful my wife and I are for the cordial hospitality offered to us by your Majesty and Prince Philip during our visit to London last Monday," he wrote in a letter to mark Trooping the Colour, the official celebration of the monarch's birthday in the UK, which always takes place in the summer, regardless of the king's or queen's actual day of birth. "We shall always cherish the memory of that delightful evening."

Ever polite, Queen Elizabeth responded: "I have received with very much pleasure Mr President the kind greetings which you have extended to me in your own name and in that of the people of the United States on the celebration of my birthday. I and my husband are delighted that you enjoyed your recent brief visit to London."

While President Kennedy returned to the city in June 1963, he did not see the Queen again. He died before he got the chance.

CHAPTER 7

A Pair of Queens

Jackie's international popularity grew following her successes in Canada and Europe, and the Kennedy administration began to see the First Lady as a diplomatic asset all on her own. So in March 1962, she undertook a diplomatic tour of India and Pakistan. Originally, Jackie had planned a personal trip to the two countries, but it was later upgraded to a "semi-official" visit, following interest from both governments.

"Ken [Galbraith, the US ambassador to India] first talked to Jack about it," Jackie later explained, "and when we talked about it at the Cape, Jack said I could bring Lee along, and it all sounded informal and fun . . . But by the time the trip had been postponed a couple of times, and so many things added to the schedule, I was almost sick before we left, thinking I just couldn't do it."

But Jackie swallowed any anxieties for the good of her country, and after a quick stopover in Vatican City for an extended private audience with Pope John XXIII, Jackie and Lee touched down in New Delhi, where they were met by Indian Prime Minister Jawaharlal Nehru, his daughter, Indira Gandhi, and a sea of people eager to catch a glimpse of America's glamorous First Lady. The crowds were larger than the Secret Service had anticipated. "The sheer number of people was astonishing to me," Jackie's Secret Service agent Clint Hill wrote.

Over the next two weeks, the women were photographed atop camels and elephants; boating down the Ganges River; dining with politicians and dignitaries, including Prince Philip's cousin Lady Pamela Hicks (née Mountbatten), whose father, Louis Mountbatten, served as the last viceroy of India; attending polo matches and cattle shows; visiting a textile showroom; handing out lollipops to hospitalized children; and taking in the sights in both countries. *Time* magazine described the trip as a "benign competition" between India and Pakistan, which have historically had an adversarial relationship, rooted in the partition of British India in 1947, which created the two new states mainly divided along the basis of religion. Given that India and Pakistan were still relatively new nations, the US was keen to use Jackie's appeal to foster relationships and strengthen ties, as a strategy in the ongoing Cold War between the democracies in the West and communism. Each country, *Time* wrote, was "trying to outdo the other in the warmth of its greetings to visitor Jacqueline Kennedy." For her part, Lee was always a few steps behind her sister. She was still in the spotlight, but Jackie was clearly the star.

The pace of their visit was arduous but not punishing. As writer Anne Chamberlin relayed to *Life*, Jackie "was not slavishly given over to Kennedy ways. One morning when a lot of Kennedys would have been up to see the sun rise over Delhi or swim 80 laps in the pool, Jackie slept late." Hundreds of thousands of people came out to see her over the course of the trip. In Udaipur they called out, "Jackie *ki jai!*" and "Ameriki Rani!"—"Hail Jackie!" and "Queen of America!"— as they saw her arrive via boat wearing a peach shift dress, coupled with a pair of white gloves and her signature multistrand pearls. Jackie's close friend Joan Braden, who covered the tour for *The Saturday Evening Post*, also noted her stateliness. "Part of the time she had seemed to me very much like a queen," she wrote, noting that her "dignity and reserve were indeed queenly." But when Braden asked the First Lady about that perception, Jackie denied feeling any different. "Isn't it funny! I always felt myself," she said. "But how can anyone look at the Taj Mahal or Gandhi's tomb, with forty-five reporters hanging on your every word, and not seem like someone you're not."

Regardless of how she felt, her trip consumed the local communities. "Nothing else happened in India while Mrs. Kennedy was here," the editor of the *Times of India* recalled. "Her presence completely dominated the Indian scene."

A HIGH POINT OF THE TRIP WAS THE VISIT TO THE TAJ MAHAL, a grieving emperor's monument to his late wife. Lee would later remember the "tremendous" crowds that greeted them. "The press was nearly out of control," she wrote. "My first glimpse of what is perhaps the greatest tribute to love will always remain indelibly imprinted in my mind. Its outline against the sky is as fine as an ink-drawn line." Jackie was so enamored by Agra's grand marble mausoleum that she made time to see it twice: once in the morning and again by moonlight. A photo of her posing alone in front of the beautiful tomb in a sleeveless printed sheath with a jeweled neckline circulated widely. Thirty years later, Princess Diana, also solo, would pose in almost the exact same spot, in an image many saw as symbolic of a failing marriage, a portrait of loneliness at a monument to everlasting love. When asked by a reporter her feelings of the mausoleum, Diana replied. "It was a fascinating experience—very healing." When asked to elaborate, she declined, saying simply, "Work it out for yourself." Later that year, she and Prince Charles announced their separation.

Jackie, on the other hand, made her devotion to her husband known during the trip. It was clear she was serving as his representative, and she made a point to emphasize her roles as a loving wife and a good mother in her conversations with the press. In Pakistan, she spoke to a crowd of seven thousand at the Shalimar Gardens in Lahore. "All my life I've dreamed of coming to the Shalimar Gardens," she said. "It's even lovelier than I'd dreamed. I only wish my husband could be with me." On the flight home, she told a reporter that while she was glad that she went on this tour of India and Pakistan, she would "never take a trip like this again without Jack," revealing that at one point during her visit to Lahore she had even pondered what she was doing "so far away and alone, without Jack or the children to see them."

"Jack's always so proud of me when I do something like this," she said, "but I can't stand being out in front. I know it sounds trite, but what I really want is to be behind him and to be a good wife and mother."

From the start, Jackie hoped that the trip "would not turn into a fashion show," but given her status in 1962 as a style icon, her wardrobe inspired breathless international press coverage, with *Life* estimating that she wore at least twenty-two different outfits over the course of the trip. One day, the publication noticed she wore five distinct looks—though it should be noted that one was for riding; Jackie changed into a pair of jodhpurs, a tweed coat, and a hunting cap to practice jumping with the palace guard in New Delhi. "She has worn only two things a second time. These rare 'repeats' are greeted with the joy of a bird watcher spotting a prothonotary warbler," Chamberlin reported. Some of the male reporters on the trip, including Phil Potter of *The Baltimore Sun* and Keyes Beech of *The Chicago Daily News*, struggled with the specifics of the outfits, asking other members of the press corps if it was accurate to call her hair a "bouffant" or how to describe the specific shade of a dress. To get a sense of the fervor around her fashions, one only has to look at how Chamberlain described the First Lady's parasols. They were "earth-shaking." Upon her arrival in Pakistan, Jackie was being described as "the best-dressed woman in the world."

Even if she didn't want the focus to be on her clothes, Jackie understood the impact her fashion would have during her time in India and Pakistan, and so she collaborated with her go-to designer, Oleg Cassini, on a slate of ensembles that nodded to both countries' cultures but remained true to her signature aesthetic. She also took a cue from Queen Elizabeth: wearing vibrant shades so that she could be seen by the crowds. "I wanted Jackie to stand out, and we both felt that the visual impact of color was important," Oleg later wrote. He kept to a palette inspired by Moghul miniatures: pinks, greens, apricot, and white. "These colors would make an impact," Oleg said, and his silhouettes were influenced by traditional regional dress as well.

As the tour was coming to an end, Jackie sent Oleg a note on stationery from the President's House in Karachi, Pakistan, telling her friend that she was in a "complete state of exhaustion" but that there was "no doubt the trip was a TREMENDOUS success." In particular, she was "delighted" by the clothes Oleg made for her.

Jackie called the trip "a dream." But she missed her children. It was difficult for the First Lady to leave John and Caroline, who were then only fifteen months and four years old, respectively, for an extended period. Fortunately, back in the States Jack made sure they followed along with their mother's travels. "The President had a large map and he ritually most evenings pointed out the different villages or places wherever Mrs. Kennedy was on that day or the following day or the day before," their nanny Maud Shaw later recalled. After spending so much time away from her family, Jackie was eager to return home, but before she flew back to Washington, she spent a few quiet days with Lee in London, recovering from the stresses of the trip.

THOUGH JACKIE USED HER TIME IN LONDON TO RELAX, THE VISIT was hardly a casual one. As US Ambassador David Bruce wrote in his diary, prior to her arrival, his office was "plagued with all sorts of details" regarding security and protocol, as well as the plan to greet the First Lady at the airport, and whether she would make an official media appearance or even be photographed during her time in the UK. The list of queries top of mind for Bruce also included more trivial topics such as: "do we know what hairdresser she may go to" and "what antique shop she may visit" as well as "a multitude of other questions that keep a corps of people busy." In the end, Ambassador Bruce and his wife, Evangeline, accompanied the Radziwills and went to pick up the two women from the airport. Upon arrival, Jackie, who was wearing a "girlish, ice-cream pink suit made of wool boucle trimmed with navy blue, and one of her famous pillbox hats to match," kissed her brother-in-law on the cheek before shaking hands with several dignitaries. Little did she know that particular bubblegum ensemble would go on to become one of the most tragically iconic outfits in American history.

Jackie gave the photographers a friendly wave before ducking into the Radziwills' blue Cadillac alongside her sister, Lee. She promptly reached into the front to greet her two-and-a-half-year-old nephew, Anthony, and hauled him into the back seat alongside them as they made their way back to 4 Buckingham Place.

Despite such a long journey, the women were in good spirits and eager to talk about their recent adventures. Jackie was keen to catch up with friends, so Lee hosted an intimate get-together that evening.

Oleg, who had been skiing at Sestriere, in Italy, was in attendance, as was Moira Shearer, the ballerina and star of *The Red Shoes*. Photographers Cecil Beaton and Benno Graziani were also there for the evening of caviar and vodka and discussion of the trip. There was dancing and silliness, too. With Oleg wearing a "makeshift turban" and Benno, a pot for a hat, they danced around the living room. Whether it was the free-flowing drinks or the knowledge that she was among her close, inner circle, Jackie was able to let loose, shedding the carefully polished exterior she maintained as First Lady. "This was the kind of gathering Jackie preferred—a few close friends in an informal family setting," Oleg wrote.

Though this trip to the UK was a private visit, unlike the travels of the previous two weeks, the press and the public didn't seem to make that distinction. Excitement for Jackie had only grown since she was last in London, and photographers and fans lingered outside the Radziwills' home in droves. American diplomat G. Lewis Jones described the trip as a "family holiday," explaining to the media, "We gather Mrs. Kennedy is not interested in going to parties or receptions." She did, however, make one exception. When Queen Elizabeth was informed of the trip, the monarch made certain to extend an invitation to the First Lady to have lunch at Buckingham Palace during her stay. Jackie, of course, accepted.

So on March 28, the crowds were waiting as the First Lady emerged from 4 Buckingham Place wearing a deep pink claret wool suit by Givenchy, a mink hat, and a soft smile. Neighbors hung out windows watching the scene while onlookers pressed up against the cars to get a better view. All the while, paparazzi kept snapping. British police, as well as Secret Service agents, were there to make sure things didn't get too rowdy, as the rapport Jackie shared with people who came to see her was not unlike the affection and coy give-and-take that Princess Diana would show her fans decades later.

"How do you feel about having lunch with the Queen?" someone shouted.

"It's a great honor, and it is very kind of the Queen to invite me," Jackie responded. She also confided in the press corps, "I'm feeling full of beans and very excited about having lunch with the Queen."

As she made her way to the street, a photographer called out, asking her to wave. "Why should I wave?" she responded, ducking into a car. "I'm not leaving yet." But then she was gone.

Jackie was silent, anxious and excited, on the short ride, but while her earlier interaction with the Queen hadn't exactly prompted a close friendship, she had nothing to worry about in returning to the palace, especially since all matters of protocol had been sorted earlier in the week, including whether or not she needed to curtsy to Elizabeth. (As the wife of a head of state, it was not necessary, especially on an unofficial solo visit such as this one.) Crowds met her once again upon her arrival at Buckingham Palace. Roughly five hundred people were gathered on the steps of the Victoria Memorial to watch her drive up to the royal residence.

The day's luncheon was an intimate party in the 1844 room overlooking the palace gardens, and the guest list was filled with familiar names, including Andrew Cavendish, Duke of Devonshire (the brother-in-law of the late Kick Kennedy), the Queen's private secretary Michael Adeane, and Ambassador Bruce, among others. Prime Minister Harold MacMillan sat next to Jackie for the meal. "She was very agreeable, and flattering," he recalled. "She assured me of the President's devotion to me!" (He had less kind things to say about the woman on his other side, Mrs. Bruce, the second wife of Ambassador Bruce. "I found her rather intense. She understands Modern Art and has theories about the Ballet . . ." he wrote in his diary.)

Whether or not Jackie's introduction to the Queen had been less than perfect the year prior, this second meeting offered them a moment of genuine connection. They talked about their shared experiences in India and Pakistan, and over the course of the meal, the similarities between these two women became apparent to anyone who cared to look closely enough. Elizabeth, a few weeks shy of age thirty-six, and Jackie, age thirty-two, were simply two young mothers in the blinding spotlight, with enormous visibility and influence but few official avenues for true political impact. Instead, they deftly practiced soft diplomacy, influencing the perception of their respective countries with a gloved wave. Publicly, they played similar roles, and privately, even if they didn't discuss it, both were intimately familiar with what it meant to be married to a proud, confident man with a wandering eye. They talked about their children, but perhaps where they found the most common ground was in their shared love of horses. Ambassador Bruce noted that the Queen spoke of little else during the lunch, but this wasn't a passing obsession for either woman.

Legend has it that Jackie's mother, Janet, first propped her up on a horse at the age of one, and that's all it took. Similarly, Queen Elizabeth's interest in the animals was sparked at age four when she was given a Shetland pony named Peggy by her grandfather King George V. But regardless of when the fascination began, for both women, it was a lifelong love and a rare personal interest.

"I think it's the Queen's only private hobby," John Warren, the Queen's racing adviser, once said. "Something that takes her away from her commitment and her duties." She was at ease with horses, and riding and watching racing gave her a brief reprieve from her public responsibilities as monarch. It allowed her to be herself, simply Elizabeth, not Her Majesty.

"When the Queen was with horses, she was a horse person," her friend the American horse trainer Monty Roberts recalled after the British monarch's death. "She didn't want to be the queen."

Jackie, too, found solace in spending time with the animals.

Speaking about her late husband, Jackie said, "He liked to see me ride—he always said Daddy told him 'Keep her riding and she'll always be in a good mood.'"

Jackie's cousin John H. Davis even drew the conclusion that her love for horses grew out of a childhood need to escape her dysfunctional family. "I did not realize it at the time, but now I believe her obsession with horses stemmed from her desperately unhappy home life," he wrote.

Jackie's Secret Service agent Clint Hill said of the two women: "They had a good relationship. I know that the press has sometimes written it otherwise, but that's not really true. The relationship was friendly, much more warm than it was cold." Hill escorted her to the luncheon, but not inside, as the palace was the purview of Scotland Yard. "They had small children and they had horses—two things that they could discuss forever," he said.

Indeed, at the luncheon, Jackie shared how she had received a beautiful sable-colored horse named Sardar from President Mohammad Ayub Khan of Pakistan. "It is my hope that every time you ride, you will remember with fondness the time you spent in Pakistan," he said. To which Jackie replied, "He is magnificent." The gift, while personal, thoughtful, and much appreciated, was something of a surprise and caused quite the logistical quagmire, as Jackie's team had been wholly unprepared to transport the animal home—much less how to navigate quarantining the horse for health and safety reasons while remaining respectful to the government and people of Pakistan. (Clint later recalled thinking, "How the hell am I going to get that damn horse back to Washington?") Like Jackie, Queen Elizabeth had received a horse from Khan, a beautiful thoroughbred bay gelding named Sultan, in 1959.

Two months after the lunch, in May 1962, the Queen recalled their conversation in a letter to President Kennedy. "It was a great pleasure to meet Mrs. Kennedy again when she came here to lunch in March. I hope her Pakistan horse will be a success," the Queen wrote, referencing Sardar. "Please tell her that mine became very excited by jumping with the children's ponies during the holidays, so I hope hers will be calmer!" She signed it, "Your sincere friend, Elizabeth R."

When Jackie arrived back at the Radziwill residence after the meal, she was met once again by a swarm of gawkers, curious to hear about her meeting with the Queen. The First Lady simply shared that she'd had a nice English lunch, revealing only that they'd talked about India and their children. "After a while, we were just two mothers," she said.

Other than that, she was tight-lipped with the media. "Her Majesty was so kind to have me there," she said. "I don't think I should say anything about it except for how grateful I am and how charming she was."

She stepped inside, closing the door and escaping the chaos. She was greeted by her sister. "Tell me everything," Lee said.

CHAPTER 8

Nobody's Kid Sister

IT CAN'T BE EASY BEING THE LITTLE SISTER OF A QUEEN—WHETHER she officially holds that title or not.

There's a natural comparison to be made between Jackie Kennedy's younger sister, Lee, and Princess Margaret. In a fairer world, perhaps Margaret would have been monarch and Lee, First Lady. They were more glamorous than their older sisters, more stylish, more outgoing. They relished attention and sought out beauty, but as fate would have it, the spotlight would always favor their siblings.

"She was marvelous," Jackie said of Lee in an interview after the tour of India and Pakistan, acknowledging how difficult it had been for her sister to be on the trip but not the focus of attention. "It must have been trying sometimes. Though we'd often ride together, sometimes I'd go ahead with the most interesting person, and Lee would follow along five cars behind and, by the time I got there, I couldn't even find her. I was so proud of her—and we would always have such fun laughing about little things when the day was over. Nothing could ever come between us."

Popular culture has long been obsessed with sisters, both real and imagined: the Mitfords, the Bennets, the Marches, the Hiltons, the Obamas, the Kardashians. And the Bouviers and the Windsors captivated the media, occupying similar roles on either side of the pond. Jackie and Elizabeth were dutiful and sophisticated, if somewhat staid, never putting a foot wrong or faltering in the public eye; Lee and Margaret were vivacious, exciting, a bit scandalous—always inspiring a newspaper headline—and unlucky in marriage, but they were *fun*.

To a degree, the same could be said of Kate Middleton and her sister, Pippa. As Kate's relationship with Prince William became serious, all eyes turned to the two Middleton girls. Kate has a younger brother, James, as well, but more often the conversation centered on Kate and Pippa, the "Wisteria sisters," as some less-than-kind publications called them. (If the gardening metaphor is lost on you, it's a play on the idea that they were thought to be . . . *ambitious* in their dating lives, social climbers akin to the aggressive vines of a wisteria plant.)

Like Lee and Margaret before her, Pippa has been described as more outgoing than her older sister, and perhaps more naturally inclined toward a life in the public eye. Early on, she was a fixture on the social circuit. In 2008, Pippa even took first place in *Tatler*'s Little Black Book of the most eligible singletons in the UK, ahead of actors, models, musicians, and blue-blood aristocrats, including Princesses Beatrice and Eugenie (who were deemed "definitely the coolest members of the royal family") and Princes William and Harry (the magazine described them simply as "hearty 'n' solid"). Kate didn't make the list. The publication wasn't entirely kind to the youngest Middleton in its rankings, hinting at the family's middle-class roots. "Catherine's li'l sis, this perma-tanned Chelsea girl confines herself to über-beefy toff types. Low-maintenance; you'll find her working out at the council gym on Chelsea Manor Street. Goes to a lot of parties, but mainly as the caterer."

When Kate eventually married Prince William in 2011, some would argue that Pippa stole the show (or at least drew some attention away from the bride) as she walked into Westminster Abbey in a form-fitting custom satin gown designed by Sarah Burton for Alexander McQueen. Dubbed "Her Royal Hotness," Pippa—or perhaps more accurately, her rear end—became an international fascination.

It's an association Pippa didn't necessarily shy away from. In her 2012 book, *Celebrate: A Year of Festivities for Families and Friends*, she fully acknowledged the source of her fame: "It is a bit startling to achieve global recognition before the age of 30 on account of your sister, your brother-in-law and your bottom," she wrote. "I certainly have opportunities many can only dream of, but in most ways I'm a typical girl in her 20s trying to forge a career and represent herself in what can sometimes seem rather strange circumstances."

She also became a regular contributor to several publications: *Vanity Fair, The Spectator, The Telegraph*, and the promotional food magazine of the British supermarket brand Waitrose. (Her columns primarily focused on fitness, sporting events, entertaining, and easy recipes . . . but often referenced her most well-known asset. "No year is complete without a bottom story, and the 'Rear of 2014' award undoubtedly goes to Kim Kardashian," she wrote in a December 2014 column in *The Spectator* titled "Pippa Middleton on Wine, Fishing and Kim Kardashian." "I must say that mine—though it has enjoyed fleeting fame—is not comparable.")

Those gigs were short-lived. Later, she penned a second cookbook, called *Heartfelt*, which benefited the British Heart Foundation, but any attempt to carve out a career for herself was met with less-than-kind press attention. "Pippa's Book a Bum-mer," teased the *New York Post* about *Celebrate*. She is rumored to have received an advance of £400,000 from publisher Penguin Books for the party-planning guide. "Pippa Middleton's Getting a Bum Deal Here," quipped the headline for a Victoria Coren opinion column in *The Guardian*. A *Daily Mail* story, headlined "I'm Not Saying It's Basic, but It's Perfect for Anyone Who Needs a Recipe for Making Ice," asked, "Would she really have gained a lucrative publishing contract to write about something she calls 'simple, creative entertaining' if her sister were not married to a member of the Royal Family?"

Pippa faced an almost impossible dilemma, one likely understood by both Lee and Margaret. "Kate married William and she had this intense level of scrutiny, all of this interest, but she had a role, she had a job to do; she was stepping into a new life and that life was mapped out for her. Whereas Pippa had this intense level of scrutiny, and James as well, but yet they didn't have a job. They didn't have a life mapped out," explained royal commentator Victoria Murphy.

While her sister's path was set out for her, Pippa had to forge her own identity under the unforgiving glare of media attention. "By all accounts, we get the impression that Pippa is the one who is slightly more outgoing, who is perhaps more suited to a career where there was an element of public speaking. She seems more comfortable with that than Kate, who is more naturally reserved," Murphy continued. "So she may have suited some kind of career in the media or some kind of public-facing role, but it's incredibly difficult for her to do those jobs because people are, for a start, people accuse her of only having those positions, of only having those opportunities, because of her sister . . . And then also everything that she does within those positions is constantly looked at through the lens of 'How would the royal family feel about this?'"

Criticism was harsh regarding Pippa's career ambitions, but the press could also be downright cruel about her appearance. "Does Pippa Dress in the Dark?" asked the *Daily Mail* in 2013, declaring not only that she lacked style and that her clothes looked like "potato sacks," but also calling her knees "knobbly" and admonishing her for not wearing a bra, describing her breasts as "loll[ing]."

"I have felt publicly bullied a little bit just when I read things,"

Pippa told Matt Lauer during an interview, which aired on *The Today Show* in June 2014. "It is quite difficult because I'm just trying to pave my way and try to live a life like any thirty-year-old." But when speaking directly about her sister, she was vague, and supportive, saying only: "Obviously she has pressures that she's taken on and things. But we spend a lot of time together. We still do a lot together as a family . . . We have a very normal, sisterly relationship. We're very close. And, you know, we support each other and get each other's opinions and things."

Pippa has since largely faded into the background, despite the fact that one day her sister will be queen. She is now married and has kids, and has seemingly left behind any ambitions for a public-facing career. She's demonstrated an unwavering loyalty to Kate, overlooking any difficulties she's encountered thanks to her sister's choice of partner. "You have to think about how discreet she has been over these years. I think what people always forget is when somebody marries into the royal family, they are marrying into the royal family, but their whole family is, that whole family's life is, completely changed forever," Murphy said.

"She couldn't really get going in a lot of the things that she might have wanted to do with her life. But now obviously she really seems to have found a great situation for herself. And in many ways you do feel that Pippa is living the life that Kate would be living had she not married into the royal family."

IN CONTRAST TO PIPPA, LEE WAS NEVER ONE TO SHY AWAY FROM the public eye. In the late 1960s, after her brother-in-law died, Lee pursued a career in acting, saying around that time, "My ambition is to be a working actress who is offered things of quality. I feel I have an intensity to bring to acting—it is just something I feel I can do, I'd like to do new plays or films. Tennessee Williams, [Truman] Capote, interesting older women, alcoholics. I have the greatest sympathy for those who end in despair."

But when she made her debut as Tracy Lord in the revival of *The Philadelphia Story*, a production that premiered in Chicago in 1967, reviews were not kind. "A new star is not born," wrote the *Chicago Tribune*. The following year, she starred as Laura in her friend Truman Capote's television adaptation of the 1944 film noir *Laura*. Again, she failed to impress. "She is just not an actress," wrote *Variety*.

Lee never acted again after that, and while her fire for performing dimmed, she didn't slink away. With the help of her friend William "Bill" Paley, the founder and chairman of CBS, she launched a half-hour TV show called *Conversations with Lee Radziwill*, in which she filmed sit-downs with her famous friends (think feminist activist Gloria Steinem, diplomat John Kenneth Galbraith, and designer Halston). She conducted six interviews, but the show didn't move forward. Later, she worked as an interior designer and as the special events director for Giorgio Armani (in addition to being his muse). She wrote multiple books, though never a tell-all, saying that "would hurt people," and she toured with the Rolling Stones. She lived a vibrant life, but she could never escape her sister's shadow.

"It's the subject you never bring up," fashion editor André Leon Talley explained in a 2016 interview with *Vanity Fair*. "I mean, there's an unspoken rule that if you're friends with Lee you don't talk about her sister at all." It's a topic she struggled with for decades. In 1976, she told *People*, "I'm nobody's kid sister." The quote ended up on the cover of the magazine. For the same story, Truman Capote gushed about his friend, but in his praise there was still a comparison to Jackie. "She's a remarkable girl. She's all the things people give Jackie [Onassis] credit for. All the looks, style, taste—Jackie never had them at all, and yet it was Lee who lived in the shadow of this super-something person."

She couldn't escape it, even in death. Despite her own accomplishments and fame, her role as a sibling eclipsed any sort of unique identity. The headline of her 2019 *New York Times* obituary read, "Lee Radziwill, Ex-Princess and Sister of Jacqueline Kennedy Onassis, Dies at 85."

THE PARALLELS BETWEEN LEE AND MARGARET ARE MORE THAN SYM-bolic; they also knew each other socially. While Jackie had married into American royalty, it actually was Lee who had more than one brush with European aristocracy. In 1953, Lee married Michael Canfield, but that marriage wasn't meant to last. It was later annulled so that Lee could marry Prince Stanisław, of the Polish-Lithuanian house of Radziwill, making Lee a true princess in her own right. That said, while formalities were by all accounts very important to Princess Margaret, Lee "didn't care about the princess thing," her good friend Alejandra Cicognani said. "She was a princess even without a title, I can tell you that. She behaved like one, but it was an addition to who she was. That title did not define her at all."

Though Princess Margaret wasn't present at the Kennedys' famous dinner at Buckingham Palace, she and Lee crossed paths on a number of occasions: at a 1982 party at the Houston home of socialite Lynn Wyatt, for example, and a rare holiday at the Radziwills' country estate, Turville Grange in Buckinghamshire. They were friendly if not close friends, perhaps joined together by the all-too-familiar feeling of what a charmed life, albeit two steps behind one's sister, could feel like.

In 2016, journalist and former *Vanity Fair* editor Tina Brown, who has written multiple books about the royal family, grouped Pippa, Margaret, and Lee together in a recap of the Netflix drama *The Crown*. "Being the younger sister of a queen bee is always a buzz kill. Just ask Lee Radziwill or Pippa Middleton," she wrote. "Younger sisters seem fated to be racier, more transgressive and more criticized. They seethe with suppressed rebellion." Of course, she was referencing a fictionalized version of Margaret with her words, one whose emotions were dramatized to suit the story, but it's undeniable that, like Lee and Pippa, Princess Margaret had a challenging relationship with both her sister and the press.

"When my sister and I were growing up, she was made out to be the goody goody one. That wasn't interesting, so the press tried to say I was wicked as hell," Margaret said in the 1960s.

Early on, after her father became king following her uncle's abdication in December 1936, Margaret began to realize that she and her sister no longer held the same positions in the rigid structure of the monarchy. Elizabeth was being groomed to become queen, and Margaret was royal, yes, but positioned lower in the family hierarchy. Her sister was heir, and she was the spare. While Elizabeth was tutored in constitutional history, Margaret's education was less extensive, and according to her lady-in-waiting Lady Anne Glenconner, that discrepancy bothered Margaret. She "always said, 'I was never educated as well as my sister in order not to be a sort of threat to her.' That's what she felt."

According to another one of her ladies-in-waiting, Jane Stevens, Margaret said this divergence in education "'was the first time I sort of thought or realized that my sister was going to be Queen and I wouldn't really be part of what she was going to do.' It hit her quite hard that their lives were going to be completely different."

While Elizabeth's future was clearly laid out, Margaret's was less so. She would have all the trappings of a royal life, the tiaras and gowns and the invitations to exclusive events, as well as the public scrutiny, but without the explicit purpose of being head of state. And that's why her lack of education bothered her. "I think she was afraid of being belittled, but what role can you have next to the Queen? I don't know," her friend Lady Jane Rayne said. "She was intelligent, but it was never put to any sort of good use. I think that's all that was expected of her. Do good work, marry somebody, and have lots of little princesses."

But her love life, too, was dictated by the rigid rules of the royal family, and no doubt there were tensions between the sisters when Margaret was not allowed to marry her first love, Peter Townsend, because he was divorced. Initially, under the 1772 Royal Marriages Act, Margaret needed to seek permission from her sister to wed. As the head of the Church of England, Elizabeth would not grant it.

Margaret and Peter were told to wait until the princess was twenty-five—but even then, Margaret would have had to give up her position in the order of succession to the throne to marry. Eventually, in 1955, she released a statement confirming that she would not give up her royal life for this man. "I would like it to be known that I have decided not to marry Group Captain Peter Townsend. I have been aware that, subject to my renouncing my rights of succession, it might have been possible for me to contract a civil marriage," she said. "But mindful of the Church's teachings that Christian marriage is indissoluble, and conscious of my duty to the Commonwealth, I have resolved to put these considerations before others. I have reached this decision entirely alone, and in doing so I have been strengthened by the unfailing support and devotion of Group Captain Townsend."

One can imagine that the frustrations Margaret felt were only made worse by her sister's ability to marry for love, choosing her "strength and stay" Prince Philip at age eighteen and never even considering anyone else, and amplified again later when Margaret's marriage to Antony Armstrong-Jones failed, culminating in divorce. But if you're looking for evidence that the sisters were close throughout their lives, it's not difficult to find. They talked to each other nearly every day. A phone with a direct line to Buckingham Palace sat atop Princess Margaret's desk in Kensington Palace. And when Margaret died in 2002, the stoic Queen Elizabeth was seen crying, in a rare public display of emotion.

WHILE *THE TELEGRAPH* HAS SUGGESTED THAT MARGARET WAS AT least at one point "subconsciously jealous" of her sister, many have detailed the explicit rivalry between Lee and Jackie. In 1962, Truman Capote, the American novelist and collector of "society swans," wrote to his friend the photographer Cecil Beaton after dining with Lee: "Had lunch one day with your new friend Princess Lee (My God, how jealous she is of Jackie: I never knew)." It started early. Even as a child, Lee realized that her father "favored Jackie." "That was very clear to me, but I didn't resent it, because I understood he had reason to," she wrote in her 2000 book *Happy Times*.

The rivalry only grew when Jackie married Aristotle Onassis in 1968, just five years after Jack died. Publicly, Lee said, "I am very happy to have been at the origin of this marriage, which will, I am certain, bring my sister the happiness she deserves." Privately, she felt betrayed, reportedly calling Capote in anguish saying, "How could she do this to me!"

Lee had reportedly carried on a relationship with the Greek shipping magnate, whom she later described as "magnetic." When asked if she had ever thought about marrying him, Lee quipped, "Who didn't?"

The nature of the sisters' relationship was complex, and any friction was far from one-sided. When Jackie died in 1994, she didn't leave any money to her younger sister, a move widely interpreted to symbolize the ongoing strife between the sisters. "I have made no provision in this, my will for my sister, Lee B. Radziwill, for whom I have great affection, because I have already done so during my lifetime," her will read. She did leave bequests for each of Lee's two children. But despite any long-standing hostility, Lee was there at Jackie's bedside the day before she died. "I love you so much," she told her. "I always have, Jacks. I hope you know it."

There is an inherent duality to sisterhood. A sister is both one's earliest competition and a true lifelong companion, someone with a shared history and, oftentimes, the ultimate confidant because the backstory to any situation can remain unsaid. Despite any animosity Lee and Margaret undoubtedly felt for their sisters, there was real love there, and a closeness prompted by a level of understanding that no one else could offer. In a world of transactional relationships, of grifters, and social climbers, it was hard for both Jackie and Elizabeth to know whom to trust. For that reason, they kept their circles intentionally small, but their sisters were always on the inside.

"Lee Radziwill was always painted as less perfect perhaps. It is difficult if you are two sisters and one has everything. One has a glistening career like Jackie did, or the Queen had everything. It must be difficult. But Princess Margaret coped with it very, very well actually, I thought," Lady Anne Glenconner said of her friend, making a comparison to Jackie's sister.

"Princess Margaret was very, very loyal. She had a difficult marriage, which was sad. But she was extremely brave, and she never dwelt, she never whined, she never complained or said 'Why me?' or 'My sister's got everything.' Nothing like that."

In fact, Margaret once said that she tried to help her sister however she could. "In my own humble way I've always tried to take some of the burden off my sister. She can't do it all, you know, and I leap at the opportunity to help," the princess told author Andrew Duncan in 1969.

As a child, Princess Elizabeth understood Margaret's social prowess, reportedly telling her nanny, "Oh, it's so much easier when Margaret's there—everybody laughs at what Margaret says." Upon ascension to the throne in 1952, Elizabeth became the embodiment of duty, of power and dignity, the symbol of a country, an empire, and a people. "My sister has an aura," Margaret once said. "I'm enormously impressed when she walks into a room. It's a kind of magic." Margaret, too, though, had her own kind of magic—a charm and a curiosity all her own—and she used it to serve her sister.

Pippa doesn't have a position within the monarchy, but that hasn't stopped her from being a source of support for her sister, particularly in recent years as Kate handled both a cancer diagnosis and treatment in the public eye. "Pippa has been something of an angel and backbone for Catherine," one source told the tabloid *Daily Express*. "She's there at the drop of a hat, helping to pick up the slack on physical tasks when needed. But it's the emotional support she provides that is invaluable to Catherine."

And when Jackie needed her the most, Lee was there. "It's just the most ludicrous talk in the world that we're rivals," Lee told *People* in 1976. "We're exceptionally close and always have been. We're together very often. In fact, endlessly."

Lee offered support when Jackie's son Patrick was born prematurely and died at just two days old in August 1963. "My impression of Lee's relationship with Jackie is that she loved her sister," Cicognani said. "There might have been a little bit of a disconnect at times, but she loved her. She is the one that rescued Jackie when she was depressed and invited her to England and consoled her after her son died, Patrick."

Just a few months later, Lee was in London with her husband Stas when she heard the news of President Kennedy's death. "It was in the evening, in London. Stas came running up the stairs, his voice and face in shock," Lee would recall many years later. "I started crying . . . uncontrollably. For hours."

But she pulled herself together and flew to DC as soon as possible. According to the First Lady's Secret Service agent Clint Hill, Lee did "everything she could to support her sister." It wasn't always easy. Lee would later claim that she "had gone through hell" to help her sister.

"She came to Washington. She got there before Stas did; a day before, to be with Mrs. Kennedy," Hill noted. And on the day of JFK's funeral, Lee was there in the background, quietly serving as a pillar of strength for her sister. After the burial, she reportedly left a note on Jackie's pillow, which read: "Good night my darling Jacks—the bravest and noblest of all. L."

CHAPTER 9

The Death of a President

On November 22, 1963, John F. Kennedy was shot and killed as he rode in a motorcade through Dealey Plaza in Dallas. News of JFK's assassination was confirmed in the UK at 7:27 p.m. local time, but unlike the iconic moment when trusted broadcaster Walter Cronkite removed his glasses to inform a shocked nation that their president was dead, Kennedy's murder was reported on the BBC by a relatively unknown newsreader, John Roberts. Roberts was on duty that night as all the network's biggest names were attending the Guild of Television Producers and Directors Awards (the precursor to the British Academy of Film and Television Arts Awards) at the Dorchester Hotel.

Queen Elizabeth was shocked and horrified when she heard of President Kennedy's death. She and Prince Philip were visiting their friends Sir Harold and Lady Zia Wernher at their lavish country house, Luton Hoo, when they got word of the tragedy. Immediately, she began drafting emergency messages to both President Lyndon Johnson and Jackie Kennedy, which were to be delivered via the Foreign Office.

"I am so deeply distressed to learn of the tragic death of President

Kennedy," Elizabeth wrote to Jackie. "My husband joins me in sending our heartfelt and sincere sympathy to you and to your family."

To the newly sworn-in Johnson, she extended her condolences beyond the Kennedy family to include the government, Congress, and the people of the United States. She had been on the receiving end of such notes eleven years prior, when her father had died. "My deepest sympathy goes out to the British people," President Harry Truman had said. "God bless Queen Elizabeth and may her father's exemplary memory provide the courage and inspiration she will need in the great responsibilities that lie before her." But while the anguish of loss is keenly felt regardless of the circumstance, the broader response to Kennedy's death was quite different from that of the King. Elizabeth's father had been sick, and his death was not entirely unexpected, in contrast to the abrupt violence of Kennedy's murder.

The way Queen Elizabeth responded to the President's assassination was similar to the reaction of her people. As the devastating details spread, a wave of grief swept over the United Kingdom. Prime Minister Alec Douglas-Home was new to his post; in his words, he had "barely taken charge of the Government when President Kennedy was assassinated," having succeeded Harold Macmillan in October 1963. Douglas-Home was struck by the depth of the British response, especially among the youth in the country. Teens in London, he said, were "just distraught, openly crying in the streets although they had never seen President Kennedy."

Certainly, there were detractors who disagreed with Kennedy's policies, but the President was widely admired in the UK. He had made an enormous impact in a very short time, and many were moved by the vitality of his administration. Not just the visual of a young family in the White House, in contrast to the series of gray-haired prime ministers in their own country, but also the hopeful commitment to putting a man on the moon and Kennedy's contribution to the civil rights movement. So when news broke of his death, people were aghast.

"Things became flat. Many people couldn't handle his loss; their true colors began to show. The carefree and exciting times vanished," Lee Radziwill said of those days right after her brother-in-law's death. Ten days before the assassination, Radziwill and her husband had dined with Queen Elizabeth and Prince Philip at the residence of the American ambassador, David Bruce. Despite the Queen being pregnant with her fourth child, Prince Edward, she "was ready and gay in conversation, as was her husband," the ambassador recalled. Little did they know, tragedy would rock the world less than two weeks later.

Following the BBC broadcast, crowds in London immediately started making their way to the US embassy in Grosvenor Square to pay tribute. People left flowers and crowded into the Chancery to sign books of condolence. For the next few days, men came straight from work, some even in stained clothes, lining up to offer even a small gesture of sympathy. Many simply inscribed their names, while others wrote short messages: "In respect and admiration of a great statesman, and courageous man," read one note. "To express my deepest distress," read another. The day after the assassination, at a performance of Chekhov's *Uncle Vanya* at the Old Vic theater, Sir Laurence Olivier asked the audience to stand for two minutes of remembrance, a silence broken only by the orchestra playing "The Star-Spangled Banner."

But amid the grief and shock and fear, there was no time to wallow. As Jackie began planning her husband's funeral, political leaders and members of the royal family were frantically discussing who would represent the United Kingdom at the memorial for Kennedy in the US, and what official tributes would look like in the UK.

Early on, there was talk of multiple services for Kennedy in the

States, including a Mass at St. Matthew's Cathedral in DC, the church where he and Jackie worshipped, and a more intimate funeral in Boston, where the President had grown up. From the beginning, it seemed almost certain that the British government and the Queen would need to be represented at the memorial in Washington.

UK GOVERNMENT CORRESPONDENCE IN THE DAYS AFTER KENNEdy's death shows the pace at which decisions were made, and how quickly both the royals and the prime minister recognized the need for a personal presence at the funeral. At 12:43 a.m., five hours after news of Kennedy's death broke, the prime minister had "it in mind to attend President Kennedy's funeral in Washington." And by 1:15 p.m. the following day, he had "definitely decided to come himself."

Queen Elizabeth, too, wanted to attend the funeral in the US, but given that she was expecting, that wasn't an option. So she did what she could. The morning after Kennedy's death, the tenor bell at Westminster Abbey tolled every minute between 11 a.m. and noon in the President's honor, and she ordered the royal court to observe a full week of mourning—a rare distinction for someone outside the royal family, and an American, no less.

It was also decided that Prince Philip would fly to the States in Elizabeth's stead, along with a delegation representing the United Kingdom. Initially, the Duke of Edinburgh thought there would be no rush to make it to the US, reportedly saying that "it would take at least two weeks to plan and execute such a funeral." But he was clearly mistaken.

Shortly after she returned to DC with the body of her slain husband, Jackie started making arrangements. She understood that a swift funeral could offer a moment of peace in the chaos, and be the first step toward healing for a nation in distress. But she was also keenly aware that these memorial services, filled with pomp and circumstance and symbolism, were a performance of grief on a world stage and would become the foundation on which the Kennedy legacy would be built.

And so, she sat at her desk on the second floor of the White House, near the windows overlooking the Rose Garden, and began to doodle, scribbling lists filled with names and reminders. The Queen was seemingly among the key guests in her notes: "Salinger, Mr. West, Clifton, Queen, de Gaulle, Bishop Hannan, Taylor, Tish," and so on. Her designs for memorial services would take inspiration from those for Franklin D. Roosevelt and Ulysses S. Grant, but perhaps most poignantly, she asked the chief usher, J. B. West, to follow the protocol and details of Abraham Lincoln's 1865 state funeral, which took place just four days after he died.

On November 24, just two days after President Kennedy's death, a select group met at London Airport to board a special British Overseas Airways Corporation plane. The group included Prime Minister Alec and Elizabeth Douglas-Home, as well as Harold Wilson (the leader of the opposition party), and Lord Andrew Cavendish (Kick's brother-in-law) and his wife, Deborah. The size of the delegation was so large that David Ormsby-Gore even apologized for "hogging space" in the church. Harold Macmillan didn't travel to DC for the service, as he was not feeling up for it. Kennedy's death, he wrote in his diary, was "a staggering blow."

Prince Philip arrived exactly on time and the group took off for Washington.

Early in the flight, Philip called his traveling companions to the front of the plane for what Deborah would go on to describe as "one of the strangest dinners of my life." At a small table, she sat next to Mr. Wilson and across from the Duke of Edinburgh, and the two men "started talking about aeroplanes . . . in such an incredible, technical way that it was quite impossible to listen to them and I found my mind wandering." (She kept her thoughts about Wilson's dirty fingernails to herself—at least until she described them in the notes of her memoir.) Her husband was nearby, eating and conversing with the prime minister across the aisle.

"If it hadn't been for such a sad sad reason, the journeys there & back would have been rather fascinating," Deborah wrote in a letter to writer and WWII hero Patrick Leigh Fermor days after returning home. "We got a lift off the Prime Minister who had chartered a Boeing 707. The passengers were him & Lady Douglas-Home, the Duke of Edinburgh, Mr. Wilson, Sir Philip de Zulueta, Sir Timothy Bligh, Sir Harold Evans, 2 girl typists, 2 detectives, the D of E's ADC & Andrew & me & 150 empty seats behind."

David Ormsby-Gore and his wife, Sissie, whose eyes were red from crying, met the party at Dulles airport in Washington, DC, and shared the latest news: Lee Harvey Oswald, the man who had been arrested for Kennedy's assassination, had been shot dead.

With that update looming over their arrival, Prince Philip and the Prime Minister Douglas-Home greeted a number of ambassadors— many from Commonwealth countries—as well as members of the British military, before the delegation piled into cars and set off for the British embassy. The procession, which was flanked by police cruisers, did not stop, not even for red lights, on the drive to the stately compound on Massachusetts Avenue.

As the group settled into the drawing room with drinks, they discussed how "chaotic" the funeral planning had been and how quickly it had come together, while across the city, people lined up to pay their respects to President Kennedy, whose flag-draped coffin was lying in state in the Capitol Rotunda. It sat atop Lincoln's catafalque.

The line of mourners doubled back upon itself for sixteen blocks as people waited in the bitter cold to spend a few moments with the late President. The enormous crowd would be rivaled perhaps only by that at the funeral of Princess Diana in 1997, or that of the Queen in 2022.

"I'll never forget coming out of the Capitol, and lined up outside were roughly two hundred fifty thousand people who had just gathered there because they wanted to walk past the President's coffin," Secret Service agent Clint Hill said. "And we saw that in London, where they lined up to walk past the coffin of Queen Elizabeth. They were just two people held in such high regard that people, the general population, wanted to be close, wanted to pay their respects."

The morning of November 25 was bright and blue and cold. At 11 a.m., Kennedy's coffin left the Capitol on a horse-drawn carriage to return to the White House one last time. There, it was met by a crowd of dignitaries—including Prince Philip and the prime minister—waiting to accompany Jackie and the rest of the Kennedy family on the short walk to St. Matthew's Cathedral for the memorial service.

There was no precedent for an American First Lady walking in a funeral procession like this one, but Jackie had refused to ride to the Mass "in a fat black Cadillac." And so, the widow, with her face covered by a traditional Catholic mourning veil, followed her husband's coffin as it traveled the half mile to the church, her two brothers-in-law, Bobby (by now attorney general) and Ted, by her side. As they set off for St. Matthew's, church bells boomed.

Wearing a black Givenchy dress and jacket paired with black gloves and pointy-toe pumps, Jackie "walked with a poise and grace that words cannot convey—as regal as any emperor, queen, or prince who followed her," wrote *National Geographic* editor Melville Bell Grosvenor, who watched the scene from a fourth-floor window. Lady Jeanne Campbell, who covered the funeral for the *Evening Standard*, wrote that Jackie had "given the American people from this day on the one thing they had always lacked—majesty."

She never looked back, but if she had, she would have seen that right behind her were her half brother Jamie Auchincloss and her brothers-in-law Sargent Shriver and Steve Smith. Not far behind them were President Johnson and his wife, as well as their two children, who rode in a limousine to the church. They were trailed by a strictly organized procession including foreign heads of state and diplomats, former presidents, Supreme Court justices, cabinet members, congressional leadership, and members of the Joint Chiefs of Staff, as well as personal assistants and close friends of President Kennedy's.

At least twenty-two presidents or prime ministers, three reigning monarchs, and princes or princesses from nine different countries could be found in the cortège, along with delegations headed by foreign ministers or ambassadors from nearly every nation with which the United States had diplomatic relations. It was believed to be the largest gathering of royals and diplomats since the state funeral of King Edward VII in 1910.

Wearing the rich blue uniform of the Royal Navy, the Duke of Edinburgh walked alongside Prince Bernhard of the Netherlands and Prince Gholam-Reza Pahlavi of Iran as they made their way to the cathedral. The procession included live music by a small regiment of pipers from the Black Watch Pipes and Drums.

Earlier in the month, at one of President Kennedy's final public appearances, the regiment had performed for the First Family and a crowd of area schoolchildren on the South Lawn of the White House, and Jackie had been "most anxious" for them to be a part of the funeral. David Ormsby-Gore arranged for nine of the pipers to travel to Washington to perform. "I hope that this is in accordance with the wishes of Her Majesty The Queen and Her Majesty The

Queen Mother as Colonel-in-Chief of the regiment," he wrote in a telegram. "It seems to me a notable gesture to both the British Army and the British People." The songs they played were far from traditional mourning ballads; rather, they filled the air with the same tunes they'd played just weeks prior—"The Brown Haired Maiden," "The Badge of Scotland," "The 51st Highland Division," and "The Barren Rocks of Aden." Although now, the mood was quite different.

As the group of world leaders made their way down Connecticut Avenue, security along the route "had their eyes and rifles firmly fixed upwards," as at the time they believed "it was from a roof that the fatal shot which killed the President had come."

Jackie walked into the church at precisely noon. The space could hold only 1,100 people, and so the service was by invitation only. Even then, there was hardly enough room. (Bobby had anticipated this problem, telling Jackie, "I think it's too small." But she wasn't swayed. "I don't care," she replied. "They can all stand in the streets. I just know that's the right place to have it.")

Prince Philip ended up sitting quite far back in the church—in fact, upon arrival, he didn't appear to have a seat, so Douglas-Home's wife made space for him. "Prince Philip, it is true, only got a place in the Cathedral when Elizabeth surrendered her seat to him," the prime minister wrote in his autobiography. "Which was emphatically not the right position for the Consort of the Queen." But he still had to pack into the pew, with his ceremonial sword crowding his neighbors.

Angier "Angie" Biddle Duke, the chief of protocol who had worked tirelessly to organize the funeral, later said, "They were jammed in like sardines. I stood throughout the Mass and suffered. Somehow we had got them all seated, but I hate to think how it was done."

The Mass was led by Cardinal Cushing, a Kennedy family friend who had married Jack and Jackie; just a few months prior, in August

1963, he had officiated the funeral of the couple's infant son Patrick. The Catholic rituals were foreign to most of the English members of the audience—and those watching on-screen. This was not only the first time many Americans saw a Catholic church service, but it also served as arguably the first globally televised live news event, with a satellite feed broadcasting portions of the memorial to British audiences.

The emotion of it all was also unfamiliar to those who had traveled from the UK. "Oh it was strange, Americans aren't suited to tragedy. They like everything to be great," Deborah Cavendish recalled in a letter sent a little more than a week after the service. "I was more or less alright in church till his friends came in & their crumpled miserable faces were too much & it was floods all the way after that. I never wanted to leave anywhere so quickly as that town." Three-year-old John F. Kennedy Jr. touched the flag covering his father's coffin before the child was led away, while Deborah stood crying. She recalled Prince Philip's "stern blue look" as he stood next to her.

While many of the Mass attendees had walked to the church in the procession, Arlington National Cemetery, where President Kennedy would be buried, was a bit farther away. After the service concluded, a traffic jam ensued as a crowd of Kennedy confidants, heads of state, royals, and diplomats milled about on the steps of the church, waiting for their cars.

Angie tried to keep the departures to the cemetery organized, but eventually protocol fell apart as rides came and went in no particular order. Relatively speaking, the ambassador's Rolls Royce arrived rather quickly, and the British delegation joined the procession to Arlington. They arrived just as the last part of the service began, as Air Force jets flew in formation overhead.

After he climbed the hill, using his sword as a sort of walking stick, Prince Philip once again stood toward the back of the crowd of mourners, behind a group of soldiers and somewhat apart from the other foreign visitors who had traveled from across the world for this brief ceremony in Arlington.

Like everything else that day, the President's interment was meticulously planned, albeit in the eleventh hour. It was Jackie's idea to mark the grave with an eternal flame. She was clearly inspired by the fire that burns unyielding at the Tomb of the Unknown Soldier at the Arc de Triomphe in Paris, but also perhaps by T. H. White's *The Candle in the Wind*, the Arthurian novel that tells the story of the fall of Camelot, using the titular flame as an allegory for the fragility of peace. The thought occurred to her as she accompanied her husband's body to the Capitol Rotunda; it "just came into my head," she said.

From there, it was on the US Army Corps of Engineers to realize the widow's vision. "They decided on Sunday they wanted the eternal flame. The funeral was on Monday. So suddenly, again a mission arrived to the Chief of Engineers, this time to produce an eternal flame by the time of the burial in the morning," Lieutenant General Walter K. Wilson Jr. recalled in an oral history. Despite the short timeline, they were able to make it happen. At the end of the burial service, Jackie, alongside Bobby and Ted, took a torch from her military escort to light the flame.

"Jackie looked tragic, with tears glistening on her veil, and Rose so very pathetic," Deborah later wrote. "The Kennedys are so good when things are going well but they are not equipped for tragedy."

AFTER THE INTERMENT, THE BRITISH DELEGATION DROVE BACK to the embassy around 4 p.m., to do what is done in happy times and in sad. "There was a great sense of sorry and emptiness everywhere. We drank a lot of tea," Deborah wrote. Not long after that, Prince Philip left to attend a reception at the White House.

A consummate hostess even on her most difficult day, Jackie threw an event for diplomats at the White House after the service at Arlington. As she rationalized it, "It would be most ungracious of me not to have all those people in our house." As they started to arrive, she asked other members of the Kennedy family to greet the foreign guests, so Ted, Eunice, Pat, and Jean started the first reception line in the Red Room. Jackie then called Evelyn Lincoln and asked her to keep Rose Kennedy company while she freshened up and removed her mourning veil and hat. "I have to comb my hair for all these dignitaries," she said.

While Angie Duke, in his role as chief of protocol of the United States, was charged with making sure no leader (and therefore no country) felt slighted, the first widow had her own way of approaching things.

Of all the dignitaries, Prince Philip was one of only four men she wanted to see in private, on the second floor of the White House in the Yellow Oval Room—the other three being Emperor Haile Selassie of Ethiopia, President Charles de Gaulle of France, and President Eamon de Valera of Ireland.

The morning of the funeral, Jackie called the White House curator, James Roe Ketchum, to have the Cézannes removed from the family quarters of the White House. "She'd decided to receive certain heads of state there—she singled out Charles de Gaulle, Haile Selassie, and Prince Philip," Ketchum said. "She knew we had just acquired a collection of aquatint views of American cities of about 1800, and she wanted those to replace the Cézannes. She thought the setting should be American."

The sorrowful occasion even made unlikely conversational partners of the Irish politician and the British prince, as Jackie spoke with Selassie and de Gaulle. But Philip's most memorable interaction with Jackie wouldn't come until after de Valera shared a Gerald Griffin poem with the Kennedy family—one President Kennedy had memorized. For the President's brother Bobby, hearing the ode to a river returning once again to its home was what broke him for the first time that day.

When Jackie saw her brother-in-law's stiff upper lip waver, her carefully polished facade also fell, and she started to cry. Ducking into her husband's bedroom for a moment alone to compose herself, she was surprised and a little embarrassed to find her son playing with Prince Philip on the floor. Philip, blushing, immediately shared that John Jr. reminded him of his own son.

"I've got one like that," he had told the Kennedys' nanny Maud Shaw earlier in the reception when he saw her chasing John Jr. down the second-floor corridor. "They're a handful, aren't they?"

"Heavens, you're right," she responded, not realizing who she was talking to. "For a moment, I was unable to place the face—and anyway, I was more concerned with taking John in hand," she would later recall, noting that he was a "kind-looking man." She continued, "It was only after another dozen steps that I suddenly remembered that lean, suntanned face. It was Prince Philip! Horrified at the way I had spoken so casually, I turned round to make some apology—but he had gone."

Jackie quickly regained her composure. "John, did you make your bow to the Prince?" she asked, dipping into her own curtsy. John, who had turned three years old that day, proudly proclaimed that he had, and any remaining awkwardness instantly vanished as the group had a laugh over his enthusiasm. Later in the evening, Angie looked back on that moment with Prince Philip and broke down, remembering how just a few years before, ahead of the Kennedys' dinner at Buckingham Palace, he had advised Jackie that she needn't curtsy to the Queen or Prince Philip, as it wasn't necessary for the wife of the head of state.

"Angie," Jackie said with a sad smile as she bent her knee upon greeting Prince Philip in her dead husband's bedroom. "I'm no longer the wife of a chief of state."

Jackie called her sister, Lee, in for a round of Bloody Marys, while Angie shared his concerns that the former First Lady needed to speak with each of the dignitaries. This was an informal repast, of course, but it was also a key moment of diplomacy for the United States, and it was important that no one feel slighted. Prince Philip suggested a receiving line. "I'd advise you, you know, to have the line. It's really quick and it gets it done," he said. She took the advice, coming downstairs to mingle with distinguished guests in a move that surprised attendees, including her family.

While several members of the British delegation stayed in Washington for a few more days, Prince Philip left that evening, flying first to New York and then on to London. Once he arrived home in the UK, Prince Philip continued to represent Queen Elizabeth at events paying tribute to Kennedy, including the official memorial at St. Paul's Cathedral on December 1. Additional other members of the royal family were also in attendance, including Princess Margaret and her husband, the Earl of Snowdon, along with Princess Marina, Princess Alice, the Duchess of Gloucester, and Princess Mary, the Princess Royal.

While the Queen was not present at the St. Paul's tribute, she hosted a smaller memorial for Kennedy in St. George's Chapel, inviting roughly 350 American servicemen of all ranks and their families into the small church on the grounds of Windsor Castle.

Exactly two weeks after her husband was assassinated, on December 6, 1963, Jackie Kennedy moved out of the White House. A letter she'd sent to her stepbrother Yusha in 1945 poignantly foreshadowed the moment. She'd written of how FDR's death had left her "dazed."

"I feel sorry for poor Mrs. Roosevelt," she wrote. "It will be awfully hard to leave the White House after all those years."

CHAPTER 10

Runnymede

By March 1965, the shock of her husband's violent assassi-nation had started to wear off for Jackie, replaced by a lingering trauma and an unyielding grief. So when Lyndon Johnson proposed that a presidential plane could take the young widow and her family to the upcoming dedication of a British memorial honoring President Kennedy, Jackie hesitated.

Ever polite, she deflected the offer in her signature breathy voice, suggesting that it might be a waste of taxpayer funds for her to em-ploy a government aircraft for such a trip. But Johnson insisted she at least consider it. "It's very important to us, and very important to the country," he said. "You just let me know how you feel after you have a chance to think about it."

It's not hard to imagine Jackie's mind immediately flashing back to the flight home from Dallas, when she stood as witness to John-son's swearing-in on Air Force One, still wearing her bubblegum pink bouclé suit stained with her husband's blood. But on the phone, in that moment, her manners concealed any fears. "Oh, listen, I just don't know what to say," she told Johnson, charming him without sharing her decision yet. "It's the nicest thing I ever heard of."

Eventually, she agreed to President Johnson's suggestion, but had one necessary request. "Please do not let it be Air Force One," she wrote to him, "and please, let it be the 707 that looks least like Air Force One inside." President Johnson obliged, and when Jackie and her two children flew across the Atlantic in May, it was on a plane that had taken her family on vacations to Cape Cod and Palm Beach a few years prior.

The mood on the flight, which also ferried Bobby Kennedy, Ted Kennedy, and a few other invited guests, was lighthearted and nostalgic, despite the melancholy reasoning behind it. John Jr., in particular, was excited to be back on "Daddy's airplane," and both he and Caroline stuffed their faces with candy over the course of the journey. As the children's nanny, Maud Shaw, recalled, "The same Air Force sergeant who had always looked after us was still in the crew, and the children recognized him as an old friend." Even Jackie seemed caught up in a moment of wistful sentimentality on the plane. "This brings back some wonderful memories, doesn't it?" Shaw heard her sigh. "There is only one person missing."

Initially, Jackie thought she could handle the children on this visit by herself, but when she realized how many events and meetings would require her attention, she asked Shaw to accompany them. As an Englishwoman, Shaw was also key in helping the children practice proper etiquette for their meeting with the Queen, who would be present at the memorial ceremony. "Miss Shaw will know what we have to do," Jackie told John and Caroline. "You just listen to her. She's English and she knows about those things."

When they finally arrived in the UK, seven-year-old Caroline confidently bounded out the door and down the stairs, ready to meet the crowd of dignitaries who had gathered to greet the Kennedy party. Jackie, wearing a white coat and black hat, followed soon after her daughter, holding on to four-year-old John as they departed the jetliner. Unlike his older sister, John was more interested in watching the other planes take off and land than in speaking with their welcoming committee.

Finally, after all the requisite hands were shaken on the tarmac, the trio made their way to Jackie's sister's home at Buckingham Place to get some rest. (Jackie appreciated that rooms had been made available for the former First Family and JFK's siblings at the American embassy, but opted instead to stay with Lee.)

After a good night's sleep, the group took advantage of Lee's proximity to Buckingham Palace and walked a few blocks to watch the Changing of the Guard.

Nearly everywhere they went, the Kennedys drew a crowd of onlookers and photographers. And so, while it was an unofficial visit to the palace, the Queen allowed Jackie, John, and Caroline, as well as Lee and her two children, Tina and Anthony (and the Radziwills' pair of pugs, Thomas and Tarquin), to watch the ceremony from inside the courtyard, outside the Privy Purse door, offering them a welcome bit of privacy. John, who was photographed carrying a loaf of bread, presumably to feed the ducks in Green Park, was "quite entranced" by the cavalrymen with all their regalia, the plumed helmets and swords. Caroline, for her part, was more interested in their horses. Later in the trip, the young girl spent time at the stables in Hyde Park and rode on the fashionable Rotten Row, graceful as ever atop a horse, just like her mother.

For the rest of the week, Nanny Shaw kept the two children busy while Jackie made appearances and caught up with old friends. A visit to the Tower of London was a real highlight for John. He wanted to hear tales of the executions from the storied Beefeater tour guides, and, as many little boys are, he was fascinated by the armory (less so with the Crown Jewels). At one point, he even crawled into a cannon, hoping to get a closer look. "The next thing we knew, we could only see his little feet sticking out of one end," his nanny recalled in her memoir. "We hurried round to the front of the gun to see his face—absolutely radiant with delight—pop out of the other end."

They also went to the London Zoo and visited their cousins' school, where Tina was so protective of John that she held tight to him until one of her teachers said, "You don't have to put your arm around your cousin. He's absolutely safe as he is."

John Jr. and Caroline remained somewhat sheltered from the somber nature of their trip, but Jackie struggled, opening up to her friend Antonia Fraser about the difficulties of widowhood. "I just thought it was such an extraordinary reaction—she had this horror as if she herself had done something wrong . . . She felt blighted by the state," Fraser later told biographer Sarah Bradford. Several other members of the Kennedy family also made time to mourn their late sister Kathleen on the trip. On May 13, the anniversary of her death, they chartered a plane to visit her grave at Edensor.

But beyond all the tourist attractions, dinners with old friends, and sojourns north, the main purpose of the trip was the ceremony at Runnymede.

IT WAS A DEDICATION MORE THAN A YEAR IN THE MAKING. ON December 5, 1963, following the enormous outpouring of grief by the British people over JFK's death, Prime Minister Alec Douglas-Home spoke with Parliament about the creation of "an appropriate British memorial to President Kennedy," noting that the Queen "has been graciously pleased to express her wish to be personally associated with whatever proposal may be decided upon." He established a committee, chaired by Lord Franks, which then met with Jackie to share its recommendations. There were also discussions with Bobby Kennedy and Dean Rusk, the US secretary of state. Simultaneously, the Lord Mayor of London, Sir James Harman, launched a national appeal for funding.

Initial suggestions for the memorial ranged from statues and religious spaces to hospitals, memorial gardens, and even a museum of American life. But symbolically, on July 4, 1964, the Kennedy Memorial Trust was established to oversee a commemoration in two parts: one "in landscape and stone" and the other as a "living memorial" in the form of scholarships for British postgraduates to study at Harvard University and the Massachusetts Institute of Technology (MIT).

Designed to foster the "special relationship" between the US and the UK, the scholarship has been offered every year since 1966 and has been granted to more than 570 British postgraduates. Ahead of the founding of the Trust, Ted Kennedy described the scholarships as the most ambitious of all the memorials to his brother, and many years later in 2001, he shared that this part of JFK's legacy is something he knows the late President "would have valued very, very highly."

But perhaps more complicated than establishing the academic award was the creation of a permanent memorial to President Kennedy. When Lord Franks spoke with Jackie about the various potential memorials, she was "deeply touched" by the idea of an acre at Runnymede, in Surrey, dedicated to her husband's memory. Queen Elizabeth, too, supported the plan, showing a "deep and direct interest in the memorial." And so the monarch bequeathed the symbolic soil in the meadow where the barons of England had forced King John to sign the Magna Carta in 1215, taking a first step toward democracy, as a gift to the American people in President Kennedy's honor. It was, and would remain, a place of history. A monument was also crafted from a seven-ton block of creamy white Portland stone taken from the same quarry that had supplied the material for St. Paul's Cathedral.

On May 14, 1965, the day of the dedication, the sun was bright and the weather uncharacteristically hot, with temperatures quickly rising into the eighties. While the Kennedy party was scattered throughout London during their stay, Bobby and Ted came first to Buckingham Place to start the trip alongside Jackie and her two children. As they had come to expect, the group was met with crowds as they piled into cars to take them to Surrey.

Strangely, as Robert F. Kennedy exited the limousine, bits of white fluff filled the air from the poplar trees—so much so that it almost looked like snowflakes. He smiled and shook Randolph Churchill's hand as John and Caroline greeted the Queen. They bowed and curtsied, just as their nanny had taught them. With practice, Caroline had mastered the gesture quickly; after all, she had previously learned it ahead of meeting the King of Saudi Arabia. John, on the other hand, struggled with the protocol. "Good afternoon, My Majesty," he would say. "That's not quite right. We have to call the Queen 'Your Majesty.' Try it again,'" his nanny would gently correct him. But on the day of the event, he didn't disappoint.

The British monarch, escorted by David Ormsby-Gore, then led the group down the path to the memorial. Jackie, Caroline, and John (holding Prince Philip's hand, perhaps recalling his playmate from his father's funeral) followed close behind them on the walk through the woods and up a series of steep granite steps. There are fifty in total, one for each state. The winding trail, which itself is made of sixty thousand granite setts, was built to be purposefully uneven, filled with bumps and irregularities, to represent the trials of life.

Near the top, it levels off, leading to a simple stone block impeccably inscribed with the following words:

"This acre of English ground was given to the United States of America by the people of Britain in memory of John F. Kennedy, born 29 May 1917, President of the United States 1961–63, died by an assassin's hand 22 November 1963."

The stone, which was carved by sculptor Alan Collins, also includes a quotation from President Kennedy's inaugural address:

"Let every nation know, whether it wishes us well or ill that we shall pay any price, bear any burden, meet any hardship, support any friend, or oppose any foe in order to assure the survival and success of liberty."

The block is just one element of the monument. Architect Sir Geoffrey Jellicoe designed the site to be striking yet informal, a quintessential example of the traditional English countryside—unmanicured and yet also not unkept. He took into account how a visitor would approach the stone, drawing inspiration from both *The Pilgrim's Progress*, John Bunyan's 1678 Christian allegory of life as a journey, and Dante's *Inferno*.

"The idea that you walked up through the wood and the path through the wood was cobbles, all the stones were actually symbols of people. Not only were you walking on a pilgrim's track, but the stones symbolize the people who would walk on there," Jellicoe explained in 1991. "What I was groping for was a parallel in landscape of Bunyan's *Pilgrim's Progress*. You approach it through the wicket gate and through the wild woods of life. That is life."

On the day of the dedication, a raised platform with seating for approximately twenty-five important guests was constructed in the meadow next to the memorial. The stage was set on a hill directly across from another platform holding three hundred people. Many, many more onlookers crowded into the nearby field to listen to the speeches; they also hoped to catch a glimpse of both the monarch and the Kennedy family, who were met with applause as they made their way to their seats.

The ceremony itself was somber but not funereal, a fact exemplified by the Kennedys' outfits. Jackie, John, and Caroline all wore shades of cream. (The former First Lady's heels undoubtedly made the walk to the site even more difficult than intended.) In keeping with the mood, the band played a mix of songs—lively marches but also "Flowers of the Forest," a traditional Scottish lament. The military presence was minimal but poignant: two sailors, two airmen, and two soldiers, one American and one British from each branch of the military.

Former Prime Minister Macmillan, who'd had a deep friendship with and an affection for the late President, spoke first after a brief introduction by David Ormsby-Gore. "None of us will ever forget that grim November day nearly two years ago when we heard the news. Sudden, unexpected, incredible, it seemed like a fantastic fiction; yet, as the remorseless story was unfolded, we were faced with the stark finality of fact," he said, describing how "every home, every family in Britain felt a sense of personal bereavement."

Prime Minister Harold Wilson also gave a speech, but it was Queen Elizabeth who emphasized the ties JFK had to the UK and would continue to have, even in death. "Bonds like these cannot be broken, and his abiding affection for Britain engendered an equal response from this side of the Atlantic," she said. "The unprecedented intensity of that wave of grief, mixed with something akin to despair, which swept over our people at the news of President Kennedy's assassination was a measure of the extent to which we recognized what he had already accomplished, and of the high hopes that rode with him in a future that was not to be."

She ended by saying, "This acre of English soil is now bequeathed in perpetuity to the American people in memory of President John Fitzgerald Kennedy, who in death my people still mourn and whom in life they loved and admired."

Serving as the representative of President Johnson, Secretary of State Dean Rusk closed the ceremony by accepting the gift of the memorial and the acre of land on behalf of the American people. "I do so with the joy, and the sadness, which shall forever mark those of us who served with John Fitzgerald Kennedy," he said. "We shall cherish this memorial to a President who shall be forever young."

For all its importance, the ceremony was a relatively short one. As David Bruce recalled in his diary, "No spectacle could have been better." But while others spoke of Kennedy's life and their grief over his death, in that moment, Jackie could not. She sat silently throughout the dedication, perfectly composed. "It was such an emotional and difficult day for me," she would later write to Johnson. "So many thoughts of all my loss surged on me again."

Before the program was set, she worried over the idea of speaking at the event, questioning how she could express the family's appreciation for the memorial. Arthur Schlesinger, who had served as a speechwriter during the Kennedy administration, even prepared a few words for Jackie to consider. But in the end, she composed a personal message of thanks to the British people that was shared with the press, which read in part: "My husband loved history, and what you have done today in his honor would please him more than my words can express . . . To all of you who created this memorial I can only say it is the deepest comfort to me to know that you share with me thoughts that lie too deep for tears."

After about one hour's time, the Kennedys left Runnymede almost as quickly as they'd arrived. Jackie, accompanied by Prince Philip, gave the memorial one last lingering look before heading back down the path. Caroline walked away from the site holding Bobby's hand; John was just behind them holding Ted's. While their nanny had been there to keep an eye on the children throughout the ceremony, seated nearby on the grandstand, her watchfulness ultimately wasn't necessary. The two children were quite well behaved, even when a bee buzzed through the crowd. Following the dedication, the whole family drove on to Windsor Castle for tea with the Queen and Prince Philip. A small group of friends later gathered at Buckingham Place to finish off the day alongside Jackie and Lee.

"It was good to see them," Macmillan said of the Kennedys, describing them as "a tempestuous, lively, gallant family, who have had sad losses—two brothers and a sister—but drive on, with courage and gaiety, treating life as a great adventure." Later, Jackie would thank Macmillan for his part in the weekend, writing of her in-laws: "All that family, and all the confusion—you cannot travel with them without it." Of her two children, she continued, "You have to have something that makes you want to live—and now I have them."

Jackie penned a letter to Prime Minister Wilson that evening, thanking him for his speech, which highlighted how President Kennedy had "brought new hope and vitality to a tired world." It was "hard" for Jackie to listen to Wilson describe her late husband's "rigour" and the innovation he brought to the role of President. "Though I had steeled myself for this day—the awful sense of waste came over me again. But I do thank you with all my heart," she wrote. "I will remember and be moved by it forever." Wilson would later reply, sharing, "The sense of loss in this country at your husband's tragic death is something that has few parallels. I am glad that we had the opportunity last week of telling you publicly of our admiration for his work and our grief at his death."

Runnymede was one of several proposed memorials to JFK in England. It has never been officially confirmed by Buckingham Palace, but the idea for the monument is believed by historians to have come from Queen Elizabeth herself. But she wasn't the only Brit eager to honor the late President—the public wanted their say, too. At the International Students House in London, a bronze sculpture was erected as the British public's tribute to the late President, commemorating both his youth and his focus on young people. The day after the dedication in Surrey, Bobby and Ted Kennedy unveiled a bust of their late brother by artist Jacques Lipchitz, paid for by more than fifty thousand subscribers of *The Daily Telegraph*, who each gave a donation of a pound or less to the appeal.

Even after they returned home, the British memorial remained on Jackie's mind. In December 1965, she privately printed one hundred commemorative red leather–bound books featuring the text of the dedicatory remarks made by former Prime Minister Harold Macmillan, Prime Minister Harold Wilson, Queen Elizabeth, and JFK's secretary of state, Dean Rusk. She gave them as a memento to those close family and friends who had traveled to the UK for the ceremony. On each one, she wrote a message to the effect of, "Thank you for coming. With memories of the last thing that we all do together for Jack. With love, Jackie." She also personalized many of the covers with the recipients' gilt-stamped initials.

But in a letter to Macmillan, she spoke more freely about her feelings about Runnymede. "For everyone else Jack has receded and it was a beautiful memorial—but he has not receded for you or for me," she wrote.

Over the decades, the space has continued to hold significance for the Kennedy family. In the 1990s, Runnymede even served as a point of frustration for John Jr. when his wife, Carolyn Bessette-Kennedy, didn't understand the importance of the grounds. "What is

Runnymede?" Carolyn called to ask her close friend, Carole Radzi-will, the wife of John's cousin Anthony, during a spring 1999 visit to London. "He wants to go to Runnymede and I want to come home. I think he was mad because I didn't know what Runnymede was," she said. Tensions were already running high between them. It was a busy work trip, but their minds were back in the states with Anthony, who was receiving treatment for cancer. Carolyn's lack of knowledge of the Kennedy legacy only added to the stress.

While John's idea of a restful day trip involved a visit to the mon-ument, Carolyn's friend Hamilton South, who had been traveling with the couple, recalled that she "was more excited about a private tour of Windsor Castle." "Besides the exquisite beauty of the castle and surrounding grounds, we got to see the royal family's breathtak-ing collection of art," he told Carolyn's biographer Elizabeth Beller. Carolyn was struck by the beauty of the paintings, but appreciated them even more because she didn't have to deal with the crowds to view them. "Carolyn was so grateful and thanked them profusely for allowing this special moment."

WHILE TECHNICALLY THE PURVIEW OF THE KENNEDY MEMORIAL Trust, the monument at Runnymede continues to be "lightly man-aged by the National Trust," allowing for the natural cycle of life and death to repeat each year. Every fall, an American scarlet oak, which grows next to the monument, turns red in November—the wood's annual commemoration of Kennedy's death.

The fiftieth anniversary of President Kennedy's passing was marked a bit more formally. In 2013, the Kennedy Memorial Trust held a ceremony at the monument to commemorate the milestone. It wasn't a gorgeous spring day, as it was for the 1965 event, but despite the strong wind and chilly temperatures, the sun was shining as a small crowd gathered once again in Surrey.

"We have come here today to honor his memory as this monument does so well, but today is a difficult day, because it is a reminder of a moment of profound sadness for my family, for America, and for the world," JFK's granddaughter Tatiana Schlossberg, then twenty-three, said during the service. She noted how, "as a lover of history, particularly British history," she knew "he would be both proud and humbled to see that his work on behalf of peace and liberty for all people is remembered in the very place where the rule of law was made manifest nearly 800 years ago."

She continued, "Fifty years after his death, as my grandfather's story begins to belong more and more to history, I can think of no better place to honor him, to tell and remember his story, and to look again, as he would have wanted us to, towards the future."

Schlossberg, who tragically passed away from cancer in 2025, was the daughter of JFK's only living child, Caroline Kennedy. She grew up out of the public eye and rarely sought the spotlight, but she served as the family representative at the event and was accompanied by Matthew Barzun, the US ambassador to the United Kingdom.

"I'm just deeply moved by the fact that the British people didn't do this because they were told to, or because they had to. They did it in the spirit of spontaneous generosity, and that's a very powerful thing—something that we need more of in both our countries," Barzun said in his remarks, delighting in the fact that he was standing on American soil in the UK. "It's a strange and wonderful thing to say."

In addition to Tatiana and Ambassador Barzun, two more people spoke: the leader of the House of Lords, Lord Hill of Oareford, and the chairman of the Kennedy Memorial Trust, Professor Tony Badger.

The group planted a symbolic oak sapling, donated to the Kennedy Memorial by the Crown Estate and grown from a thousand-year-old parent tree in Windsor Great Park. Then four wreaths were laid on the memorial, one by each of the speechmakers.

No member of the royal family was present at the anniversary event, though the Queen had been invited and did consider attending. "In the end she didn't come, but she did send warm wishes, which I think was genuine. It wasn't just boilerplate stuff that people say when they turn down an invitation," recalled Johnny Grimond, who was trustee of the Kennedy Memorial Trust at the time.

That said, the ceremony at Runnymede came a few months after Prince Harry paid his own respects to President Kennedy. On May 10, 2013, during a "true whirlwind" of a tour to the US, Prince Harry visited the eternal flame at Arlington, kneeling to lay a bouquet of flowers on JFK's grave. When he stood, he bowed his head, spending a few moments in quiet reflection.

The visit to the cemetery was an emotional one for Harry, a soldier himself. In particular, he was touched by the practice of laying a wreath on the tomb of the unknown soldier. As he wrote in his 2023 memoir, *Spare*, "I'd laid dozens of wreaths before, but the ritual was different in America. You didn't place the wreath on the grave yourself; a white-gloved soldier placed it with you and then you laid your hand singly, for one beat, upon the wreath. This extra step, this partnering with another living soldier, moved me."

In 2016, Prince William hosted a reception for the Kennedy Memorial Trust at Buckingham Palace. "My grandmother would very much like me to pass on some words to all of you," he said in a speech. "In 1965, my grandmother, Her Majesty The Queen, inaugurated the memorial to President Kennedy, which stands at Runnymede, on land bequeathed by her to the people of the United States.

Her Majesty spoke that day of the extent to which we recognized what President Kennedy had already accomplished, and of the high hopes that rode with him, in a future that was not to be. So I am honored, half a century on, to be here this evening and pay tribute to a man whom my family continues to hold in the highest esteem."

CHAPTER 11

Eligible Royalty

JOHN F. KENNEDY JR. IS THE CLOSEST THING THE UNITED STATES has had to a crown prince. The morning after the 1960 election, JFK gave his acceptance speech alongside a very pregnant Jackie at the Hyannis Armory, a few miles away from his family's famed compound. He committed himself to the presidency, "to the long-range interests of the United States and to the cause of freedom around the world," ending his statement with, "So now my wife and I prepare for a new administration and for a new baby. Thank you." John F. Kennedy Jr. was born less than three weeks later, and by the time he was three months old, he was living in the White House.

The press was enamored. There hadn't been a baby in the First Family in decades, and both John Jr. and his older sister, Caroline, made frequent appearances on television and the covers of magazines—respected news publications and more salacious supermarket tabloids alike. Articles even then suggested that the Kennedys were the US equivalent of a royal family. And many of Kennedy's supporters had been young World War II veterans with children, not unlike the President himself. They could identify with him and with Jackie in a way they hadn't connected with past presidents and first ladies, and they were captivated by stories and photos of Caroline and John Jr.

(who was eventually given the nickname John-John by the press, though those close to him never actually used the moniker).

But the attention on her children quickly became too much for Jackie, who wanted to preserve their privacy as much as possible. As early as April 1961, she requested a ban on outlets photographing her children playing on the White House lawn, instead opting for carefully controlled photo shoots. Jackie would then curate which images were released to the press. A former photojournalist and a shrewd storyteller, she understood more than most the power of a photo on the political conversation, but by October 1962, she declared a "major effort to be made this year to keep children out of papers and magazines."

"If press has questions about children—what does Caroline want for Xmas—do for birthday etc—say 'Mrs K is very sorry but she doesn't want to give any info. about the children this yr,'" she wrote in a memo to press secretary Pamela Turnure. While she was an active participant in the Kennedys' symbiotic relationship with the papers, she didn't hide her disdain for journalists and how they went after her family. Jackie "waged a three-year war of independence with the press," recalled journalist Helen Thomas, who covered the Kennedy administration. The First Lady, she said, "treated the press corps like so many foreign invaders." (Per Thomas, when Jackie was asked what her German shepherd puppy named Clipper liked to eat, Jackie replied simply: "Reporters.")

After the Kennedys left the White House, the public's fascination with John continued. People were invested in his life and his happiness, and even as he grew up, he remained America's son—that little boy who spent his third birthday at his father's funeral, saluting the casket. John also became something of a heartthrob, and before the age of thirty, he had been named *People*'s Sexiest Man Alive. A string of high-profile romances and rumored flings with the likes of

Sarah Jessica Parker, Madonna, and Daryl Hannah kept him in the news, as did his struggles with the New York bar exam following his graduation from law school. "I'm clearly not a major legal genius," he said, making light of the situation after failed attempt number two.

Eventually, he passed the exam on his third try, in 1990, but John wasn't destined to be a lifelong lawyer. He put in four years at the New York DA's office before he turned his attention to a more entrepreneurial pursuit: launching his own publication. Following the 1992 election, Kennedy and his cofounder Michael Berman saw an opportunity to "change the definition of a political magazine," and the idea for *George* was born.

"The way Americans were accessing information about politics and politicians was changing. Candidates were appearing on late night talk shows, on talk radio, on sitcoms, and there was a kind of a leveling process. And while the rest of media clearly had caught up with that, we felt that political magazines per se hadn't," John told TV host Larry King, explaining his decision to step away from the law. "And so while you had all this interest on it that you really could point to with statistics and facts, we thought, well, here's an opportunity to do a different kind of political magazine."

A media venture was a curious choice for someone whose complicated relationship with the press literally dated back to the day he was born, but the irony was not lost on John. *George* was his way of creating an identity for himself, one that existed in conversation with his family's history, but on his own terms. It was also his way of taking back a bit of control of his public narrative. If John needed to, he would always have a place where he could make an unfiltered statement to the public. After shopping the concept for almost a year—everyone wanted to take a meeting with John Jr.; fewer people were willing to invest in a political magazine—David Pecker, then CEO of

Hachette Filipacchi Magazines (who would later go on to become better known for his friendship with Donald Trump), offered them a deal. And in September 1995, they published their first issue of *George*.

The tagline? "Not just politics as usual." The goal? To be to politics "what *Rolling Stone* was to music and what *Sports Illustrated* was to sports," in the words of publisher Elinore Carmody. But there's a reason *George* was often referred to as simply John F. Kennedy Jr.'s magazine. Senior editor Richard Bradley, who was hired ahead of the first issue, described the publication as a "psychobiography in semimonthly installments." John wasn't only the name behind the project—though certainly his involvement helped sell advertisements and copies on the newsstand. He was actively involved as an editor, shaping what stories were told and how. In a way, he was taking after his mom, who went on to have a second career in book publishing but who didn't live to see *George* hit newsstands; she passed away on May 19, 1994, at the age of sixty-four from non-Hodgkin's lymphoma. "I think that my mother would be mildly bemused," John said of Jackie at the official launch of *George*. "I think that she'd be glad that she wasn't standing up here, and I think that she'd be very proud."

Editing the magazine was also his way of engaging with the modern political discourse while embracing and interrogating his father's legacy. From the beginning, a staple of each issue of *George* was John's interview. These weren't just Q&As with pop singers or Hollywood actors, or even always the issue's cover star. He would sit down with someone he found interesting, whether that was segregationist George Wallace (President Kennedy's old political rival), evangelist Billy Graham, journalist Cokie Roberts, former Vice President Dan Quayle, or the North Vietnamese general Võ Nguyên Giáp. At first glance, there isn't an obvious connection between his interview subjects. But "John's interviews were really his own research about the expectations and the demands and, maybe most of all, the sacrifices of public life—what would he have to say goodbye to if he chose to go into politics? The interviews allowed him to ask other people's advice without explicitly asking other people's advice. Frankly, most of the interview subjects were people the other editors would never have recommended," Richard explained. "He chose to interview these people because he had questions about his own future, and he thought they might have some answers."

In the early days of the magazine, John was particularly interested in interviewing one of the rare people who could understand the level of press attention and scrutiny he faced on a daily basis: Princess Diana.

IN 1995, FEW WOMEN IN THE WORLD WERE MORE FAMOUS THAN Princess Diana. Separated from Prince Charles but not yet divorced, Diana and her romantic life were of unending interest to the public and the press, both in her native England and in the United States. (Interestingly enough, during a 1996 conversation with Iain Calder, the editor in chief of the *National Enquirer,* John asked if he would have run photos from Charles and Diana's wedding night. "Not if it was in the bedroom," he responded. "Readers would think that was an invasion of privacy." Calder would, however, be fine with printing images of a royal "covert frolic on a beach.") Unlike the (usually) private Kennedys, the Windsors had also used the media as a battleground, with both Diana and Charles collaborating with journalists to reveal details about the demise of their relationship, each making sure their side of the story was known.

An issue of *George* with Diana on the cover would be guaranteed to sell—both to advertisers and on the newsstand. Not to mention, she fit the ethos of the burgeoning publication.

"It seems obvious why he would've wanted her on the cover, because he was trying to capture the intersection of political life and celebrity life in his magazine. Lady Di, at that moment, was a perfect example of that because she was a symbol of the intersection of those things. She was a celebrity, a royal who had a defined role, but she also had a personal and political mission. She had ideas about how she wanted to help the world. She had her own feelings about her service, at least that's the perspective that I got from her," John's close friend artist Sasha Chermayeff, who had known him since his boarding school days, said. "She was loved by America, too. We loved her, everybody loved her."

John and Diana were uniquely matched. They were glamorous, beautiful, and charismatic—but there was substance there, too. They were also both so often underestimated, by the public and the people around them. Editorially, a conversation between them was an interesting prospect.

"He was America's equivalent of Diana," said British photographer Platon, who often worked with John at *George* magazine. "They both had this quiet aura in the media, that they don't have to ever shout about who they are and what they do. They just give you this shy look, that you are just drawn to it. And you can't fake that. That's not built by marketing companies and PR companies. That's not a strategy. That's real.

"Both had complicated legacies and history that had already passed, even when they were at their prime. And they didn't seem to go begging for attention. They knew that they had this quiet power that you can't cultivate. It's just there. And I can't tell you how many celebrities wish they had an ounce of that aura."

Initially, John sent Diana a letter asking for a meeting, and per her private secretary Patrick Jephson, she was "keen on the idea."

And so calls were made, and a date was arranged for John to meet with Diana at the Carlyle hotel during her visit to New York in December 1995. She was going to be in the city to receive a humanitarian honor at the annual United Cerebral Palsy Awards gala. The trip also came one month after Diana's bombshell interview with *Panorama*, in which she spoke at length about the failed state of her relationship with Prince Charles. "We agreed that she would find time in her program in New York to meet him. Nobody wanted it to be public," Patrick remembered, so the encounter was set for midday, when, in theory, the hotel would be the least busy.

John and Diana weren't complete strangers, but they also weren't as close as the media sometimes assumed. "I always think that people imagine that we have a bat phone on my desk and Diana's desk and Princess Stephanie's and we can pick it up and the other will answer," John once said joking. But while they were hardly confidants, they had met before. About a decade prior, they'd both attended a luncheon at Bunny Mellon's farm in Virginia during the 1985 royal visit to DC. "She has the most unusual upwards glance, really seductive," he said at the time to his friend Billy Noonan, noting that she also had "the most unusual blue eyes." But ten years later, this meeting wasn't a date—or really even a social call. John was there on business. He wanted to ask Princess Diana to pose for the cover of *George*.

John was excited, but he was also "annoyed about everybody hinting about how this would be a marriage made in heaven if they could be together," Sasha said. "The classic, still continued, idea that monarchies must come together for the good of the families."

And from the very beginning, John expected someone to leak the details of this encounter to the press.

"When you're talking about people that are that famous, it's interesting just if they're spotted on the street," Richard Johnson, the gossip columnist who edited the *New York Post*'s Page Six in the 1990s, said. "Photographers will start taking pictures. They don't have to be doing anything." A photo proving a rendezvous between the People's Princess (a term bestowed on Diana after her death by British Prime Minister Tony Blair) and America's Prince (as John was already referred to in the press) in the summer of 1995? That would have been a guaranteed front-page story.

At first, it was suggested that he should wear a disguise to the meeting to throw off any photographers, but that wasn't how John operated. He was someone who took the subway to work and rode his bike through the streets of Tribeca in New York City. He tried to live his life as normally as he could, even if someone managed to snap a picture. "We were laughing and carrying on: 'Oh, go in as this' or 'Go in as that,'" recalled John's executive assistant and close friend RoseMarie Terenzio. "And finally he was like, 'I'm not going anywhere in disguise, that's the stupidest thing ever.'"

In the end, he opted for a smart navy blue suit. "Nothing extravagant, not full-tilt-boogie JFK Jr., but on the cusp," RoseMarie described. John decided that RoseMarie should accompany him to the meeting ("Rosie, come with me. If I go in by myself and I leave by myself, if anyone sees me, there's gonna be all kinds of speculation. You know, *They were caught at The Carlyle*."). And the day of, they were driven to the hotel in John's Saab.

Princess Diana always stayed at the Carlyle. Located on New York's Upper East Side, the luxurious hotel has an English charm. And it has long been a royal favorite for visits to New York City. James Sherwin, the manager of the hotel at the time, only added to the appeal. He had at one point worked for Lady Elizabeth Anson, a cousin of Queen Elizabeth's, and understood Diana's need for privacy completely, describing the hotel's discretion as "extraordinary." "It was not as big as many of the other New York hotels, so you could control it in a slightly different manner," he said.

John, too, was intimately familiar with the property and its security; he had lived there with his mother and sister in the years following his father's death.

When they arrived at the Carlyle, John and RoseMarie simply walked off Madison Avenue right through the hotel's front door, unfettered by the crowd of press, who just so happened to be waiting at the other entrance.

"I had remembered that the last time I had been to the Carlyle for an event, there had been no photographers at the front entrance," RoseMarie said. "So I told John, 'Don't go in the side entrance, because if anyone does leak it beforehand, people will expect you to go in the side. So walk in the front door.'"

Patrick was there to meet John in the corridor between the foyer and the bar. It was dark, so from a distance, Patrick didn't recognize the tall man as he approached, but John immediately extended his hand. "John Kennedy," he said, introducing himself despite the fact that everyone in the room—and practically everyone in the world—knew exactly who he was. He always did that. "He was very, very polite. I would say modest. There was no swagger to him. He was quite right and proper," Patrick said.

They made their way to the elevator, leaving RoseMarie in the lobby. Princess Diana greeted them in the penthouse suite—much like John, she was dressed smartly. "It was a working meeting. Business attire," Patrick said.

Once in the room, the pair sat down at a table to talk. Tea was served, or maybe it was champagne—that detail has been lost to history, but regardless of the drinks, John appeared nervous.

"He was quite in awe of her," Patrick said. "Not uncomfortable, but he certainly seemed to be on his best behavior," and acutely aware that he was asking Diana for a favor. Diana, on the other hand, was unfazed. "She was very cool—and jolly, you know, and smiley and welcoming."

Despite the nerves, John didn't delay in making his pitch. He perched on the edge of his chair and asked Diana to appear on the cover of *George*. (Recollections differ as to which issue the ask was for. As Richard put it, "I suspect that invitation would've been, 'Whenever the heck you want to.'")

John had brought along with him several ideas for the cover shoot. His creative director Matt Berman (unrelated to his cofounder) had mocked up sketches of Diana on tracing paper in Magic Marker to show her what the photograph might look like. One featured her wearing a three-corner hat like one from the Revolutionary War; another, oddly enough, showed her in the back of a limousine with the window rolled halfway up, in an attempt to avoid photographers. "I remember sending him over to the Carlyle. I made a little package for him with all the sketches of how we might do her on the cover. So there was one with a George Washington outfit, of course, but then we did other ones," Matt Berman recalled.

While *George* was still in its infancy, its visual identity was quickly solidifying. The magazine would become known for having its cover stars dress up as George Washington or other iconic figures from American history. Barbra Streisand, for example, posed as Betsy Ross; Harrison Ford took on the persona of Abraham Lincoln in his cover shoot; Robert De Niro's Washington look came complete with the founding father's actual sword, a gift to JFK during his presidency.

Controversially, for an issue pegged to President Bill Clinton's fiftieth birthday, Drew Barrymore posed on the cover in a slinky nude dress—a not-so-subtle nod to Marilyn Monroe's birthday serenade to President Kennedy. John's mindset was "Why is it OK for everyone else to play with the political iconography of my family and I can't? It's my family, it's not offensive to me. Why should it be offensive to you?" In his editor's letter for that issue, he wrote simply, "And on our cover, Drew Barrymore reprises what may be the most memorable 'Happy Birthday' sung in the history of American politics. Cheers."

But unfortunately, this particular conversation about the cover of *George* was over before it started. Prior to John even opening his mouth to ask about doing an interview and a photo shoot, Diana had already made up her mind to turn down the opportunity. She needed the magazine to be a success before she'd publicly front it—and even with a Kennedy at the helm of the publication, that was hardly a guaranteed prospect.

While Diana was no stranger to collaborating with the press, a cover story with her would have been quite the get, and she didn't like the possibility that John was planning to trade on her fame in order to get his magazine off the ground. So once he finished making his case, Diana shot a sly glance over to Patrick before politely saying no.

"Well, you know, this is all very nice, John. Thank you. But I hope you'll forgive me if I don't take up the opportunity this time, but would love to maybe for your fiftieth or your hundredth issue or something," she said.

While he was disappointed, John understood that the decision was final, and so conversation quickly turned to other things.

They had both spent time with the Catholic nun Mother Teresa, so they talked about her mission. And part of the reason Diana had taken the meeting in the first place was to ask John about his upbringing. She wanted to raise Harry and William the way Jackie had raised John and Caroline. "I'm hoping he'll grow up to be as smart about it as John Kennedy, Jr.," Diana would say about her eldest son to journalist Tina Brown years later, weeks before her death. "I want William to be able to handle things as well as John does." Diana had long looked up to Jackie and saw parallels between their lives.

She was "very intrigued" by her, Brown's *Vanity Fair* successor Graydon Carter said, noting that during a dinner Diana "kept asking questions—she wanted to know how Jackie Kennedy was treated by the Kennedy family because, I think, she felt there were parallels between how Jackie was treated and the way she was treated by the royal family."

Perhaps less significantly, the appointment with John was also a ploy by Diana to make her sister-in-law Sarah, the Duchess of York, jealous. By this point, Diana and "Fergie," as she was known, had become rivals of sorts, and the redheaded soon-to-be ex-wife of Prince Andrew apparently had a crush on JFK Jr. "The Princess's wish to meet America's most eligible bachelor owed more than a bit to the fact that he was at the time a particular pin-up of Fergie's," Patrick later wrote. Fergie would eventually visit the *George* offices, mingling and taking pictures with editorial staffers, but it seems unlikely that she met with John. "It was brief," RoseMarie said. "I don't remember exactly how it came about. I think she was doing meetings for Weight Watchers in the city." The duchess appeared in the September 1996 issue in a small way. She was featured in a photo highlighting her visit at Hale House in New York City, a "facility for drug-addled and HIV-positive infants. In the caption, *George* noted that she was following "her former sister-in-law Diana's benevolent instincts."

In the end, John and Diana spent "a pleasant enough" hour or so together. "I remember he felt like it was more fun than he had expected in the royal meeting, a little more genuine," Sasha said. "I think he liked her, put it that way." And despite later rumors that the couple had an affair that was consummated at the Carlyle that day in a "moment of pure lust," Patrick said he remained in the room the whole time. "I stayed in the room throughout and was not aware of any mad, passionate activities," he said. "My observation was, it was a kind of mutual sounding-out. It was a kind of appraisal, and it wasn't overtly flirtatious, but it was friendly."

Prior to the meeting, Patrick and Diana had discussed how long to let the conversation go on. When it reached that point, Patrick interrupted, apologizing, and saying something like, "We've got to get ready for the next thing," giving the princess an out.

As John made his way back downstairs, Diana turned to Patrick and said "words to the effect of 'That went well, and it was the right thing to do.'"

"I can't remember the words, but there was a degree of sympathy. I think she might have spoken about the famous picture of him as a little boy. And she had sympathy for him growing up with the name and being the object of public fascination. These were things that she could relate to. I definitely picked up a sense of sympathy, of concern, for him. She didn't see him as the rest of the world saw him. As this big, famous, handsome guy. She saw him, I think, as rather vulnerable because he had grown up in public," Patrick would later recall.

But while the ask to appear on an early cover was denied, John didn't leave the hotel entirely empty-handed; Diana wrote him a note, which read, "Thank you so much, but not right now." And again she had agreed to consider appearing on a future cover of *George*, possibly enjoying the tease of being able to say yes in principle, but that they'd have to wait.

As John exited the hotel, his assistant asked the obvious question: "Well, how was she?"

"She's tall, taller than I thought," he said. "She's very nice, shy, a little coy. But she's not going to do it."

"I could tell he was disappointed that she said no," RoseMarie said.

And with that, they trekked back to midtown to the *George* offices. "What was she like?" a chorus of editors asked upon their arrival. As he dropped the imagined cover sketches back on Matt Berman's desk, John said, "Well, she said no, but she had a great pair of legs!" From there, John kept things light, never lingering on the disappointment.

"At the end of the day, all he cared about was getting a yes to the cover of *George*," RoseMarie said. "Everything else was kind of, whatever."

Cindy Crawford in a midriff-baring George Washington–meets–pinup girl ensemble was featured on the cover of the debut issue of *George*, which John revealed at a press conference at Manhattan's Federal Hall in September 1995. When the suggestion of Crawford initially came up, John's future wife, Carolyn Bessette, insisted it was the right call. "She's all-American, a self-made woman, sexy, strong, and smart," Carolyn said, in an opinion shaped by her years of working in fashion PR. She was right. The image was instantly iconic, and it set a precedent for the magazine. But despite the inherent Americanness of *George*, John continued to think about how Princess Diana could be a part of the magazine, and she was still mentioned within its pages quite often. In the August 1997 issue, for example, Marla Maples appeared on its signature "If I Were President" page, answering the question "What foreign problem would you like to solve?" with "Princess Di's peace of mind." The September 1997 issue, which went to print a few weeks before Diana's untimely death, included a photo of her alongside Elizabeth Dole at a Red Cross event for land mine survivors. The two women were also pictured together in the final issue John edited. The image helped illustrate a profile of Dole.

John never gave up on the idea of putting a British royal on his cover. He stayed in touch with Diana, asking her for an interview more than once. In February 1997, she penned him a letter, thanking John for sending her issues of the magazine, but once again, she had to "regrettably" turn down his offer. But it wasn't an outright refusal.

Once again, she suggested that she'd be in touch when a conversation might be appropriate. She finished off the note by writing, "I hope"—with "hope" underlined—"the media are leaving both you and Carolyn alone. I know how difficult it is, but believe it or not, the worst paparazzi are here in Europe!"

"I think she saw in him a fellow victim, if you can put it that way, of life in the public eye and difficulty of knowing who to trust," Patrick said. "And I think that that did create a connection between them. I wouldn't call it a bond, but an affinity, a recognition of each other's unusual hardships and difficulties."

John was also interested in pursuing Prince Charles for *George*. According to society columnist Aileen Mehle (who was better known by her pen name Suzy), in 1998 John and his wife, Carolyn, attended a private dinner thrown by Charles at Kensington Palace, during which John asked the Prince of Wales to appear on the cover of *George* to mark Charles's fiftieth birthday in November of that year. A photo of the Prince of Wales had appeared within the pages of *George* before; a 1997 issue notably featured the iconic image of Charles meeting the Spice Girls. But like his ex, Charles was hesitant to collaborate with Kennedy, and once again, John was turned down by the House of Windsor. To appear on the cover of a magazine or a tabloid via a licensed photo was one thing; to pose for a cover shoot and presumably consent to an interview with John was another. Per Mehle, the request was "graciously met by something that sounded like 'um, uhm, hum, we'll see, um, uhm, hum.' After all these years, [Prince Charles] is an expert at avoiding the pinning-down process."

George did eventually reach its fiftieth issue before closing in 2001, but it never had a royal cover star. Tragically, by the time the magazine printed its final edition, both Diana and John were dead.

The Vanishing Lady

THE FRENCH INTERIOR MINISTER ANNOUNCED PRINCESS DIANA'S death a little before 5 a.m. local time on August 31, 1997. She and her boyfriend Dodi Al Fayed had been killed in a car crash in the Pont de l'Alma tunnel in Paris. Their driver was intoxicated, and he lost control of the car after paparazzi on motorcycles started pursuing the couple. They slammed first into the tunnel's center divider, then its right wall. While Dodi and the driver died at the scene of the accident, the princess later succumbed to major chest and lung injuries at Pitié-Salpêtrière Hospital. She was thirty-six years old.

The outpouring of grief and the onslaught of media coverage following Princess Diana's death were instantaneous, and not long after the news broke in the US, John's phone rang. It was *George*'s executive editor, Elizabeth "Biz" Mitchell, calling to discuss how the magazine would cover the tragedy. Some sort of tribute story would be expected in the next issue, and the team needed to formulate a plan—quickly. "We'll talk about it," John told Biz, delaying the conversation. She put a meeting on the calendar, but he simply didn't show up. When John finally arrived at the magazine's office, he brushed Biz off once more. "I can't do it right now," he told her. "I don't see why this needs to be a story."

"Instead of talking about Diana with the editors, he started cleaning out his office files, throwing them into a big dumpster. I think he thought, *This is going to push my wife over the edge even more*," RoseMarie Terenzio would later write of this moment. Carolyn was already troubled by the paparazzi's invasive pursuit of photos of her and John. To hear that Diana, who just a month prior had sat one pew in front of her at their mutual friend Gianni Versace's funeral, had died being chased by photographers would have been distressing fuel for Carolyn's anxiety and frustration about the press.

It was clear to everyone close to John that Diana's death weighed heavily on him in those early days. Yes, the two had met, but his reaction seemed to be about more than that. They were two of a kind—in terms of their fame, their impact, how beloved they were by the people, and also how pursued they were by the press. "My reaction was, 'Oh my gosh, now there's only one of them left,'" *George* editor Richard Bradley recalled. "It's like the existence of white dolphins in the Yangtze River. If there are two of them, there's hope. But if one dies . . ."

Multiple people have said that John "hesitated" in planning *George*'s response to Diana's death. He was not only personally rattled but also felt that anything the magazine did would be seen as a statement about his relationship to the paparazzi—and his wife's. But Biz pushed the topic. "I told him you can't just completely ignore it," she said.

Eventually, John reluctantly conceded that Diana's passing was "too central" to the cultural conversation and "too commercial" for *George* to completely disregard it. Biz was right; they needed to do something to memorialize the princess in the next issue. So John reached out to the photographer Platon. Instead of a straightforward obituary, *George* commissioned a photo essay of the public's reaction to Diana's death.

"It was entirely Matt Berman's concept," RoseMarie recalled, crediting *George*'s creative director. "Because John didn't want to do anything about it, Matt came up with this idea to have a photographer go and photograph all of the flowers and all of the tributes in front of Buckingham Palace instead of doing an image of her, because I think he felt like everybody's going to do that."

"It was obviously an enormous story, and we were just trying to find our own way to illustrate it," Matt Berman said. "And so the idea was for him to go and just give on-the-streets reportage of what the feelings were and what the grieving looked like. So instead of us publishing historical pictures of her, it was a nice way to show a sensitive take on that moment in time by showing the people who loved her, documented."

Diana's death—like President Kennedy's—thrust the world into a period of overwhelming sadness. This heartbreak was, of course, felt most intensely by those in the UK. In what has been described as both "mass hysteria" and the edge of a shared "nervous breakdown," people in London quickly gravitated toward royal residences. They created impromptu tributes outside Princess Diana's home at Kensington Palace, but also Buckingham Palace and St. James's Palace, where her body would eventually lie in state. As people came to terms with what had happened, there was quite literally weeping in the streets.

"I just feel disbelief more than shock," Fiona von Schank, a student who brought two roses to leave at Kensington Palace, told CNN the day Diana died. "It's amazing that this woman who finally seemed to have just about found some happiness has now died so tragically." In total, an estimated sixty million flowers were left at these makeshift memorials, as were a sea of candles, cards, flags, and stuffed animals. The tokens served as physical manifestations of the raw emotion people felt about the princess's death.

"It's completely unprecedented. It's an occasion that is unique possibly in the history of the world and certainly in anyone's experience here," said David Welch of the Royal Parks service, who oversaw the cleanup of these memorials. The English also did what they do best, queuing for hours to sign books of condolence. At their peak, wait times lasted more than twelve hours. But the response to Diana's death was also decidedly un-British in its deviation from the stereotypical "stiff upper lip" mentality many associated with the culture. Britain was mourning publicly, with abandon.

The royal family, at least at first, wasn't quite sure how to handle this almost explosive reaction. Initially, Queen Elizabeth stayed silent, focused on her grandchildren instead of her subjects. Meanwhile, headlines began to question "Where Is Our Queen?" as well as admonish "Your People Are Suffering, Speak to Us Ma'am" and "Show Us You Care." Eventually, she did address the nation, in her words, "as your Queen and as a grandmother."

"I want to pay tribute to Diana myself. She was an exceptional and gifted human being. In good times and bad, she never lost her capacity to smile and laugh, nor to inspire others with her warmth and kindness. I admired and respected her—for her energy and commitment to others, and especially for her devotion to her two boys," she said, clarifying that her attention in the days following Diana's death was focused on William and Harry. "This week at Balmoral, we have all been trying to help William and Harry come to terms with the devastating loss that they and the rest of us have suffered."

While the Queen was widely criticized for her lack of emotional response to her former daughter-in-law's death, she shared a more intimate perspective on her grief in a letter to her lady-in-waiting Lady Henriette Abel Smith. "It was indeed dreadfully sad, and she is a huge loss to the country," the Queen wrote. "But the public reaction to her death, and the service in the Abbey, seem to have united people round the world in a rather inspiring way."

John wanted the *George* tribute to focus on the "spirit of the nation," and Platon was directed to skip the official ceremony held at Westminster Abbey, where the royal family, celebrities, international monarchs, and heads of state flocked to pay their respects. Instead, Platon documented how people were engaging with the more makeshift memorials on the street. It was a difficult ask, given the circumstances of Diana's accident. Grief bloomed into anger, with many blaming journalists, and in particular photographers, for the tragedy. "You've got to remember that when Diana died, she was hounded by paparazzi," Platon said. "It sounds weird now, but walking around at that time on the streets photographing mourners and bereaved people who were really upset with a camera, it's like I was walking around with a weapon."

But Platon used his "Englishness" to connect with his subjects, and the story that resulted was a feature titled "The Lady Vanishes: The People's Funeral for Diana, Princess of Wales." (The headline that ran on the issue's cover was a bit more clever and provocative, in hopes of capturing more newsstand buyers: "Exclusive: Diana Photos of the Mourning After." It was sandwiched between two other attention-grabbing cover lines: "Washington's Best & Worst Dressed" and "Paul Newman & John Kennedy Want You to Find the Most Generous Company in America.")

One of Platon's images shows two British rockers tearing up as Diana's cortège rolled by, grieving "the loss of their improbable heroine." Another of his pictures documents the seemingly endless sea of mourners in London's Hyde Park. There hadn't been a plan in place for Diana's funeral, but it quickly became apparent to everyone involved that the public would need a space to participate, so huge screens and speakers were set up on the lawn. The hymns had even been printed in the newspapers that day so that everyone watching, even those outside, could sing along.

"It was a very moving experience because it was not just about Diana dying. Very few people actually knew her personally, but there was some phenomenon happening on the streets. And you can't predict it," Platon said, likening the scene to the queue of people who waited to see Queen Elizabeth's coffin in September 2022. Another image shows a trio of young people in the hours before the funeral: One is lying on the ground; all three appear inconsolable. Elisabeth Kübler-Ross, the psychiatrist and author of *On Death and Dying*, is quoted as calling the reaction to Diana's death a "worldwide *depression*."

"For a few days, everyone was gentle with each other; everyone was compassionate; everyone was feeling the same thing," Platon said. "So I captured that, came back with all these pictures."

His photos of collective grief ran in the November 1997 issue of *George*, accompanied by quotes about Diana and her untimely death. "It was incredibly moving. To me, it was more evocative than a photo of her because it really spoke to the outpouring of grief and how loved she was. How much she meant to people,'" RoseMarie recalled.

Several of the reflections featured in the spread centered on Diana's relationship with the media and the history of the paparazzi. Richard Boulter, a representative of the charity Halo Trust, recalled that Diana was quite "relaxed" as she walked through an active minefield with the organization. "In fact, it amused her to be there, because she could be sure there would be no photographers lurking in the bushes," he said. "It's amazing that she had to walk into a minefield to get away from the photographers."

In contrast, Roy Gleenslade, a former editor of the *Daily Mirror*, spoke perhaps to what John had realized when he asked Princess Diana to be on the cover of *George* two years prior: that she was a "guaranteed seller" when it came to the newsstand. "We sold more copies whenever we featured pictures and stories about her," he said, speaking to both Diana's frustration with how the royal machine worked with the British press and to her own savvy methods of working with the tabloids. Diana devised a media strategy that involved encouraging her friends to serve as sources, using photos to send a message both to her in-laws and the world, and, as he put it "colluding with the very newspapers that made her life a misery."

While this issue of *George* is hardly a dedicated tribute edition, the memory of Diana infuses its pages in big and small ways. In his editor's letter, John compared her life and death to that of Mother Teresa, who had passed away just days after the royal did. He shared his memories of a trip to Calcutta and the work he had witnessed there. "What I saw was that by sheer force of will, [Mother Teresa] was able to transform the lives not just of the poor whom she aided but of the rich whom she relentlessly solicited," he wrote, describing the three days he spent with her as "the strongest evidence this struggling Catholic has ever had that God exists."

He didn't mention that he and Diana had once spoken about the nun in the penthouse of New York's Carlyle hotel, instead noting that the "muted" reaction to Mother Teresa's death, compared with the international grief over Diana, revealed "a truth about human nature." He wrote, "Both women gave comfort to the poor and sick. Yet their deaths affected the world so differently." After reflecting on privilege, beauty, and goodness, there was the morose foreshadowing of John's contemplation of what it means to die before your time, as he described the tragedy of Diana's death as "made ever more acute since she was young."

George editor Richard Bradley would look back on John's letter with sadness, calling it "both a remembrance and a prophecy." As he described it, "Mother Teresa and Lady Diana represented the two extremes of John's existence, the call to service and the lure of celebrity."

The editors also used the tribute to Diana as a way to investigate privacy laws in the United States, putting a *George* spin on the issue of paparazzi. Slotted between an article about George Bush's new presidential library, a profile of Barbara Walters, and a feature on the high-stakes world of salmon fishing was a "rant" from lawyer Martin "Marty" London about celebrities' legal right to privacy when it comes to being photographed. Martin, who is best known for representing Vice President Spiro Agnew in relation to the criminal charges brought against him in 1973 (leading to Agnew's plea of no contest to a single felony charge of tax evasion and later his resignation from his position in the Nixon administration), was acquainted with John through his mother, Jackie. In 1972, he represented Jackie in a harassment lawsuit against famed New York paparazzo Ron Galella. In the case, Jackie testified that Galella made her life "intolerable, almost unlivable, with his constant surveillance." She won, and a judge ordered him to stay twenty-five feet away from her and thirty feet away from her children. In *George*, Martin argued that laws, particularly regarding photographers, needed to adapt to modern times with recognition of "generally accepted notions of privacy." He also suggested that the agencies that pay said photographers should be held accountable for the bad behavior of the paparazzi they employ. New legislation proposed in California regarding photographers and celebrity privacy also received a short write-up.

While John was able to work with the team at *George* to pull together an issue that memorialized the princess and stayed true to its brand, outside the office, both John and his wife, Carolyn, were deeply affected by Diana's death. Carolyn could not tear herself away from the television coverage, watching and wondering if she, too, would meet a similar fate, given how ruthlessly the paparazzi pursued her and John. "I think it scared her. I think it shocked her, because she was human and she was really empathetic. It scared her about having children," RoseMarie said. "She was afraid of something happening if she was out with a child and John wasn't around."

Her reaction worried John. "I'm not sure what I'm going to do about Carolyn," he told his lifelong friend William Sylvester "Billy" Noonan. "She's really spooked now."

The day of Diana's funeral, the couple were in Hyannis Port on Cape Cod. For some reason, John kept playing the Rolling Stones' song "You Can't Always Get What You Want," and Carolyn was "in a world of her own."

At dinner with Kathy McKeon, Jackie's former personal assistant, Carolyn fully broke down. She was terrified of how the media played a role in the car crash that killed Diana, and also of the prospect that paparazzi might now come after them with renewed fervor. Diana was dead, but America's prince and princess were very much alive. Sensing how upset Carolyn was when conversation turned to Diana, John asked Kathy to explain how his mother used to deal with photographers.

"When she was up here, she'd leave the gate smiling, give them one good picture, and they'd let her go," she said, but Carolyn wasn't interested in playing the photographers' games. "No," she almost shouted back. "I hate those bastards! I'd rather just scream and curse at them." She explained how she constantly felt pursued by the photographers, almost hunted.

"They were grunting and groaning and pushing each other. They were almost on top of me," she said, recalling one horrible experience when they trapped her in an elevator. "It was just awful. I can't take it!"

"You gotta just take it easy," John said, trying to comfort his wife.

Carolyn wasn't used to the attention, but it was all John knew. He didn't realize how hard life in a fishbowl could be, because he had built up strategies for navigating the press over decades. Plus, he was one of them now. John had also miscalculated the media's interest in his life with Carolyn. He thought that after their wedding—a quiet, private ceremony on Cumberland Island off the coast of Georgia on September 21, 1996—journalists would lose interest. "John believed once he got married, the press would leave him alone," his friend Steve Gillon said. "He'd no longer be America's most eligible bachelor. He'd be another married guy. And just the opposite happened."

Carolyn had reached a breaking point and began isolating herself, scared to venture out for fear of encountering photographers. That anxiety only intensified after Diana died, with friends recalling her becoming paranoid and reclusive, limiting her and John's social circle. "She just didn't want to leave the apartment," John's friend Sasha said. "She didn't want to go out and be followed."

THE ANXIETY CAROLYN FELT ABOUT THE PRESS WAS SOMETHING she battled for the rest of her life. One of the reasons John learned to fly was so that he and Carolyn could travel discreetly. He'd loved aviation from the time he was a boy, but flying commercially was challenging. As for taking a private plane? "It wasn't really his style," one of John's *George* colleagues said. And so, he got his pilot's license.

On July 16, 1999, Carolyn, her sister Lauren, and John boarded a small single-engine plane at New Jersey's Essex County Airport. The plan was for John to drop Lauren off on Martha's Vineyard before continuing on to the Cape. His cousin Rory, the youngest of Bobby Kennedy's children, was getting married in Hyannis Port. But they never made it. The plane crashed into the ocean that night.

In the end, there was a cruel parallel between what killed the People's Princess and how John and Carolyn died: All three of them were pursuing privacy. Sasha echoes the connection: "Like Diana's death, John's death, Carolyn's, and Lauren's were all related to the same exact thing, which is getting away from the press. . . . I also think the overbearing obligation of showing the right face for the media was driving the escape from public scrutiny," she said. "Constant pressure from the tabloids, and other journalists, left Princess Diana, like John and Carolyn, scrambling for privacy. They might still be alive if they hadn't been under pressure to always appear a certain way—for their families, for the countries that they represented in a public manor. . . . It was all related to the same exact thing, which is getting away from the press and showing the right face for the press," she said, calling out the "Kennedy family wedding" for needing "a certain veneer. It needed to have a certain facade for the American people and for the world, I suppose. That was the priority."

Not long after Diana's death, Platon spoke with John about seeing the public mourn the princess so passionately, with such an impressive display of emotion. "I remember saying to him, 'I wonder if this would ever happen in America,'" Platon recalled. John responded, "I doubt it." But Platon remembered, "When he died, it *did* happen in America."

CHAPTER 13

The Public Funeral

AT FIRST, NO ONE WAS WORRIED WHEN JOHN AND CAROLYN DIDN'T show up on time. The duo wasn't particularly known for being punctual, so at first no one panicked when they didn't land at Barnstable Municipal Airport as scheduled. But as the hours ticked on, it became clear that something was very wrong.

John's friend Dan Samson had been waiting up for the couple, expecting them to walk through the door around 10 p.m. or so. By 11:30, he started calling friends, family, and the Coast Guard. At 1 a.m., he knocked on Senator Ted Kennedy's door.

RoseMarie Terenzio was staying at John's apartment while he was away, fielding phone calls of her own. She, too, got in touch with Senator Kennedy, and around 2 a.m., the police knocked on the door of the Tribeca loft, looking for John and Carolyn.

The news that they were missing broke to the public early in the morning. "And then—I just remember the phone started ringing off the fucking hook," RoseMarie said.

The television coverage was relentless as America collectively held its breath, hoping the Kennedy family would be spared another tragedy. Lacking any other critical hard news story at the moment, the twenty-four-hour television news cycle focused on John and Carolyn (and to a much lesser degree, Lauren), offering updates on the Coast Guard's search as well as a maudlin loop of paparazzi coverage of the couple paired with emotional footage of John throughout his life, including the iconic visuals from his own father's funeral.

In Hyannis Port, Senator Kennedy started the day with a swim, joined by Father Gerry Creedon, an Irish priest from West Cork and a friend of the Kennedy family's, who was visiting Cape Cod for the wedding. The plan had been for Father Gerry to say Mass that morning for Rory; her fiancé, Mark; and her mother, Ethel.

But the wedding was postponed indefinitely. Instead, that morning, the Kennedys gathered at their compound to hope and to pray in a private service under the white tent intended for a celebration. About fifty family members were joined by three priests in prayers "for the safety of the loved ones, as well as for Rory and Mark," family spokesman Brian O'Connor said at the time. As *The New York Times* reported, "At the end of the service, Senator Edward M. Kennedy could be seen holding the communion chalice, offering wine to Ethel Kennedy, the widow of Senator Robert F. Kennedy, their daughter Rory Kennedy, and other family members."

It was an abrupt shift in mood from the evening before. Everyone had been so excited for Rory, who was no stranger to tragedy, to finally have a happy ending. Ethel and Bobby's youngest child never met her father, as she was born after his assassination. "There are a lot of people in the family who don't see each other too often," Brian said, describing the scene at the house. "They're still catching up. A somber mood is going on. Mrs. Kennedy is showing great spirit and pulling everyone together. She is the leader in this household."

Indeed, Ethel took on the role of matriarch in the family, making sure everyone was fed and looked after, while Ted served as family patriarch, once again stepping into a role he never wanted, but one that was thrust upon him after the deaths of his older brothers.

Father Gerry shared that while some speculated, asking "What if they hadn't held the wedding in Hyannis?" and "Is it ever going to stop?"—referring to the seemingly unending list of tragedies endured by the Kennedys—there was already an overarching feeling of acceptance. After all, they were a family who knew how to mourn.

Later that afternoon, debris from the plane washed up on shore: Lauren's suitcase containing her business card, and a prescription bottle labeled with Carolyn's name.

President Clinton also made a statement, thanking the Coast Guard for their efforts and offering prayers to the Kennedy and Bessette families.

"For more than 40 years now, the Kennedy family has inspired Americans to public service, strengthened our faith in the future, and moved our nation forward. Through it all they have suffered much, and given more," he said. "At this difficult moment, we hope the families of these three fine young people will feel the strength of God, the love of their friends, and the prayers of their fellow citizens."

Sunday evening, after two days of searching, the Coast Guard changed its mission to one of recovery as opposed to rescue. "I have spent some very painful moments with the families tonight," Admiral Richard Larrabee said in a news conference around 9:45 p.m. "They have been very understanding all along, and very appreciative of what we have been trying to do, and it was very difficult for me to share this information with them. But I think they understood it."

Throughout the search, makeshift memorials popped up at sites of significance to the Kennedy family, like the John F. Kennedy Presidential Library and Museum in Boston, the John F. Kennedy Hyannis Museum on Main Street, and the John F. Kennedy Memorial overlooking Lewis Bay. But the largest was at the Tribeca apartment where John and Carolyn lived in New York City. Thousands of mourners gathered in disbelief on North Moore Street, leaving behind a growing pile of flowers, flags, stuffed animals, balloons, candles, newspaper clippings, and handwritten notes. "Goodnight sweet prince," read one prominent sign left alongside the door. In equal sentiment, there were cards asking John to "come home" and to "rest in peace."

"He was a Kennedy, but that was just a name," Jennifer Torres of Brooklyn said to *The Washington Post* at the impromptu shrine. "He took the subway, he roller-bladed, he biked all over the city. He was one of us."

On July 21, Navy divers recovered all three bodies from the wreckage. John was found in the cockpit, and all three of them were still strapped into their seats. Autopsies eventually concluded that they died upon impact from multiple traumatic injuries sustained in the crash. One year later, a report from the National Transportation Safety Board attributed the probable cause of the accident to pilot error, specifically "the pilot's failure to maintain control of the airplane during a descent over water at night, which was the result of spatial disorientation. Factors in the accident were haze and the dark night." Like his father and his uncle, John was now frozen in time.

"We are filled with unspeakable grief and sadness by the loss of John and Carolyn and Lauren Bessette. John was a shining light in all our lives and in the lives of the nation and the world that first came to know him when he was a little boy," Senator Kennedy said in a statement on behalf of his family.

The Bessette family also issued a statement of their own, saying, "Each of these three young people—Lauren Bessette, Carolyn Bessette Kennedy, and John F. Kennedy Jr.—was the embodiment of love, accomplishment, and passion for life. John and Carolyn were true soul mates. . . . We take solace in the thought that together they will comfort Lauren for eternity."

By the time the news broke, thousands of cards and letters had already arrived in Hyannis Port, addressed simply "To the Kennedy family," offering condolences.

While there had been discussions of John being buried in the family plot in Brookline, Massachusetts, there would have been no room for Lauren, and Carolyn's mother was adamant that her two girls stay together. "I don't want the girls separated. I want them together," she said. Per the Pentagon, Lauren and Carolyn's family requested that the two women be buried in the same ceremony as John. So the three passengers' remains were cremated, and on July 22, members of the Kennedy family, including Caroline, as well as relatives of the Bessette sisters, boarded a Navy destroyer to scatter the ashes of their loved ones in the waters off the shore of Martha's Vineyard.

At the time, Senator Kennedy confirmed this was in line with John's wishes for his remains; a family member also shared that they hoped to avoid making a spectacle of his final resting place.

After some debate among Kennedy family members, the memorial Mass for John and Carolyn, which followed the burial, was also planned to be by invitation only. Eventually, it was decided that the service would be held on July 23 at the Church of St. Thomas More, the small (at least by New York City standards) neighborhood parish where Jackie had once worshipped on the Upper East Side. All in all, it could hold only 350 people, meaning that each of the guests had a close relationship with John, with Carolyn, or with them both.

Even with a reduced capacity, mourners included political figures and prominent names from the Kennedy administration along with friends and family members. President Clinton was in attendance alongside Hillary and their daughter, Chelsea, as was John's childhood hero, Muhammed Ali. Wyclef Jean sang "Many Rivers to Cross."

Two eulogies were given: one by Senator Kennedy, who was all too familiar with the task, and the other by Carolyn's friend Hamilton South. Several of the couple's loved ones provided readings; for example, before the service, Carolyn's mother shared a passage from *Facts of the Faith*, a collection of sermons by Henry Scott Holland. John's sister selected a poignant verse from Shakespeare's *The Tempest*, beginning with the line "Our revels now are ended" and ending with "We are such stuff as dreams are made on, and our little life is rounded with a sleep."

Caroline was there with her husband and their three children, Rose, Tatiana, and John. Jackie's longtime partner, the last love of her life, Maurice Tempelsman, and her sister, Lee Radziwill, were also in attendance. Three of John's aunts—Jean, Patricia, and Eunice—were among the many, many Kennedys who filled the pews.

Initially, the staff of *George* was allotted only five tickets, but RoseMarie Terenzio fought for them all to be included.

"Caroline said I could pick five from the *George* staff and I said that that was unacceptable," RoseMarie would later recall. "He spent ten hours a day with them for five years. She said okay. I made sure that every single person from *George*, all forty, were invited, because those were John's people."

The intense media interest, combined with a limited guest list, created a morbid demand for access both to the Mass and to the separate service held for Lauren and Carolyn in their hometown of Greenwich on July 24. As Carole Radziwill put it, the "tragedy whores" came out "in full force" after John and Carolyn's death. "They're voyeurs. They feed like coffin flies on drama, embroiled in virtual grief and the illusion of heartbreak. They all have stories they want to tell, *insist* on telling, proclaiming their link to tragedy. Emotional rubberneckers. I didn't like them at twelve, and I hated them at thirty-five," she wrote in her memoir. "Everyone wanted an invitation to the funerals. It seemed to be the hottest ticket in town. These are all small transgressions, really. Carolyn and I would laugh if she were here, but she is not."

Unlike the funerals of his mother and father, John's memorial was not televised. But despite the fact that cameras weren't rolling inside the church, the scene continued to capture the twenty-four-hour news cycle, as broadcasters meticulously documented the arrivals and provided color commentary throughout the hour-long service. Footage from outside the church was interspersed with vintage clips of John, conversations with Kennedy biographers, and person-on-the-street interviews with New Yorkers paying their respects to John at his Tribeca apartment.

As *The New York Times* reported, "The fact that the onlookers could see little and hear nothing seemed irrelevant to their compulsion to be there."

"We're not here to gawk," explained twenty-four-year-old Heather Sheehan, who came up from Philadelphia for the service with her mother, Kathleen, who had attended RFK's funeral at St. Patrick's Cathedral. "We're just here to show the Kennedy family our support," she told the *Cape Cod Times*. Ultimately, they were blocked by a police barricade, but they were still happy they'd made the trip.

"From the first day of his life, John seemed to belong not only to our family, but to the American family," said Senator Kennedy. "He had a legacy, and he learned to treasure it. He was part of a legend, and he learned to live with it."

But while John had come to terms with his role in the American story, neither he nor his loved ones ever felt entirely comfortable with the ownership that other people felt over him or his family, especially in death. And following John's passing, his friends struggled to process the general public's outpouring of grief for someone they didn't know, in tandem with their own intimate feelings of profound loss.

"It was so public," RoseMarie said, noting that John's and Carolyn's faces were all over newsstands. She recalled going out to dinner with *George* staffers but being afraid to talk about John's death because they didn't want it to "end up in the media."

"People don't know that we're actually in mourning and we're holding a funeral basically amongst ourselves," she said. In the face of all that, "It was strange to have to pull your personal grief back in."

THE REACTION TO THE DEATHS OF JOHN AND CAROLYN MIRRORS the response to Princess Diana's less than two years prior.

In US history, there are few images as iconic as the photograph of three-year-old John F. Kennedy Jr. saluting his father's casket. In the United Kingdom, the same could be said of the image of fifteen-year-old Prince William and twelve-year-old Prince Harry stoically walking behind their mother's coffin. To be or to love a Kennedy or a Windsor is to share your grief with the world. But while John hardly remembered his father's funeral and rarely spoke about it, Prince Harry has opened up many times about the lasting trauma of walking in Princess Diana's funeral cortège.

"My mother had just died, and I had to walk a long way behind her coffin, surrounded by thousands of people watching me while millions more did on television," Harry said in a 2017 interview, speaking about the performance required of him after his mother's death. "I don't think any child should be asked to do that, under any circumstances. I don't think it would happen today."

It was Prince Philip, ever aware of the optics, who convinced his grandsons to do it. "I seem to remember him saying that in fact, it was a question of, 'If you'll do it, I'll do it,'" Princess Anne said in an interview after her father's death. "And that was him as a grandfather saying to them, 'If you want me to be there, if that's what you want to do and if you want me to be there, I will be there.'" Prince William has described it as a collective family decision—though not an easy one. "There was that balance between duty and family, and that's what we had to do," he said.

So on the day of Princess Diana's funeral, Princes William and Harry walked through the crowd-lined streets of London alongside Prince Philip, Prince Charles, and Diana's brother, Charles Spencer. "Come morning, bright and early, off we went, all together. Uncle Charles on my right, Willy to his right, followed by Grandpa. And on my left was Pa," Harry wrote in *Spare.* "I noted at the start how serene Grandpa looked, as if this was merely another royal engagement. I could see his eyes, clearly, because he was gazing straight ahead. They all were. But I kept mine down on the road. So did Willy. I remember feeling numb."

It provided the public with a performance of grief they found enormously sympathetic, in contrast to the way Queen Elizabeth had initially reacted to Diana's death, by trying to protect her grandchildren. In the end, the only thing that calmed the anger felt toward the Queen for not immediately paying tribute to her late former daughter-in-law was the Queen's nod and bow as Diana's coffin passed.

As Harry struggled to process his grief, the fact that so many people who had never met his mother were mourning so fervently with anger and sorrow only made it harder.

"It was very, very strange after her death, you know, the sort of outpouring of love and emotion from so many people that had never even met her," Prince Harry said years later, recalling the collective, almost compulsive keening in the wake of his mother's tragic passing. "And I was thinking to myself, 'How is it that so many people that never even met this woman, my mother, can be crying and showing more emotion than I actually am feeling?'" The disorientation wasn't simply because of his age. Despite her experience working with bereaved people, Julia Samuel, a grief therapist and Diana's close friend, also could not comprehend the disconnect between the passionate emotion displayed by strangers following Diana's death and her own intimate sadness over a personal loss. "I remember clearly the shock I'd felt when she died," she would later recall. "The pain and subsequent fury of missing her and wanting her back. My confusion when millions of people who didn't know her were sobbing hysterically in the streets."

That dissonance in grief was something John understood—and when Carolyn heard the news of Diana's death, she urged him to call William and Harry to offer his condolences. John was one of the few people who could truly empathize with what Diana's sons were going through—having to put on a brave face while publicly mourning. Not only because of his experience at his father's funeral, and just a few years later at that of his uncle Bobby, but also because he was still fresh in his grief over his own mother. But after thinking about it, he decided against calling the princes, given that they were not particularly close.

Even though he didn't reach out to the Windsors directly, Diana's death, and the communal grief and almost contagious catharsis that followed, stirred up memories for John. In 1994, three years before Diana died, Jackie had passed away from non-Hodgkin's lymphoma. She was buried alongside Jack and Bobby at Arlington National Cemetery in Washington, DC. But for John, her burial wasn't a poignant moment to say goodbye. It was a performance for a national and an international audience, just as the memorials to his father and his uncle had been.

"He was really, really, really taken down by his mother's death," John's close friend Sasha Chermayeff recalled. "I remember, so distinctly, him saying how he had to protect himself from expressing himself because the funeral was being filmed, the burial of his mother was being broadcast. So his energy went into psyching himself up to not express anything that he was going through.

"His take on his mom's funeral was, 'I don't want everybody to see this. I don't want everybody to know how I feel. I'm not going to cry in front of a million people, or ten million people, or a one hundred million people. I'm not doing any of this.' There's Jackie O being laid down with two assassinated men, and it's pretty intense, and it has a lot of meaning for all of us. But the personal side of it, it's just messed up because of the way that they have to conduct themselves in the face of what they really feel. Having really deep feelings about your mother's loss is something that we can't project as an image of grace—or certainly not grace without pain, or a grace without tears," Sasha continued. John's sister, Caroline, considered the relative intimacy of his funeral to be a final gift to her brother, who struggled to find privacy when he was alive.

King Charles is said to regret the decision to have his two sons walk behind their mother's coffin, but at the same time, the royals continue to live by the mantra that public duty trumps private emotion. All the family's most significant life milestones—be they marriages, births, or deaths—must be shared. Such is the covenant the royals have with their subjects. So after Queen Elizabeth died in September 2022, King Charles was seen wiping away a tear as he and his wife, Queen Camilla, greeted public mourners outside Buckingham Palace.

At the monarch's state funeral a few days later, Prince William's nine-year-old son, George, and seven-year-old daughter, Charlotte, sat in the front row as the world watched.

A Signature Style

Before Meghan Markle even met Prince Harry, she was already thinking about her ideal wedding dress. Back then, she wasn't the Duchess of Sussex, but rather a successful working actress. Her character on *Suits*, Rachel Zane, was getting married, and Meghan revealed to *Glamour* that she helped select the on-screen bridal look.

"I weigh in on all of Rachel's outfit choices," she explained, sharing how she had looked at options with her close friend Jessica Mulroney and the show's stylist, Jolie Andreatta. Eventually, they decided on an Anne Barge V-neck gown with a cinched waist and delicate beaded detailing. The dress "just screamed 'Rachel,'" Meghan said but admitted it wasn't her personal style. "I have the luxury of wearing beautiful pieces of clothing every day for work, so my personal style—wedding or not—is very pared down and relaxed," she said. "Classic and simple is the name of the game, perhaps with a modern twist. I personally prefer wedding dresses that are whimsical or subtly romantic."

When the interviewer asked about her favorite celebrity wedding dress, Meghan quickly responded, "Carolyn Bessette Kennedy," calling the iconic silk crepe Narciso Rodriguez slip dress "everything goals."

On May 19, 2018, Meghan walked down the long aisle of Windsor Castle's St. George's Chapel on the arm of Prince Charles in a sleek bateau-neckline gown with three-quarter sleeves, a fitted waist, and a soft train by Givenchy's Clare Waight Keller. It certainly wasn't an exact replica of Carolyn's cut-on-the-bias bridal look, but the effortless inspiration was there. "I knew at the onset I wanted a bateau neckline. I wanted a cropped sleeve. I wanted a very timeless, classic feeling," Meghan later said in audio recorded for an exhibit about the royal wedding displayed at Windsor Castle.

It was a picture for the history books, and Meghan was focused on her gown "being absolutely perfect for the occasion." The design was also steeped in symbolism, with flowers from every Commonwealth nation embroidered on her veil. For Meghan, the sole Black member of the royal family, it was a subtle reference to the role she could play in maintaining relationships between the UK and Commonwealth nations, many of which are former British colonies. To offer even more significance, the veil featured two extra flowers: wintersweet, which grows in front of the Nottingham Cottage at Kensington Palace, where the couple lived at the time, and the California poppy, in honor of Meghan's home state. Stalks of wheat were also embroidered throughout to represent love and charity.

The ceremony gown was one for the ages, but there is arguably a more apt comparison to be made between Carolyn's iconic look and Meghan's reception dress.

After a daytime celebration at Windsor Castle, complete with champagne, cake, and a performance of "Tiny Dancer" by Elton John, the royal bride had a change of wardrobe. To the evening re-

King George VI and Queen Elizabeth, the future Queen Mother, attend
an event at the residence of Ambassador Kennedy and his wife, Rose.

Rose Kennedy with her daughters Kathleen
and Rosemary before being presented to
the King and Queen in 1938.

(left) Joe Kennedy Jr., Kathleen Kennedy,
and John F. Kennedy walk toward
the Houses of Parliament on
the day the UK entered World War II.

Before marrying JFK,
Jacqueline Bouvier
worked as a photojournalist
for the *Washington Times-Herald*.

Queen Elizabeth II and Prince Philip wave to the crowds
following the Queen's coronation in June 1953.

Kate Middleton and Prince William pose for photographs to mark the announcement of their engagement to be married.

Jacqueline Bouvier's 1953 wedding to John F. Kennedy was a public spectacle similar to Princess Diana's 1981 marriage to Prince Charles, albeit on a different scale.

On June 5, 1961, British royalty met the American kind when President Kennedy and his wife, Jackie, visited Buckingham Palace.

During Jackie's 1962 diplomatic tour of India and Pakistan, cameras captured the First Lady outside the Taj Mahal. Thirty years later, Princess Diana would take a photo in almost the exact same spot.

There are few photos as iconic as that of John F. Kennedy Jr. saluting his father's casket. The same could be said of the image of Princes William and Harry stoically walking in their mother's cortège.

Prince Philip is pictured here among the foreign dignitaries in President Kennedy's funeral procession.

Eunice Kennedy Shriver visits with Prince Philip during a reception at the White House following President John F. Kennedy's funeral.

Queen Elizabeth greets JFK Jr. during the inauguration of
the Kennedy Memorial at Runnymede in May 1965.

The Kennedys and the Radziwills take in the Changing
of the Guard ceremony at Buckingham Palace.

The former "Fab Four"—Kate, William, Harry, and Meghan—reunite in Windsor following the death of Queen Elizabeth II.

President John F. Kennedy delivers his famous Moonshot speech at Rice University in September 1962.

Prince William meets Jack Schlossberg, Tatiana Schlossberg, and Caroline Kennedy outside the John F. Kennedy Presidential Library and Museum.

The Duke and Duchess of Sussex speak with Kerry Kennedy at the Robert F. Kennedy Human Rights Ripple of Hope Gala.

The Duchess of Sussex has long been a fan of Carolyn Bessette-Kennedy's classic style.

ception at Frogmore House, Meghan wore a "lily white high neck gown made of silk crepe," as Kensington Palace described it at the time. Created by Stella McCartney, it evoked the essence of Carolyn's sleek and sexy bridal look. Meghan paired the dress with a messy updo and simple heels, and on her right hand, she wore an aquamarine ring that had belonged to Princess Diana.

Unlike the Sussexes' highly public nuptials, which were attended by hundreds of aristocrats and celebrities, John and Carolyn's wedding was a secret affair.

Only forty of their closest family and friends were in attendance, and almost unbelievably, the press didn't find out ahead of time. "It was wonderful to have no press around," said one guest. "We were so excited to have fooled everybody."

Their humble wedding ceremony in an eight-pew church with no air-conditioning couldn't have been more different from the Sussexes' televised vows in St. George's Chapel, a broadcast that reached nearly two billion people. But Harry and Meghan managed to carve out a private moment on their wedding day—members of the press were not invited to the couple's evening reception, and over the years, few specifics have come out about the event.

"In the end, this was a wedding, an actual wedding, between two people who are real people that fell in love. And people who know them know that this is a private moment that was not allowed to be private," Janina Gavankar, Meghan's longtime friend, said at the time.

For both Meghan and Carolyn, their weddings were one final moment to embrace their individuality before joining families that also function as institutions. While Meghan shared her daytime ceremony with the public, the nighttime party was just for her.

"The role that she's taken on is very austere, it's very serious, and I think there's a great weight that she has acquired through that and she takes it very seriously," Stella said of working with Meghan. "It was the last moment that she could reflect the other side to her . . . the joy and the human within her."

Even as Meghan's aesthetic shifted to fit her new position within the British monarchy—from a relaxed look to a closet full of prim silhouettes and classic accessories—her affinity for Carolyn's style was still evident. She wanted to "blend in" and often chose to wear neutrals, so as not to upstage any other member of the royal family. At her first official engagement with Prince Harry, in December 2017, for example, Meghan paired a black turtleneck with a camel skirt and slouchy boots, a look that seemed to nod to Carolyn's first experience with the press after her honeymoon in 1996.

A source close to Meghan says she didn't intend to re-create Carolyn's outfit. "Meghan's style is very American classic. She's a master of simple elegance, and I think Carolyn was the OG of that," the source said. "Meghan knows her style and what she likes, and I think that's really rooted in who she is. She's not necessarily like, 'I want to emulate a specific look.'"

But even if the homage was unintentional, it still contributed to the "American princess" narrative surrounding Meghan, one that re-surfaced in 2019, when she arrived on the red carpet of the Endeavor awards wearing a high-waisted black skirt with a crisp white button-down shirt. The bespoke Clare Waight Keller for Givenchy ensemble was almost identical to what Carolyn had worn to a fundraiser for the Whitney Museum in 1999. Media outlets were quick to draw comparisons between Meghan and Carolyn, both their senses of style and their life experiences, illustrating how fashion is one of the most important storytelling tools royal women have in their arsenal.

For women in the royal family, styling an outfit is about so much more than simply selecting clothes. Given that royal women are seen—and photographed—far more often than they are heard, their ensembles can send a powerful message through the press. This is most apparent on royal tours, when they use a sort of sartorial diplomacy to pay tribute to the host country. During an official visit to Japan in 1986, Princess Diana wore a bold polka-dot dress, reminiscent of the "circle of the sun" flag, as a sign of respect for the nation. Similarly, on a more recent royal tour of Canada, Kate arrived at an event sporting a dress in the country's signature crimson coupled with the Queen's glimmering maple leaf brooch, the same one Elizabeth wore during her 1951 tour of the US and Canada.

Royal women also frequently wear clothes or accessories from local makers, such as when Kate wore a cream-colored sundress from the Australian brand Zimmermann during a 2014 visit to Sydney, and when Meghan opted for a wrap dress from the Malawi-made fashion label Mayamiko on her 2019 royal tour of southern Africa.

At home in the UK, the royals carefully craft a visual narrative that often links the past to the present, always cognizant that these images live not only on the internet and the front pages of newspapers but also in the annals of history. When Queen Camilla wears the Greville tiara, it ties her to the Queen Mother, the most recent queen consort; similarly, when Prince George wears an outfit of Prince William's, it associates the two heirs to the throne (while also suggesting that by using hand-me-downs, the royals are, if not thrifty, at least cognizant of funding).

While all these women have access to custom designs, they sometimes chose to wear pieces off-the-rack. Just as being photographed in vintage jewelry or a design paying homage to an allied country can help shape the discourse, so, too, can wearing an affordable and easily shoppable look. Nothing screams relatable like a literal princess wearing J.Crew.

For young royals, Diana often serves as a reference point. She is remembered as the People's Princess for a reason, and the public still thinks of her with love and affection, so it only makes sense that both Meghan and Kate would want to evoke her memory. Of course, Kate's diamond and sapphire engagement ring, which once belonged to her mother-in-law, is a clear visual allusion. Kate often wears styles that can be immediately identified as inspired by Diana, whether that means favoring the tiara most closely associated with the late Princess of Wales or channeling her penchant for polka dots.

Similarly, Meghan often chooses jewelry that once belonged to her mother-in-law to punctuate important moments in her own life. For her first official event following the announcement of her pregnancy, she wore Princess Diana's gold butterfly earrings. Meghan's engagement ring, too, features a nod to Diana. The large center stone was sourced from Botswana, where Harry and Meghan spent their third date, but two of the three diamonds are from Princess Diana's collection. "Not being able to meet his mom, it's so important to me to know that she's a part of this with us," Meghan said of her ring in the couple's first sit-down interview with the BBC.

It's a strategy that Carolyn Bessette-Kennedy employed as well. Like Meghan and Kate, Carolyn never met her famous mother-in-law, but she owned a few pieces of her jewelry—a necklace featuring a bird in a cage and her Cartier Tank watch, to name two. (Presumably, John's sister, Caroline, inherited the bulk of that collection.) Carolyn's engagement ring, a platinum band featuring round sapphires and diamonds, was a near perfect copy of one of Jackie's rings. On rare occasions, particularly at events with ties to the late First Lady, Carolyn made it a point to showcase jewelry with ties to Jackie. For example, at a 1998 Municipal Art Society gala at Grand Central Terminal honoring Jackie's legacy, Carolyn wore one of her bracelets. It was a fitting tribute, given that Jackie often used her style to shape perception.

EVEN IN HER TEENAGE YEARS, WHEN MOST GIRLS FEEL AWKWARD, Jackie understood the power that beauty could provide a woman. While at Miss Porter's School, she honed an acute understanding of when to conform and when to set herself apart from the fashions of the crowd, eschewing the omnipresent white raincoat of the day or choosing a cloth coat over an extremely popular fur one. And she always had an eye for beautiful things, noting a classmate's jeweled brooch or the sophisticated perfume she often borrowed from her friend Nancy "Tucky" Tuckerman.

Perhaps it's something Jackie learned from her mother, who emphasized appearance, sometimes ruthlessly, above all else. Jackie noted her mother's attention to aesthetic detail in an application for *Vogue*'s Prix de Paris essay competition in search of editorial talent. "I have no idea how to go about describing myself but perhaps with much sifting of wheat from chaff I can produce something fairly accurate," Jackie wrote of herself in 1951. "As to physical appearance, I am tall 5′7″ with brown hair, a square face and eyes so unfortunately far apart that it takes three weeks to have a pair of glasses made with a bridge wide enough to fit over my nose. I do not have a sensational figure but can look slim if I pick the right clothes. I flatter myself on being able at times to walk out of the house looking like the poor man's Paris copy, but often my mother will run up to inform me that my left stocking seam is crooked or the right-hand top coat button is about to fall off. This, I realize is the Unforgivable Sin."

The ability to deploy style, beauty, and glamour as assets was key to Jackie's influence on her husband's political career—but that wasn't always the case. While lifestyle journalists praised her campaign style (a July 1960 opinion piece in *The New York Times* even predicted, "If her husband is elected, she can qualify as one of the most glamorous White House hostesses in United States history"), the press was broadly quite critical of Jackie's fashions, often bemoaning her love of French designers. It was even reported that she and her mother-in-law spent upwards of $30,000 a year on clothes in Paris, a claim that Jackie denied, cheekily replying, "I couldn't spend that much unless I wore sable underwear."

She also joked, "I'm sure I spend less than Mrs. Nixon on clothes," and called the criticism of her wardrobe "dreadfully unfair," saying, "They're beginning to snipe at me about that as often as they attack Jack on Catholicism."

Jackie didn't understand the controversy over her clothes—or at least publicly, she feigned confusion. "All the talk over what I wear and how I fix my hair has amused me and puzzled me," she wrote in one of her Campaign Wife columns, a few weeks before election day. "What does my hairdo have to do with my husband's ability to be president?"

But once Jack clinched the Oval Office, Jackie worked to ensure her wardrobe wasn't seen as a blight on her husband's presidency. She never sacrificed her style, but as she wrote in a letter to designer Oleg Cassini, "I refuse to have Jack's administration plagued by fashion stories of a sensational nature—and to be the Marie Antoinette or Josephine of the 1960s." Jackie vowed to wear clothes made in the United States, promising she would "resort to muumuus if it will save Jack from embarrassment." (Never mind that these American garments were sometimes line-for-line replicas of European designs, including from Chanel.) It didn't hurt that her father-in-law was footing the bill, as opposed to the American people. "With great foresight, [Joe Kennedy] wanted to wipe out any possibility that the First Lady's new wardrobe might be used against them politically," Oleg later recalled.

And so Jackie's deft use of aesthetics became a "political tool," as JFK's speechwriter Arthur Schlesinger put it. "The things people had once held against her—the unconventional beauty, the un-American elegance, the taste for French clothes and French food—were suddenly no longer liabilities, but assets." Through her clothes, makeup, and hairdos, she projected a sense not only of youthful vitality but also an appreciation of culture and the arts. Throughout the years, many people, including fashion editor Hebe Dorsey, have noted that her embrace of beauty "helped to break down a certain Puritanism that had always existed in America and that insisted it was wrong to wear jewelry, wrong to wear fancy hairdos, wrong to live elegantly and graciously." With her wardrobe, she began to reshape how the world saw America, and in doing so, she began to carve out the role of First Lady as a position of soft power.

Jackie was also curating a visual identity for herself—one of sophistication and majesty that would long outlast the Kennedy presidency. To name one richly symbolic choice: Her preference for hair jewelry at formal events, where she sometimes placed brooches in her bouffant, was no coincidence. It was the closest a modern First Lady could get to a tiara.

Jackie worked with Oleg Cassini to curate her image. He was a friend of the Kennedy family, and the brother of Igor, who so many years prior had proclaimed Jackie Debutante of the Year (albeit behind the nom de plume of society columnist Cholly Knickerbocker). "We spoke of how fashion is a mirror of history; we discussed the message her clothes would send—simple, youthful, elegant—and how she would reinforce the image of her husband's administration through her presence," the designer later wrote of their approach to

Jackie's wardrobe. "You have an opportunity here," he told her, "for an American Versailles."

It's not uncommon for first ladies to work with a stylist or a singular designer. Royal women, too, often seek out a collaborator for their most iconic looks. Queen Elizabeth had Norman Hartnell in her early years and later relied on dressmaker Angela Kelly. Princess Diana had Catherine Walker, and Kate, at least thus far, has had a close relationship with several designers. Jenny Packham and Emilia Wickstead stand out, but perhaps no one has helped shape her royal aesthetic as much as Sarah Burton, the former creative director of Alexander McQueen.

"When we look back on the relationship between Kate and Sarah Burton, I think it's important to consider where the House of McQueen was when Kate selected Burton to design her wedding dress. Alexander McQueen died by suicide in February 2010. His passing plunged the celebrated brand into uncertainty. Although Burton had worked closely with McQueen for more than a decade, she still had a sizable task in front of her: to both prove herself a worthy successor and keep the business afloat," explained American journalist and royal fashion commentator Elizabeth Holmes.

"I have long felt, given where the brand was at, it was incredibly generous for Kate to select the label to make her wedding dress. She could have had any design house in the world make her something fabulous. The choice was a huge vote of confidence in Burton and a massive moment of global recognition for the British fashion house. Burton delivered flawlessly. The resulting McQueen gown was breathtaking. Technically, it fit perfectly. It also delivered on the princess promise—romantic and grand enough for the fairy-tale setting of Westminster Abbey. But it still allowed Kate, who captured the world's attention as a commoner marrying a prince, to shine through."

Holmes added, "The relationship between Kate and Burton that unfolded in the years to come was mutually beneficial. Kate continued to use the considerable conversation around her wardrobe to boost the visibility of Alexander McQueen. Burton, for her part, nudged Kate to a more fashion-forward and sophisticated place. The High Street pieces she wore in those early years helped her maintain her relatability. But it was important, too, that she reach for something a bit more royal when the moment called for it—like the stately military-inspired coats or the headline-grabbing gowns."

While Kate and Sarah have a true partnership, Jackie was hands-on in selecting what she wore, and some even say that she deserves all the credit for her fashions. "To sum it up, Jackie actually designed her own clothes," Kennedy family confidant Lem Billings later recalled, describing how she would pore through fashion magazines and sketch ideas. "It was Jackie. Cassini happened to be somebody whom Jackie knew and somebody who was perfectly happy to have Jackie tell him exactly how she wanted things. Also, he liked the same simple lines which she liked. The clothes that Cassini made for Jackie were Jackie's concept of what she wanted to wear. She would go through the fashion magazines for ideas. She knew what she wanted."

As it turned out, it's what Americans wanted, too. Long before "the Kate effect" or "the Meghan effect" on fashion, there was "the Jackie effect"—a phrase often repeated in US publications and that traveled to places as far flung as Poland and the USSR. The week of President Kennedy's inauguration, *Life* magazine published an article proclaiming that the incoming First Lady's style was "setting a national pace."

"College girls copy it casually, suburban matrons faithfully," the *Life* article read. "Millinery shops are being fortified with the largest collections of pillboxes in history. Fashion ads twinkle more mischievously with Jackie's unmistakable wide eyes. Her bouffant hairdo is becoming a by-word in beauty salons. All in all, the shy, beautiful First Lady's fashion followers are building up quite a bandwagon."

Jackie's aesthetic was distinct yet uncomplicated, and it could be emulated at multiple price points, making it accessible to the masses—both in the US and around the world. The fashion industry quickly shifted to make the most of a new muse. As *Ladies' Home Journal* put it, "Jackie's slightest fashion whim triggers seismic tremors up and down Seventh Avenue." Much like the way Princess Diana's fashion would go on to shape the Sloane Ranger style of the 1980s, with its posh-coded style signifiers—statement blazers, loafers, feminine dresses, and pearl necklaces (think British preppy)—Jackie's look came to encapsulate American fashion in the early 1960s.

When a sitting First Lady wears a dress by a new designer, it's the kind of career-making marketing that money can't buy. That was true in 2009 when Michelle Obama wore a Jason Wu gown to the inaugural ball, and it was true back in 1962 when Jackie Kennedy was photographed wearing a dress from Lilly Pulitzer. In Pulitzer's words, Kennedy's endorsement caused the brand to take "off like zingo," and the vibrant patterned shift instantly became an "if you know, you know" shorthand for a kind of old-money, preppy aesthetic.

The women of the modern-day royal family are all too familiar with that ability to move product. While they don't shape trends in the same way Jackie or Diana did, Meghan's and Kate's profound economic influence is undeniable.

Take the dress Kate wore to announce her engagement to Prince William. The royal blue wrap style sold out in just five minutes once the brand was identified. "That morning I'd gone to yoga as usual, and then I got a call from a friend telling me about the royal engagement," recalled Daniella Helayel, then the lead designer of Issa. "It was all very exciting. We didn't have a TV at the studio, and this was pre-Instagram, but we soon knew Kate was wearing Issa because at four o'clock the phones began ringing and didn't stop. It was bonkers." (While Kate's support was initially a boon for the small label, the surge of sales and a lack of capital to finance exponential growth stressed the brand financially. Helayel left the company in 2013, and eventually it shuttered in December 2015, only to be revived by the department store House of Fraser.)

It was the beginning of "the Kate effect" in earnest, which became a powerful economic force, particularly within the British fashion industry. It also spawned a cottage industry of bloggers and social media accounts on both sides of the pond dedicated to identifying and chronicling the wardrobes of royal women—and offering readers a way to take home a piece of the glamour of the modern monarchy. "If they wear something, people will buy it," Christine Ross, a royal commentator and former royal blogger, said simply.

A royal endorsement is a confirmation of quality and sophistication—these women can afford anything, and still they choose a moderately priced brand. But there's also an intangible element for consumers. The average person won't ever attend a formal state dinner or wear a tiara, but they can afford a pair of Superga sneakers (an under $100 favorite of Kate's) to add a touch of majesty to their everyday life.

When Meghan joined the royal family, she quickly proved that she, too, could move merchandise, and thus "the Meghan effect" was born. But Meghan was more prepared for that level of influence than her sister-in-law had been. In her pre-royal life, Meghan wasn't only an actress on *Suits*—she also ran a lifestyle blog called *The Tig*, which highlighted her favorite products. She saw the impact she could have with her fashion and leaned in.

Both Meghan and Kate are keenly aware of the messages their clothes send, but they approach the impact of their fashion differently. Kate, for her part, can be quiet about publicly identifying the clothes she wears in an effort to keep the conversation focused on charitable efforts, and the brands she works with are tight-lipped about their involvement (presumably because she asks them to be). By contrast, Meghan has always been forthcoming about acknowledging and even shining a spotlight on the companies she's aligned herself with sartorially. This was the case even before she stepped away from the confines of royal life.

"The Princess of Wales does not want you to talk about her fashion, but knows you're going to anyway, whereas Meghan knew you were going to talk about her fashion and made it easier to," Ross said. "The Duchess of Sussex was much quicker to send out a press release. Meghan would wear something and the company was able to promote it and do all these interviews about it. Kate wore something from the same brand and they were asked to be discreet."

In her post-royal era, Meghan has fully embraced the role of influencer, to the cheers of her fans and the general disdain of her critics. Following the March 4, 2025, premiere of her Netflix entertaining series, *With Love, Meghan*, the Duchess of Sussex created a ShopMy page linked to her social media accounts, where she not only verified the clothes she wore and the products she used but also earned a commission from the sales she drove by utilizing affiliate links. (She has since shuttered the account.)

In 2025, she launched As Ever, her own line of products, which began with a curated selection of British-inspired pantry staples at a high but not exorbitant price. Think teas, fruit spreads, and baking mixes. She started with a line tailor-made for middle-class Anglophiles living in America, but it's not hard to imagine a future where she returns to fashion with a charitable line mimicking her 2019 Smart Set collection, which operated on a one-for-one model to provide women in need with workwear. Or perhaps more likely, she could try her hand at selling accessories or even launching her version of a celebrity beauty brand. In fact, in May 2025, she vaguely told *Fast Company*, "Fashion is something I will explore at a later date, because I do think that's an interesting space for me."

Meanwhile, Meghan and Kate's late mother-in-law continues to shape the fashion industry from the grave. Diana and Carolyn Bessette-Kennedy are two of the most notable "ghost influencers," a phrase coined by *The New York Times* in 2023. While Diana had an enormous impact on trends and the fashion industry at the height of her fame, she continues to serve as a muse not only to designers but also to a new generation online that wasn't even born when she first arrived in the public eye as the shy nursery school teacher dating Prince Charles.

Like clockwork every spring and fall, as soon as thermometers hit a balmy sixty degrees, the internet declares it "Princess Diana Season," referencing an oft-posted picture of the royal wearing a sweatshirt paired with bike shorts. The mention of a "revenge dress" instantly conjures images of Diana in the black off-the-shoulder gown she wore to turn heads (and make headlines) the very same evening Prince Charles had confessed his affair on national television. Her iconic black-sheep sweater (the symbolism speaks for itself) sold for $1.1 million at Sotheby's in September 2023, a few years after the preppy lifestyle brand Rowing Blazers collaborated with the original designers, Joanna Osborne and Sally Muir of Warm & Wonderful, to create an authentic re-creation. The sweater has become a perennial bestseller.

"We're in this era of Instagram and mood-board culture,"

explained *Business of Fashion* editor (and former *People* magazine royals reporter) Diana Pearl. "People generally like to have a feeling of personality attached to their clothes and fashion choices."

Diana, Queen Elizabeth, and Jackie Kennedy regularly serve as easily recognizable inspiration for modern runway collections; one rarely needs to peruse the show notes to spot the references. It makes sense that brands would lean on the aesthetics of these widely admired women to help craft a brand identity and to ultimately sell clothes. While Carolyn Bessette-Kennedy, too, has long served as a fashion muse, in recent years, as the "quiet luxury" trend aligned perfectly with a wave of '90s nostalgia, her look has become increasingly popular.

"Khaite, The Row, these brands are totally, totally influenced by Carolyn," said Selima Salaun, the designer behind Carolyn's signature oval sunglasses. Decades after Carolyn first sported the shades as a form of sartorial protection from the prying lenses of photographers, demand remains high. "Everything she wore, people want to have," Salaun said. "Her style is timeless. She didn't live long enough to make a mistake. She passed away too young."

Carolyn's largely neutral wardrobe filled with classic, polished pieces wouldn't look out of place in the modern day, and as Meghan Markle proved, it doesn't.

"If you look at a photograph of Carolyn walking down the street twenty-five years ago, it could be today and she would still look great. She wasn't into trends. She had a very clean, simple, tailored look, but also with a bit of a bohemian flair," RoseMarie Terenzio said. But part of the appeal, she argues, lies in the mystery of the woman behind the looks. Carolyn was beautiful, but she remains largely unknown.

"There wasn't social media. There weren't cell phones with cameras. So we're not bombarded by images. There's no fatigue for John and Carolyn, because there wasn't this massive social media world that we live in now," RoseMarie said.

Pearl agreed. "There are very few interviews out there with Carolyn Bessette," she said, noting that her clothes are "all we really have from her."

The Dark Side of a Fairy Tale

Royal sit-downs are a rare event, and, when deemed necessary, they almost always offer history-making revelations. In 1994, during Prince Charles's conversation with journalist Jonathan Dimbleby, the then heir to the throne publicly admitted his infidelity. These programs also almost always punctuate an ongoing narrative with a sound bite. Perhaps more than anything else, Princess Diana's 1995 appearance on *Panorama* is remembered for her iconic quip about there being "three of us in this marriage"—in reference to her husband's affair with Camilla Parker Bowles. And in 2019, the reaction to Prince Andrew's disastrous interview with *Newsnight*'s Emily Maitlis about his association with convicted sex offender Jeffrey Epstein effectively forced the royal out of public life.

Harry and Meghan's highly anticipated interview with Oprah Winfrey in March 2021 was no exception. It came almost exactly a year after the Sussexes said goodbye to royal life. They had finished their final public engagement, an appearance at the annual Commonwealth Day Service held at Westminster Abbey, and bid farewell both to the UK and their official jobs within the institution of the

British monarchy just as the world started to shut down amid the COVID-19 pandemic.

Twelve months later, they were still practicing social distancing as they sat in wicker chairs across from Oprah, ready to answer her questions. Both Meghan and Oprah were quick to point out that they were at a neighbor's house; the lush yard behind them was not their own. According to the longtime television host, nothing was off-limits in the conversation. Clearly feeling it necessary to set the record straight, she also clarified that Harry and Meghan were not paid for the appearance on the program.

Oprah initially spoke with Meghan alone. Pregnant with her second child, and dressed in a black silk Giorgio Armani dress embroidered with a lotus flower, a plant symbolizing rebirth and resilience, the duchess recounted the difficulties she had faced during her time as a working royal. Harry joined her later and, over the course of the two-hour conversation, the Sussexes laid bare their reasons for stepping back from their roles within the royal family.

Deftly moving from one newsworthy topic to the next, Oprah asked about everything from the Sussexes' courtship and wedding day to Harry's grief over the death of his mother to the sex of their new baby, but the clear focus of the interview was on their exit from royal life.

Harry and Meghan discussed the racism Meghan faced from certain publications and from social media as well as a conversation Harry had had with a family member "about how dark [their son Archie's] skin might be when he's born." (While the Sussexes didn't share who made the comments, they did clarify that it was not the Queen or Prince Philip. Prince Harry would later say that he didn't see this discussion as racist, citing "the difference between racism and unconscious bias" in a 2023 ITV news interview with journalist Tom Bradby.)

The oft-memed question from Oprah—"Were you silent or were you silenced?"—came amid a dialogue about Meghan feeling as if she'd lost her voice and her ability to advocate for herself when she joined "The Firm," as the institution of the royal family is sometimes called. Meghan's answer? "The latter."

Meghan spoke candidly about how different life in the royal family was from what she had assumed it would be. "There was no way to understand what the day-to-day was going to be like," she said. "It's easy to have an image that is so far from reality, and that's what was so tricky over those past few years, when the perception and the reality are two different things and you're being judged on the perception but you're living the reality of it. There's a complete misalignment and there's no way to explain that to people." But most shocking was Meghan's description of the suicidal ideation she experienced while pregnant with Archie and her claim that when she sought professional help for her struggles, the Palace did not support her.

"I didn't want to be alive anymore. That was a very clear and real and frightening, constant thought," Meghan said. In his memoir, Prince Harry recalled the moment he came home to Meghan uncontrollably crying. "She choked out that she didn't want to do this anymore," he wrote. "Do what?" he recalled replying. "Live," she said. But they carried on. The evening of her breakdown, they attended an event for Sentebale, the charitable organization Prince Harry co-founded. (In 2025, he resigned as patron of the organization following an internal dispute between the charity's trustees and the chair of its board.) "We *cannot* be late," Harry recalled thinking. "They'll skin us alive! And they'll blame her."

Meghan recounted that same evening to Oprah. "These are the thoughts that I'm having in the middle of the night that are very clear," she said, "and I'm scared, because this is very real. This isn't some abstract idea. This is methodical, and this is not who I am. But we had to go to this event, and I remember him saying, 'I don't think you can go.' And I said, 'I can't be left alone.'"

She explained how she reached out to "one of the most senior people" within the hierarchy of the monarchy about the possibility of receiving inpatient treatment only to be told "that it wouldn't be good for the institution." It's unclear if she was speaking about a member of the family or someone who worked behind the scenes—one of the palace courtiers or the "men in grey suits," as both Princess Diana and Prince Harry described them. Meghan herself would explain that distinction to Oprah: "There's the family, and then there's the people that are running the institution. Those are two separate things."

When that failed, Meghan sought help from the royal family's human resources department. "I remember this conversation like it was yesterday," she recalled, "because they said, 'My heart goes out to you, because I see how bad it is, but there's nothing we can do to protect you because you're not a paid employee of the institution.' . . . This was emails and begging for help, saying very specifically, 'I am concerned for my mental welfare.'"

She disclosed that she had surrendered her keys, driver's license, and passport when she joined the royal family. "I couldn't, you know, call an Uber to the palace," she said. And while she acknowledged that some people were sympathetic, even admitting that the abuse was "disproportionately terrible what we see out there to anyone else," Meghan said, "nothing was ever done, so we had to find a solution."

For the Sussexes, that solution was ultimately walking away.

"Everybody who gets married knows you're really marrying the family. But you weren't just marrying a family, you were marrying a 1,200-year-old institution, you're marrying the monarchy. What did you think it was going to be like?" Oprah asked Meghan fairly early on in the program.

"I would say I went into it naively because I didn't grow up knowing much about the royal family. It wasn't part of something that was part of conversation at home. It wasn't something that we followed," Meghan responded.

Oprah pressed on. "But you were aware of the royals and, if you were going to marry into the royals, you'd do research about what that would mean?"

"I didn't do any research about what that would mean," Meghan said.

"You didn't do any research?" Oprah repeated.

"No. I didn't feel any need to, because everything I needed to know he was sharing with me," Meghan answered, referencing Prince Harry. "Everything we thought I needed to know, he was telling me."

More than seventeen million people tuned in to watch Oprah interview the Sussexes that night. Journalist and former *Real Housewives of New York City* star Carole Radziwill was one of them. On Twitter, she called attention to what Meghan had said about being unaware of what joining the British royal family would actually be like.

Carole immediately drew a parallel between Meghan and her late friend Carolyn Bessette-Kennedy.

"I just watched the M&H sit down. Wow," she tweeted that night. "I love how people say Meghan knew what she was getting into . . . people said the same thing about Carolyn Bessette when she married into the Kennedy family. You could never know. Meghan said it right the perception is nothing like the reality."

As one of Carolyn's closest confidants (and the widow of John F. Kennedy Jr.'s cousin Anthony Radziwill, a prince in his own right),

Carole would know. She saw firsthand how Carolyn dealt with the invasive tactics of the paparazzi, and how hard it was for her to live up to not only the expectations of the Kennedy family but also the assumptions the public had about who John's wife would be.

Of course, Carolyn was familiar with the Kennedys and the outsize role they played in American history and culture but, as she had once told Carole, "It's not like they gave me a handbook." Still, Carolyn had tried her best to fit the mold. "She tried to tuck herself in neatly that first year," Carole recalled in her memoir, *What Remains*. "But it wasn't so much learning the rules as it was about learning they weren't for her. The glass wall and you're constantly bumping into it."

Meghan, too, says she did her best to fit in with her in-laws. "I tried so hard," she said in her and Harry's Netflix docuseries *Harry & Meghan*. "That's the piece that's so triggering," she continued, teary-eyed. "Because . . . it still wasn't good enough, and you still don't fit in."

When the Oprah interview aired, some online were skeptical of Meghan's claims that she didn't research the royals before marrying Prince Harry, citing blog posts on her lifestyle blog *The Tig* as proof that she was at least familiar with the British monarchy. Journalist Tina Brown, for example, called the comment "disingenuous." "It would seem to me if that's true, reprehensible, quite honestly," Brown said. "Because it's a serious thing to marry into that family." But even if Meghan had googled royal history and protocol, it's unlikely that would have prepared her for her experience within the royal family.

Certainly, there are people today who would balk at a comparison between Meghan Markle and Carolyn Bessette. But like Carole, John's former assistant RoseMarie Terenzio saw the similarities between Meghan's situation and what Carolyn went through. "As humans, we sit there and say, 'We think we know what to expect.' But when you get there, there are surprises," RoseMarie said. "It was something that she was not prepared for, not because she didn't know who John was. It doesn't matter what's in your head, when you're experiencing it, your emotions and your entire being has the experience. So, you could sit there and say that about anything. I could read a book about skiing, but if I've never skied, I really don't know what it's like."

Just as Carolyn didn't receive a handbook on how to thrive within the Kennedy family, there was no text given to Meghan explaining step-by-step how to be a princess, and how to ingratiate herself with the royals, the public, and, critically, the press. *Diana: Her True Story*, which journalist Andrew Morton wrote in collaboration with Princess Diana and published in 1992, noted something similar: "The popular myth paints a homely picture of the Queen Mother clucking around Diana as she schooled her in the subtle arts of royal protocol while the Queen's senior lady-in-waiting, Lady Susan Hussey, took the young woman aside for tuition in regal history. In reality, Diana was given less training in her new job than the average supermarket checkout operator."

"There was no guidance," Meghan told Oprah. "There were certain things that you couldn't do. But, you know, unlike what you see in the movies, there's no class on how to speak, how to cross your legs, how to be royal. There's none of that training. That might exist for other members of the family. That was not something that was offered to me."

"So, nobody tells you anything?" Oprah asked. To which Meghan replied simply, "No."

That isn't quite true. Her husband, who had been born into this family, should have been the one to help her. He was the one providing that "guidance" and support. But Harry, despite having grown up accustomed to the harshest glare of the spotlight, was unprepared for the scrutiny and abuse his wife would face.

"I went into this incredibly naive," Harry told Anderson Cooper during the promotion tour for his memoir. "I had no idea the British press were so bigoted. Hell, I was probably bigoted before the relationship with Meghan." When Cooper probed deeper, asking, "You think you were bigoted before the relationship with Meghan?" Harry replied: "I don't know. Put it this way, I didn't see what I now see."

John, too, even with all his years in the public eye, didn't anticipate what Carolyn would go through. "John felt that, 'Once I'm married, I'm no longer the world's most eligible bachelor, and people will move on. Once I'm married, the interest will die down, because I'm not eligible anymore. I can't be all that.' And it was the exact opposite. It just became more and more intense," RoseMarie said. The press required Carolyn to embody an ideal of Camelot.

John's close friend Sasha Chermayeff also saw the similarities between Meghan's and Carolyn's experiences. Just as America felt a protectiveness for and an ownership of John's life, and the right to an opinion on his choice in a partner, the UK, and more broadly the world, felt similarly about Harry—and, for that matter, Prince William. An emotional attachment exists, and for some, a parasocial relationship. The sad twelve-year-old forced to walk behind his mother's coffin had grown up and found happiness, and the public was invested in that love story, but they also felt they were owed a certain amount of access to what they imagined to be his fairy-tale life.

"The comparison was obvious, because I saw how hard it was for Carolyn. It was just so hard for her," Sasha said. "Immediately, I picked up on the fact that the way that Meghan was being judged, and had to be, and was under that immediate pressure, that the most important thing was to satisfy this image for this family, which is representing something larger."

Maria Shriver, the daughter of Eunice and niece of President Kennedy, hinted at those pressures to appear perfect in the public eye when she tweeted after watching the Oprah interview: "It's true what Meghan Markle told Oprah, we don't know what goes on in people's lives behind closed doors. That's something we can all remember."

But Meghan and Carolyn weren't the first women to struggle with both the expectations and the spotlight that come with marrying into these families.

While Jackie was accustomed to the attention and criticism inherent in being a politician's wife, she was less comfortable with the scrutiny she faced as President Kennedy's widow. In the years after her husband's tragic death, she made efforts to live a more private life, but the public's fascination with her never waned.

For years, she was relentlessly pursued by paparazzo Ron Galella, who terrorized Jackie both in New York and abroad. As she testified in court of his behavior: "It caused me anguish. It caused me fear for my safety, for the safety of my children. At times it caused me terror, distress, no peace, no peace of mind, fear for what was going to happen to them and to me when we would encounter him again."

Eventually, a judge barred him from taking her picture. As journalist Andrew Goldman wrote in *Town & Country*, Galella was the proto–celebrity paparazzo, in effect paving the way for the photographers who would torment Princess Diana: "Galella's unrelenting pursuit of his subjects helped spawn an entire industry that treats celebrities as prey. Princess Diana's 1997 death highlighted the real-world danger of celebrity stalking, but back in the '60s and '70s, when Galella was staking out Jackie, his pursuit was seen as a cultural curiosity, more rascally than predatory. Conversations about consent and the traumatic effects of a man pursuing a woman against her will were still, for the most part, decades away."

In addition, Jackie surprised both the press and the public when, just five years after President Kennedy's tragic assassination, she married Aristotle Onassis, the Greek shipping magnate twenty-three years her senior.

"The Reaction Here Is Anger, Shock and Dismay" read one headline from *The New York Times* in October 1968. "I'm terribly disappointed. She could have done better," said Miss Ann Farber to the paper. "To us she was royalty, a princess, and I think she should have married a prince. Or at least someone who looked like a prince." Many saw the marriage as an indication that Jackie was abandoning Camelot.

But as the Windsors are all too familiar, marrying into a royal family is no easy feat.

Kate Middleton felt the pressures, and the harassment, too, when she started dating Prince William. Her middle-class roots were fodder for the tabloids for years; they had a field day with the fact that her mother had been a flight attendant, and Kate gave up her privacy when their relationship became public knowledge, well before they were engaged to be married.

"Waity Katie" was a popular moniker for her in the tabloid press, as she and William dated for roughly eight years before formalizing their engagement. Kate was also hounded by photographers, inspiring a royal family spokesperson to issue a rare statement on Prince William's behalf, which read simply: "Prince William is very unhappy at the paparazzi harassment of his girlfriend."

Kate's experience joining the royal family differed from Meghan's in a few key ways. First, as a white woman, Kate didn't face the racist abuse Meghan was subjected to—from the more subtle bias found in social media posts negatively commenting on her hair to an article calling out her "exotic" DNA. But crucially, Kate's courtship with Prince William was also much longer than Meghan's with Harry. Kate had time to get used to the rules, both said and unsaid, that come with marrying into the royal family and the machinations of how the institution works . . . and the press had time to get used to *her*, as well. She had also grown up in the UK, meaning that she was not only familiar with the royals culturally (and the no-holds-barred way they were covered by the media) but also had her family and her support system close by. It was nothing like the whirlwind, cross-continent romance of Harry and Meghan.

Royal commentator Victoria Murphy cites the rise of social media and the fast pace of internet news coverage as other reasons why Meghan faced a more difficult entrée into royal life than her sister-in-law. Stories about Kate, she said, "would pop up every few weeks perhaps. And so it never got to that stage of this enormous, overwhelming mounding of coverage that just built and built and built and built and built. And that's what happened with Meghan." Murphy also pointed out that it wasn't only the publications writing about Meghan, as they had about Kate. Internet users could then comment on the stories, often anonymously, and further the abuse: "Meghan was the first person to marry into the royal family in such a high-profile way in the modern social media age. And I feel that that had a huge impact on how overwhelming that experience was."

But the fact that Meghan wasn't the first woman to have a difficult time in joining the royal family was in itself an issue for Harry. "For the family, they very much have this mentality of, 'This is just how it is. This is how it's meant to be. You can't change it. We've all been through it,'" he told Oprah. For Harry, this wasn't acceptable.

Harry writes in *Spare* that his brother and father were "furious" when he put out a statement publicly confirming his relationship with Meghan, which also called out "racial undertones of comment pieces" (notably in *Spare*, he mentions the *Daily Mail* story "Harry's Girl Is [Almost] Straight Outta Compton," with the subhead "Gang-Scarred Home of Her Mother Revealed—So Will He Be Dropping in for Tea?") as well as the "outright sexism and racism of social media trolls and web article comments."

"My statement made them look bad," he suggests in the memoir. "They felt as though they didn't have a chance or weren't able to do that for their partners," he further clarified to Cooper. "What Meghan had to go through was similar in some part to what Kate and what Camilla went through. Very different circumstances, but then you add in the race element, which is what the British press jumped on straight away."

Throughout *Spare*, Harry lays out his perception of the hierarchy within the royal family, often pointing out how unfair it was to him as the second-born son of a future monarch, but in this instance, his being further down the line of succession worked in his favor. He and his wife could leave royal service without uprooting a centuries-old institution. A few steps away from the throne, he could criticize the press without entirely upending the delicate symbiotic relationship the royals maintain with the media. But for William and Charles, things have always been more complicated. It's why Camilla's public rehabilitation—from vilified mistress to queen—was a slow-going, carefully orchestrated campaign designed to win over both the public and the press. Prince Harry even alleges that Camilla "sacrificed [him] on her personal PR altar," suggesting she leaked stories about her soon-to-be stepchildren to curry favor with journalists.

But while Harry acknowledges "the pain and suffering of women marrying into this institution," broadly speaking, the specific comparison he continues to make is between his wife and his late mother. The specter of Diana, hounded literally to death by paparazzi, was never far from his mind. "I didn't want history to repeat itself," Harry said in his Netflix docuseries. "I was terrified."

Prince Harry has minced no words in sharing how he feels about the media and the role he feels the tabloid press played in his mother's death. He draws a direct parallel between what Diana and Meghan experienced during their time in the royal family. Harry saw the choice to step away from the royal family as a way to save his wife, when he could not save his mother.

Princess Diana's funeral is often remembered for its visuals: the two young men walking behind their mother's coffin, the sea of flowers outside the gates of Kensington Palace left there by a hysterical public, the card addressed to "Mummy." But Earl Spencer's eulogy, too, has left an indelible mark on history. He simultaneously paid tribute to his sister and reportedly angered Queen Elizabeth by describing Diana as "someone with a natural nobility who was classless and who proved in the last year that she needed no royal title to continue to generate her particular brand of magic" and by saying, "I pledge that we, your blood family, will do all we can to continue the imaginative way in which you were steering these two exceptional young men so that their souls are not simply immersed by duty and tradition but can sing openly as you planned."

He also made a point of calling out the press: "It is a point to remember that of all the ironies about Diana, perhaps the greatest was this—a girl given the name of the ancient goddess of hunting was, in the end, the most hunted person of the modern age."

Princess Diana's relationship with the media was complicated. The tabloid "hacks," as they call themselves, pursued her relentlessly, but she was also a collaborator, especially when she wanted to shape the narrative around her marriage to Prince Charles. She shrewdly curated relationships with journalists to ensure her side of the story was told, even going so far as to secretly work with Andrew Morton on *Diana*, which laid bare both the breakdown of her marriage and her struggles within the royal family.

"It is an undisputed fact that the Princess connived with the media and exploited it for her own interests," wrote Sir David English, the head of Associated Newspapers, who, after Diana's death, was tasked with crafting a new code of practice for the industry, "just as much as we exploited her for ours."

Diana's landmark sit-down on BBC with Martin Bashir was remarkable for the revelations she offered about her relationship with Charles and his affair with Camilla and for her candor in speaking about mental health. Like her daughter-in-law would do twenty-five years later, Diana revealed her challenges publicly, and she noted the lack of support she received from the royal family. "Well maybe I was the first person ever to be in this family who ever had a depression or was ever openly tearful," she said. "And obviously that was daunting, because if you've never seen it before how do you support it?" She also admitted to self-harm and spoke about her eating disorder. "It was a symptom of what was going on in my marriage. I was crying out for help, but giving the wrong signals, and people were using my bulimia as a coat on a hanger: they decided that was the problem—Diana was unstable." (In 2021, an independent inquiry revealed the deceptive way Bashir had convinced Diana to do the interview, and the BBC issued an apology.)

Diana also knew the power of a photograph. There's no doubt that she was aggressively hounded by photographers. But even while she was fuming at their relentless presence, she was also determined to present herself in the best light possible—sometimes literally.

She was keenly aware of what the media wanted, Dickie Arbiter, who at varying times served as press secretary to Queen Elizabeth as well as then Prince Charles and Princess Diana, explained: "She would let them know where she was, ensuring they got the picture they wanted."

Sometimes that was to shine attention on a particular charity or cause, as she did when she famously strode across an active minefield in Angola in 1997. She knew full well the publicity an image like that would generate for the then-controversial issue. But other times, it was a bargaining chip, the only one she had with the photographers. So she negotiated. Her approach echoed the way Jackie would work with photographers to give them the images they needed to sell their papers. Both women employed the self-preservation strategy of "I'll give you one good photo if then you'll leave me alone."

There is nuance, but for Harry, the issue is black and white. Prince Harry blames the press, and in particular photographers, for his mother's death. "To see another woman in my life, that I love, go through this feeding frenzy, that's hard," he said in his docuseries, adding, "It is basically the hunter versus the prey."

A few days after Harry and Meghan's interview with Oprah was broadcast around the world, Queen Elizabeth responded to the allegations made in the program with a brief statement, which read: "The whole family is saddened to learn the full extent of how challenging the last few years have been for Harry and Meghan. The issues raised, particularly that of race, are concerning. Whilst some recollections may vary, they are taken very seriously and will be addressed by the family privately. Harry, Meghan and Archie will always be much loved family members."

Despite the heartfelt message issued on behalf of the Queen promising that the Sussexes would remain "much loved family members," to say that Harry and Meghan's conversation with Oprah accelerated a rift between Harry and his brother would be an understatement.

The Windsors were a house divided long before Harry and Meghan sat down with Oprah. But a televised airing of grievances—in a family whose unofficial mottoes include not only "Keep Calm and Carry On" but also "Never Complain, Never Explain"—threw fuel on the fire. The Sussexes' statements about family drama once kept behind closed doors escalated a simmering conflict into a full-on public feud.

Four days after the Oprah interview aired, Prince William became the first royal to personally speak to the press about the interview. He and Kate were visiting a school in East London when they walked past a group of reporters. One shouted out, "Sir, have you spoken to your brother since the interview?"

William replied: "No, I haven't spoken to him yet, but I will do." The reporter asked another question: "Can you just let me know is the royal family a racist family sir?" As he walked on, William turned to say: "We're very much not a racist family."

CHAPTER 16

An Earthshot

EVEN BEFORE WILLIAM AND KATE TOUCHED DOWN IN BOSTON IN November 2022, they found themselves dealing with a PR crisis. The day before their inaugural international trip as the Prince and Princess of Wales, and their first visit to the United States in eight years, news broke that racist comments were made to a guest at Buckingham Palace by a representative of the royal family.

Ngozi Fulani, the founder of domestic abuse charity Sistah Space, had been attending a reception at the palace thrown by Queen Camilla when Queen Elizabeth's former lady-in-waiting Lady Susan Hussey, whom King Charles had appointed as "Lady of the Household" following the Queen's death, repeatedly asked her questions to the effect of "Where do you really come from?" Fulani, who is Black, was born in the UK. She likened the questions to "an interrogation," and said she felt like she was being asked to "denounce [her] British citizenship." Buckingham Palace swiftly issued an apology to Fulani, and Lady Hussey stepped down from her position, a role that was largely symbolic, but did involve helping King Charles host events. Eventually, Fulani and Hussey would meet face-to-face once again, with Hussey apologizing personally.

But in the meantime, that didn't stop the incident from making international headlines. In particular, some media outlets drew parallels between Meghan Markle's observations of racial bias in the royal family and Fulani's experience. It should be noted that Harry later spoke about his and Meghan's relationship with Lady Hussey and the press's reaction during an interview with Tom Bradby. "I'm very happy for Ngozi Fulani to be invited into the palace to sit down with Lady Susan Hussey um, and to reconcile, because Meghan and I love Susan Hussey. [Meghan] thinks she's great," he said. "And I also know that what she meant—she never meant any harm at all. But the response from the British press, and from people online because of the stories that they wrote was horrendous."

While the Prince and Princess of Wales were not directly involved in the situation, a Kensington Palace spokesperson was eager to get ahead of the story, promptly issuing a statement to the press, many of whom were already in Massachusetts to cover the royal tour to the US. "This is a matter for Buckingham Palace but as the Prince of Wales's spokesperson, I appreciate you're all here and understand you'll want to ask about it. So let me address it head-on," he said. "I was really disappointed to hear about the guest's experience at Buckingham Palace last night."

He continued, "Obviously, I wasn't there, but racism has no place in our society. The comments were unacceptable, and it is right that the individual has stepped aside with immediate effect."

A racism scandal was far from how the Waleses were hoping to begin their visit, and while it threatened to overshadow the trip, a Palace source insisted that the Waleses wouldn't "be distracted by other things."

"Our number one focus this week is the Earthshot Prize."

The Earthshot Prize, which spotlights and supports innovative climate solutions through funding, as well as networking and partnership opportunities, is the crown jewel, so to speak, of Prince William's charitable endeavors. In late December 2019, he announced that every year, for a total of ten years, from 2021 to 2030, a one-million-pound prize would be awarded to five winners, one in each of the following: Protect & Restore Nature, Clean Our Air, Revive Our Oceans, Build a Waste-Free World, and Fix Our Climate. The annual award cycle culminates in a flashy gala with celebrity attendees (think Emma Thompson, David Beckham, Billie Eilish, and David Oyelowo), illustrating how this project clearly draws inspiration from both of William's parents.

King Charles has been a vocal environmentalist for decades at this point. He has a notable history of fighting against climate change, promoting sustainability and organic farming, and campaigning for conservation. William had engaged in this kind of work for years in tandem with his father, but the Earthshot Prize marked the establishment of his own major effort in the space. "Earthshot has really almost shifted William's legacy in a way," said journalist and royal commentator Victoria Murphy. "He was definitely involved with environmental projects beforehand. But it wasn't until he launched Earthshot that I think people really sat up and were fully aware of just how much he wanted to make the environment a cornerstone of his work." And using star power to shine the spotlight on a less-than-sexy cause? That's straight out of Princess Diana's playbook. But while the strategy for Earthshot is influenced by royal precedent, the award's name was clearly inspired by a much more American idea: President Kennedy's famous Moonshot.

A FEW MONTHS INTO HIS ADMINISTRATION, IN MAY 1961, PRESIdent Kennedy proclaimed to Congress and to the world that America would send a man to the moon, and bring him back home, by 1970. "I believe," he said, "that this nation should commit itself to achieving the goal, before the decade is out, of landing a man on the moon and returning him safely to Earth." It was a challenge he echoed the following year in his famous address at Rice University: "We choose to go to the moon in this decade and do the other things, not because they are easy, but because they are hard."

Jack made a habit of visiting NASA sites throughout his administration. He was a master of the photo op and of keeping the Moonshot top of mind for both the press and the American people. "John F. Kennedy was handsome, debonair, and press savvy," historian Douglas Brinkley wrote in his book *American Moonshot*. "Often, when he visited Cape Canaveral, Florida, or Huntsville, Alabama, or Houston, Texas, to inspect NASA sites, he wore dark sunglasses, which gave the visits a touch of Hollywood glamour. Because he was six feet one in height, sitting in a cramped Mercury, Gemini, or Apollo capsule for a photo op was not an option. So he mastered the art of looking upward at rockets."

President Kennedy's suggestion that America might send a man to the moon was almost unfathomably ambitious. The pursuit of a manned lunar landing was politically and scientifically risky, not to mention exorbitantly expensive. But in the end, it worked. On July 20, 1969, within the decade timeline that President Kennedy had proposed, Neil Armstrong became the first man to step foot on the moon, planting the American flag. Jack didn't live to see the Apollo 11 lunar landing, but more than sixty years later, his Moonshot legacy continues.

It's not uncommon to hear it referenced by philanthropists and politicians hoping to make "one giant leap for mankind," despite significant odds. For example, President Joe Biden's Cancer Moonshot;

Stanford University's "moonshot effort" to 3D print a human heart; and the Google division called "X, the Moonshot Factory," which has worked on projects ranging from the creation of autonomous driving cars to the exploration of geothermal energy as a means of heating and cooling homes.

While the linguistic idea of adding the suffix "-shot" to the end of a word or phrase has become common parlance, the name of Prince William's award is no coincidence. The heir to the British throne was influenced by how President Kennedy's dream of putting a man on the moon inspired the technology and innovation that made it a reality. "It seemed crazy. We'd only just launched the first satellite. Putting a man on the moon that quickly seemed impossible. But this simple challenge encompassed so much. He called it a goal to 'organize and measure the best of our energies and skills.' In taking that 'giant leap for mankind,' the team behind the Moonshot united millions of people around the world—that this crazy ambition wasn't so crazy after all," William said of the original Moonshot during a TED Talk in October 2020.

Now, he continued, "we need Earthshots. We must harness that same spirit of human ingenuity and purpose and turn it with laser-sharp focus and urgency on the most pressing challenge we have ever faced: repairing our planet." The thematic connection to the Moonshot makes sense, but it's more than that. Much like how Jackie drew on the imagery of Camelot to craft the Kennedy myth, with the name Earthshot, Prince William is leaning on the Kennedy legacy, perhaps to broaden the appeal, given the international focus of the project, and to generate American support and interest.

That month, he revealed more details about the prize with a splashy video and press rollout. He initially launched the award through the Royal Foundation, the organization that oversees his and Kate's philanthropic pursuits (it formally became an independent charity in July 2022) and assembled a prize council of notable names like famed environmentalist Sir David Attenborough, actress Cate Blanchett, and the Colombian singer Shakira. Initially, the Kennedy family was not involved in a major way. In fact, leadership at the John F. Kennedy Library found out about the Earthshot Prize when the rest of the world did—but they immediately knew they wanted to collaborate with the royal on the project.

The inaugural awards ceremony was set to take place in London in fall 2021, but given the international nature of the program, the plan was for the event to move to a different city each year. It didn't take long for the JFK Library to launch a campaign to bring Earthshot to Boston.

In April 2021, Prince William held a virtual meeting with President Kennedy's only living child, Caroline Kennedy, and in September of that year, the John F. Kennedy Library Foundation joined Earthshot as a Global Alliance Partner.

"Over the past 60 years I have watched each new generation find inspiration in my father's decision to send a man to the moon—not just inspiration for mankind or for America, but for their own lives," Caroline said. "It is a great tribute to President Kennedy that The Earthshot Prize has been inspired by his moonshot to take on the most important challenge we face today—repairing the planet. My family and the JFK Library Foundation look forward to partnering with Prince William and The Earthshot Prize on this exciting initiative."

In December, Caroline sent a personal letter to the royal. "Next year is the 60th anniversary of my father's moonshot speech," she wrote, "and it would mean so much to celebrate that anniversary with the winners of The Earthshot Prize."

The efforts paid off. The team working with Prince William on Earthshot was sold on Boston, given the symbolism of the Kennedy connection, but before they committed, they wanted to better understand the ecosystem of sustainable innovation in the city and how they could tell that story during a royal visit. So in spring 2022, Rachel Flor, the executive director of the JFK Library Foundation, toured a representative from the Royal Foundation around the city, giving them a taste of what William and Kate's itinerary could look like and introducing them to leaders in the local climate space.

Multiple cities had been in contention to host the awards ceremony, but the visit sealed the deal.

"It was important to the Earthshot Prize not only to have that history, but that the city itself was an example of that spirit," Flor later said in an interview. "Clearly, they left impressed with what they saw."

British Consul-General Peter Abbott then hand delivered a letter from Prince William to Boston Mayor Michelle Wu at City Hall. "At first, the mayor was surprised," her chief of staff, Tiffany Chu, said. "At that point, she hadn't gotten many hand-delivered letters to the office."

"We undertook a fact-finding mission earlier this year, visiting Boston, and believe there is a strong and compelling story to tell of the City's mission to become truly environmentally friendly," Prince William wrote. "It is the Prize's ambition that every Bostonian knows the Winners of the Earthshot Prize 2022 will be announced in their city, and that those around the US, and indeed world, see Boston as a leading City which is embracing a more sustainable and green agenda."

Wu, who had campaigned on the promise of a "Green New Deal" for Boston, was a fitting partner for the project, and once she and her staff confirmed the message was legitimate, she was honored and ready to get to work. "We thought, 'This is an amazing opportunity to shine a spotlight on Boston.'" Chu said. The office of the mayor then collaborated with the Royal Foundation, the JFK Library Foundation, and a burgeoning host committee—which included representatives from a variety of local charities, environmental and climate-focused initiatives, and research organizations, as well as honorary members like John Kerry and then–Massachusetts Governor Charlie Baker—on planning the royal visit.

Prince William's team "wanted to make sure that they could hear voices from a lot of different perspectives. They wanted to highlight specific neighborhoods in Boston that might not always be on the front page of the *Globe*," Chu explained.

"There is no more important Moonshot today than repairing the planet and no better place to harness the Moonshot spirit than the city of Boston," Caroline Kennedy wrote in a statement officially announcing the decision. "It is a great tribute to President Kennedy that The Earthshot Prize will partner with the JFK Library Foundation to host the 2022 ceremony in Boston and inspire a new generation with the possibility of a sustainable future."

"In Boston, we're not just aiming to improve Boston's ability to tackle climate change—we're setting an example for how imaginative, community-driven climate leadership can reshape what's possible. We are honored and excited that Boston has been selected to host the 2022 Earthshot Awards," Mayor Wu added. "This is an opportunity to shine a global spotlight on our efforts to combat climate change and demonstrate that, together, we can meet the urgency this moment demands with innovative solutions that protect our planet and future generations."

But in the few short months between when Boston was announced as host city and when William and Kate arrived at Boston

Logan International Airport on November 30, 2022, the royal family had gone through a transformation.

THIS VISIT TO THE US WAS ALWAYS GOING TO BE AN IMPORTANT one for Prince William. Members of his staff (as well as the British ambassador to the US, Karen Pierce) had taken to calling it his "Super Bowl" moment; he was showcasing Earthshot on an international stage. "Our goal is to become a global brand and we are one year into it," said the charity's chief executive, Hannah Jones, at the time. "It's very early days."

The tour marked the first time William had set foot in the US since his brother had moved to the country, reigniting coverage of the ongoing family feud, and offering William and Kate the opportunity to try to win over Americans in a strategic charm offensive—one bolstered by their alignment with one of the country's most prominent social and political families, the Kennedys.

Most significant of all, on September 8, 2022, Queen Elizabeth had died after more than seventy years on the throne, prompting enormous changes for the British monarchy. Charles became king immediately; and Prince William, the face of the institution's future. The visit to Boston would be William's first trip abroad as Prince of Wales, setting the tone for this new era of the British royal family.

And he was met, too, with a public more educated on the royal family's history, and more interested in the interpersonal drama of its most prominent members, thanks in no small part to the popularity of Netflix's *The Crown*. Fans of the series, no doubt, could be found in the crowds gathered outside city hall to welcome the royal couple to Boston. Despite biting winds and pouring rain, thousands lined up to see the royals on their first night in the US. In fact, the Prince's team had requested a last-minute shift in the layout of the event to give these well-wishers a better view.

"We wanted to make sure the press could see the royal family well, and so we initially set up the risers right in front of the speakers' podium at City Hall Plaza," explained Chu. "The day before, we heard feedback from the royal family's team that they would rather speak directly to the people instead of only to the press. So we rearranged the setup of the event." Despite the weather, the space was filled with onlookers holding umbrellas and waving British flags as they tried to catch a glimpse of William and Kate.

"It was that Moonshot speech that inspired me to launch the Earthshot Prize with the aim of doing the same for climate change as President Kennedy did for the space race. And where better to hold this year's awards ceremony than in President Kennedy's hometown, in partnership with his daughter and the foundation that continues his legacy," William told the crowd. "Boston was also the obvious choice because your universities, research centers, and vibrant start-up scene make you a global leader in science, innovation, and boundless ambition."

The inclement weather didn't dampen excitement over the royal visit, but the welcome ceremony wasn't without controversy. During the event, Reverend Mariama White-Hammond asked the audience to "consider the legacy of colonialism and racism," drawing attention once again to the incident involving Lady Hussey and Ngozi Fulani at Buckingham Palace.

When later asked if the speech was a deliberate statement about the royals, the reverend said she hadn't heard about the ongoing scandal, noting, "As a person of African descent I often begin anything I say with a land acknowledgment, I want to bless this space and acknowledge the beauty and the painful history." The press, however, drew parallels.

Caroline Kennedy was supposed to join William and Kate at the kickoff event, but her flight into the city kept getting delayed because of the rainstorm, so she met up with them instead at a Boston Celtics game later that evening. While the royals were warmly welcomed at the reception at City Hall, the crowd's reaction to them at TD Garden for the basketball game that night was decidedly mixed. Whenever the couple—who were seated alongside Massachusetts Governor-Elect Maura Healey, as well as former Celtics player Thomas "Satch" Sander and two of the team's owners, Wyc Grousbeck and Steve Pagliuca—were shown on the big screen, their image was met with a smattering of boos amid cheers and a chant of "U-S-A."

Given Boston's deeply felt ties to Ireland, and its long-held association with the casting off of a British king during the American revolution, some animosity or simply apathy from its citizens toward the royals was to be expected. While many people were generally excited to see Will and Kate, the royals encountered some anti-monarchy protests during their visit. But Celtics coach Joe Mazzulla had the most viral response to their attendance at the game. When asked how he felt about the royal family being in the arena, Mazzulla replied with his own question. "Jesus, Mary, and Joseph?" The reporter then corrected: "The Prince and Princess of Wales," to which the coach replied: "No, I only know one royal family. I don't know too much about that one."

Undeterred, William and Kate further engaged with the community on the second day of their trip, touring Greentown Labs, an incubator for start-ups focused on solutions to climate issues; visiting Roca, an outreach program focused on helping high-risk youths; and taking a very chilly walk around the Boston Harbor waterfront to see how the city is contending with rising sea levels while discussing the vulnerabilities the city faces with respect to climate change with local officials, including Mayor Wu.

On their third and final day in the US, the prince and princess briefly parted ways. Kate spent time at the prestigious Center on the Developing Child at Harvard University discussing research on early childhood development, a focus of much of her charitable work, while Prince William joined Caroline Kennedy and two of her children for a tour of the JFK Presidential Library and Museum.

Caroline was at ease as she arrived that afternoon, greeting the crowd of photographers and reporters as if they were old friends, before heading inside with her son, Jack Schlossberg, and her daughter Tatiana. (At this point, Jack had yet to become the social media provocateur he is today, but he had still shared his excitement about Earthshot coming to Boston multiple times. That said, the event was more aligned with his sister Tatiana's interests. Prior to her untimely death in 2025, she made a career writing about climate change as a journalist for publications including *The New York Times* and authored the book *Inconspicuous Consumption: The Environmental Impact You Don't Know You Have*.) They reemerged a few moments later to welcome Prince William to the impressive I. M. Pei–designed building.

Caroline led the group through the museum's exhibits, showing William ephemera from her father's campaign, before directing the Prince and her children into a room filled with memorabilia related to the space program. In particular, they spent a few moments looking at JFK's Moonshot speech, complete with his handwritten notes.

At every turn, Caroline acknowledged the press documenting the visit. "Our friends are waiting," she said to William and her children with a laugh. In contrast, her royal companion appeared completely focused on the task at hand, choosing to ignore the reporters and cameras, as is his typical modus operandi. Caroline seemed comfortable, at home in the library. The stakes were higher for William.

As the group walked down one final hallway, Caroline Kennedy paused in front of a photo of Queen Elizabeth and said, "There's the one from your grandmother." It was a solo portrait signed "Elizabeth R, 1961," presented in a silver frame. Prince William smiled as he looked at the black-and-white image and said, "Oh yeah, 1961." A placard underneath read, "Signed photograph of Her Majesty Queen Elizabeth II, presented to President and Mrs. Kennedy during their visit to Buckingham Palace." More than sixty years later, the families were reunited once again.

Following a private lunch, during which Prince William paid tribute to "the man who inspired our mission," the royal briefly met with President Biden on the waterfront outside the library. The two men posed for a photo and were expected to discuss shared climate goals as well as the prioritization of mental health issues. William also thanked Biden for traveling to London for his late grandmother Queen Elizabeth's funeral in September. "They both shared warm memories of Her Majesty," a spokesperson for the royals said.

Later that evening, the JFK Library was bathed in green light as William, Kate, members of the Kennedy family, and a roster of celebrities walked the green carpet at the MGM Music Hall at Fenway for the visit's main event: the Earthshot Prize awards. Kate wore Diana's necklace; Caroline and her children were there to help celebrate. The year's winners included Notpla, a London-based start-up creating a plastic-free packaging alternative out of seaweed and plants, and the Indigenous Women of the Great Barrier Reef, a group of Indigenous rangers encouraging a new approach to conservation in Queensland,

Australia. The royal tour of Boston ended on a high note, after the controversy at Buckingham Palace and simmering tensions between the Sussexes and the rest of the royal family threatened to hijack the media narrative surrounding the trip.

But this collaboration between William and Caroline was more than just another coming together of the Windsor and Kennedy dynasties; it was the meeting of those who are tasked with carrying these families' legacies into the twenty-first century. While Caroline has numerous cousins who bear the Kennedy name, as the only living child of JFK and Jackie, she's the keeper of the flame, so to speak. As his generation's heir to the throne, Prince William holds a similar if even more defined role within his own family.

Caroline and William exist in a different world than their parents and grandparents did, one increasingly questioning the role dynasties should play in politics and public life. As they seek to bring their families into the modern day, they must also reckon with the more unsavory aspects of their relatives' pasts—issues including infidelity and questionable business associations, and in the case of the Windsors, a heritage with ties to slavery and colonialism—while carving their own places in history.

They are the de facto spokespersons for their respective clans, with both the press and the public looking to them whenever any family member is in the news—whether that's the elevation of Robert F. Kennedy Jr.'s antivax opinions, given his role in the Trump administration, or the ongoing conversations about the man formerly known as Prince Andrew and his association with Jeffrey Epstein, or the long-simmering tensions between the California-based Sussexes and the UK-based members of the royal family.

Notably, Prince William didn't see his brother Harry during this visit to the United States. (At the time, anonymous sources told multiple royal reporters that the release of a trailer for the Sussexes' new

Netflix documentary while Prince William was on tour in the US was seen as a "declaration of war" by those in the Wales family camp.) But a few days after the Waleses headed back to the UK, the Sussexes had their own interaction with the Kennedys, at the Robert F. Kennedy Ripple of Hope Award ceremony, where they were honored by RFK's daughter Kerry for, as she put it, taking a "heroic" stand against structural racism in the British monarchy.

CHAPTER 17

A Ripple of Hope

PRINCE HARRY LOOKED UNCOMFORTABLE FROM THE MOMENT HE arrived at the Ripple of Hope Award gala in New York City. While his wife beamed for photographers, reporters began bombarding Harry with questions. "Do you have a message for your family, Harry?" one asked. "Are you putting money before family?" another asked twice. Harry quickly walked away without answering, murmuring only "so many questions" as the couple made their way down the blue carpet holding hands. For her part, Meghan smiled as journalists tossed easier queries her way, like "Where is your dress from?" (She didn't respond at the time, but the cream long-sleeved, off-the-shoulder dress was custom-made by Louis Vuitton. She paired it with a black Givenchy clutch, drop earrings, and an aquamarine cocktail ring that once belonged to Princess Diana.)

Harry has never been shy about his disdain for the media, and in particular, how he blames the paparazzi for his mother's death. "In this role and this job, every single time I see a camera, every single time I hear a click, every single time I see a flash, it takes me straight back," he said in a 2019 interview with ITV's Tom Bradby, calling his grief "a wound that festers" and sharing that being pursued by photographers, even in a generally safe setting like a press line, is "the worst reminder of her life as opposed to the best." That contempt only escalated when he saw Meghan subjected to what Kensington Palace described as a "wave of abuse and harassment," and specifically "the smear on the front page of a national newspaper; the racial undertones of comment pieces; and the outright sexism and racism of social media trolls and web article comments," even before they officially confirmed they were dating.

"Prince Harry is in a really tough position because he's openly stated he doesn't like the press; he doesn't like the media; he doesn't like photographers. That's not to say that he doesn't have a lot of admiration and appreciation for real, factual journalists. But I think overall, it has to be jarring for somebody like him who's experienced what he's experienced, what his mom has experienced, when those people are shouting at him," a source close to the Sussexes said when asked about this appearance. "At the same time as a public person, which he knows he is, he understands it's kind of par for the course. But I don't think there will ever come a time where there's a red-carpet situation where we say, 'Wow, Harry's really thriving.' That would be disingenuous."

On that rainy December 6, 2022, evening, Harry was bearing the brunt of the attention, and the criticism, over the Sussexes' new Netflix program. A few days before the Robert F. Kennedy Human Rights organization event—and notably, in the middle of Prince William and Kate's visit to Boston for the Earthshot Prize—the streaming giant dropped a first look at *Harry & Meghan*, a much anticipated six-part documentary about the couple directed by Liz Garbus. The initial trailer promised new details about the Sussexes' romance, the discord within the royal family, their issues with the British press, and ultimately the decision to step back from their senior royal roles. A second trailer, which zeroed in on Meghan's struggles in joining the royal family, dropped a few days later on the morning before the

RFK foundation event. "No one knows the full truth," Harry says dramatically at the end of that preview. "We know the full truth." The series was the first project set to come from the Sussexes' exclusive multiyear production agreement with Netflix, a contract rumored to be worth $100 million. And while, as Garbus described, *Harry & Meghan* is "personal and raw and powerful," it is very much from the perspective of its title subjects, and another avenue for them to tell their side of the story.

On the evening of the gala, speculation reached a fever pitch over what Harry and Meghan would reveal about royal life and how the Windsors act and speak behind closed doors. Reporters asked guests about the royals, and the docuseries, hoping for a quote to fuel the trending story. Yetunde Beutler, the CEO of French beauty brand Essènci, wrote on Instagram that she was "hounded by the press to answer questions about Harry and Meghan" as well as "racism within the monarchy" on the carpet.

"I think there is a lot that needs to be done," she said when asked by a journalist about racism in the royal family ahead of the event. "I think there is a lot that needs to be done within the royal family, and I think there is a lot that needs to be done within the European societies."

For his part, actor Alec Baldwin, who emceed the evening, feigned ignorance when asked about the Netflix program, saying, "Is there another documentary coming out about them? You assume I know all this stuff I don't know." In another interview, when asked what he admires about Prince Harry, Baldwin noted that he "handles difficult circumstances with the press without having too much difficulty." TV personality Gayle King, too, was asked if she thinks the British royal family is racist at the gala. She responded: "No I do not. And neither do they," referring to the Sussexes.

The timing of the event was opportune; the Sussexes' decision to leave the confines of the British monarchy and to be vocal about their experiences within it were two of the reasons they were being honored by Robert F. Kennedy Human Rights in the first place.

When the Ripple of Hope Award was initially announced in October, the organization noted that the Sussexes were being recognized for "their work on racial justice, mental health, and other social impact initiatives through their Archewell Foundation." The honor, which launched in 2007, recognizes political and social leaders, international business innovators, and celebrities using their fame to enact change. It draws its name from a speech given by Robert F. Kennedy in 1966 in South Africa during apartheid. "Each time a man stands up for an ideal, or acts to improve the lot of others, or strikes out against injustice, he sends forth a tiny ripple of hope," he said. "And crossing each other from a million different centers of energy and daring those ripples build a current which can sweep down the mightiest walls of oppression and resistance." Previous winners include Dr. Anthony Fauci, Colin Kaepernick, Nancy Pelosi, Barack Obama, Joe Biden, Bill Clinton, Desmond Tutu, Bono, and Taylor Swift. In addition to Harry and Meghan, the 2022 class of honorees featured the cofounder and managing partner of Siris Capital Group, Frank Baker; the CEO of Bank of America, Brian Moynihan; and, perhaps most notably, Ukrainian President Volodymyr Zelenskyy.

"When The Duke and Duchess accepted our award laureate invitation back in March, we were thrilled. The couple has always stood out for their willingness to speak up and change the narrative on racial justice and mental health around the world," Kerry Kennedy, president of Robert F. Kennedy Human Rights and the seventh child of the late Robert F. Kennedy and his wife, Ethel, said in a statement shared with the announcement. "They embody the type of moral courage that my father once called the 'one essential, vital quality for those who seek to change a world that yields most painfully to change.'"

The organization also commended Harry and Meghan's "lifelong commitment to building strong and equitable communities, advancing the global dialogue around mental health, and advocating for a better world—both on and offline," detailing their work supporting Afghan refugees, advocating for paid parental leave in the US, and championing vaccine access, among other initiatives.

Following some skepticism over the choice to give Harry and Meghan the award—including from RFK's son and Kerry Kennedy's brother, Robert F. Kennedy Jr., and the Kennedy biographer David Nasaw—Kerry further explained the decision to honor the Sussexes in an interview with the Spanish news outlet *El Confidencial*'s *Vanitatis*. She highlighted their "moral courage" and their "heroic" stance against "structural racism," comparing the Sussexes to RFK.

"When my father went to South Africa in 1966, he spoke in front of a white audience and said that the problem in this generation is talking about racial justice. He also spoke of moral courage, saying that few would have the courage to question their colleagues, family and their community about the power structure they maintained," she said, per a translation, which was later verified by a representative of RFK Human Rights. "And this is what Meghan Markle and Prince Harry have done."

"They went to the oldest institution in U.K. history and told them what they were doing wrong, that they couldn't have structural racism within the institution; that they could not maintain a misunderstanding about mental health," she continued, referring to the monarchy. "They knew that if they did this there would be consequences, that they would be ostracized, they would lose their family, their position within this structure, and that people would blame them for it. They have done it anyway because they believed they couldn't live with themselves if they didn't question this authority. I think they have been heroic in taking this step."

As news about the Ripple of Hope Award circulated, the media was quick to push forward a narrative of Kennedy family members aligning with one side of the family or the other in the ongoing "royal feud." "Kennedy Cousins Choose Their Sides in Royal Rift Between Sussex and Wales," read one headline. "Camelot Divided," read another.

But Harry and Meghan don't see it like that. A source familiar with their thinking shared that Prince William's working relationship with Caroline Kennedy didn't play a role in the Sussexes' acceptance of this honor, and when Harry and Meghan agreed to attend the gala and to receive the Ripple of Hope Award, they reportedly weren't familiar with William and Kate's plans to be in Boston and working in collaboration with the JFK Library just days before the event.

"There's no animosity or feeling like there's not enough room or space at the table for both of them. Both having a relationship with the Kennedys is a great thing; it's not a bad thing," the source shared. (Likewise, it wasn't an issue for the JFK Library Foundation that both these events were happening in close proximity.)

While the Kennedy connection wasn't the only reason Harry and Meghan agreed to accept the award and appear at the dinner, the Sussexes' respect for the family, and their history of service, did impact their decision to say yes. Harry, in particular, related to the organization's mission of preserving the legacy of Robert F. Kennedy, someone who passed away tragically and far too young.

"He's very protective over his mother, and keeping that legacy alive, that's something that is shared between both the Sussexes and the Kennedys," a source said. "Being part of a historical family comes with an additional set of responsibilities."

Harry is also aware of the long-standing relationship between the two families and quite familiar with the iconic images of his grandmother Queen Elizabeth with JFK from his 1961 visit to Buckingham Palace. As someone making his new home in the US, he found it "really meaningful" to be acknowledged by the family. But at the core of the Sussexes' willingness to partner with the Kennedys was alignment of the work between Archewell and RFK Human Rights.

After walking the carpet, and successfully dodging any and all interviews, Harry and Meghan made their way to the ballroom of the New York Hilton Midtown. Tickets for the event began at $2,500 and went all the way up to $1 million for an opportunity to sit at the "head table," presumably with the Sussexes, as well as access to a VIP reception, additional tickets for guests, and recognition during the dinner service.

Eventually, Harry and Meghan joined Kerry onstage for a conversation. "As my brother Douglas said earlier tonight, you're the Kennedys of England," Kerry joked, as she introduced the couple. The line got a laugh from both Meghan and the crowd (Harry merely raised his eyebrows), before the trio began their discussion of a new collaboration between their organizations. They were launching a new category in the Robert F. Kennedy Human Rights' annual Speak Truth to Power video contest for young filmmakers: the Archewell Foundation Award for Gender Equity in Student Film.

"We are honored to receive the RFK Ripple of Hope Award this year, and to partner with the Kennedy family in the creation of The Archewell Foundation Award for Gender Equity in Student Film," the Sussexes later said in a statement about the initiative. "Our hope with this award is to inspire a new generation of leadership in the arts, where diverse up and coming talent have a platform to have their voices heard and their stories told."

Beyond the announcement, much of Harry and Meghan's talk with Kerry focused on young people, as opposed to issues regarding race.

In fact, the line most publications focused on the next day came from Prince Harry, speaking of fatherhood. "We don't get out much because our kids are so small and young, so this is completely unexpected. But it's nice to share date night with all of you," he joked. Meghan also referenced spending time with Kerry's daughter, Michaela Kennedy-Cuomo. "We spent some time with Michaela, I don't know where she is, but she's great," she said, speaking of "how energizing it is to be with this generation who are so confident, so hopeful." When posting on Instagram about the awards, Michaela shared that Harry and Meghan are "two of the people whose courage and resilience" inspired her most, calling them both her "personal heroes." She also thanked them for "their strength and leadership in choosing authentic self-expression despite mass bullying and gaslighting by the press and structural discrimination surrounding race and mental health," and shared that she had given the royals and their children, Prince Archie and Princess Lilibet, beaded bracelets for "protection, peace, and joy."

The Sussexes' conversation with Kerry also focused on Meghan's decision to speak so openly about her mental health struggles. "That wasn't an easy decision to make, as you can imagine, but I don't want anyone to feel alone," Meghan said. "I think we all need to, in many ways when we can and if we feel brave enough to, to just speak honestly about your own experience. And it gives other people the space and the courage to do the same. . . . You don't see a way out. But ultimately, if you feel like there's someone else that has a lived experience, they've gotten to the other side, you can be an example of resilience. You can be an example of 'There is a happy ending.'"

At the end of the conversation, Kerry presented Harry and Meghan with a gift, a black-and-white photograph of Princess Diana taken and signed by Harry Benson, the famed photojournalist who had chronicled Robert F. Kennedy's 1968 presidential campaign on film and was there the night the senator died. "I was in my hometown of Glasgow, Scotland, when Princess Diana arrived for one of her charity events," Benson said of the image. "I was standing next to a Scottish photographer who covered all her visits to Scotland and he said to me, 'Don't bother taking any photographs until she comes closer and sees the little girl standing on the other side of the barrier. Diana will stop and bend down to say hello and that will be your picture.' And he absolutely was right."

The Sussexes were touched by the gift, which Meghan immediately described as "beautiful," and they took great care in bringing the picture back to Montecito after their trip to New York. It's important to both Harry and Meghan that their children feel Princess Diana's presence in their California home.

Two days after the gala, *Harry & Meghan* revealed how another famous picture of Grandma Diana hangs in Archie's nursery. In one poignant scene in the docuseries, baby Archie is looking up at a Patrick Demarchelier black-and-white portrait of his grandmother, in which she wears a strapless dress, a vibrant smile, and a tiara.

"Hi, Grandma. That's Grandma Diana," Meghan tells her son. Touchingly, "Grandma" was one of Archie's very first words.

"It's the sweetest thing," Harry previously shared, "but at the same time, it makes me really sad because she should be here."

Media Moguls

An oft-repeated criticism of the Sussexes is that they want both publicity and privacy. When they stepped away from their official roles in the royal family, citing the intrusive press as a key reason, they didn't slink off to California to pursue a life entirely out of the spotlight. Instead, they seek out attention via appearances, documentaries, TV shows, and books—but on their terms.

Post–royal life, the couple quickly signed a multimillion-dollar deal with Netflix, with their most successful programs focusing on themselves. (*Harry & Meghan*, their 2022 Netflix docuseries about their relationship—from their early dates to their decision to leave the royal family—quickly became the streamer's biggest documentary upon its debut, with 81.6 million hours viewed in its first four days on the platform.) A separate deal with Spotify was less fruitful, yielding only a twelve-episode podcast hosted by Meghan, a holiday special, and a number of behind-the-scenes rumors about how difficult it was working with the couple. In June 2023, a joint statement released by the Sussexes' Archewell Productions and the audio company revealed that they had "mutually agreed to part ways" but that they were "proud of the series [they] made together."

In October 2020, roughly half a year after they left the UK,

Meghan spoke for a virtual *Fortune* summit about her social media usage. "For my own self-preservation, I have not been on social media for a very long time," she shared. "I had a personal account years ago, which I closed down, and then we had one through the institution and our office that was in the U.K. that wasn't managed by us— that was a whole team—and so I think that comes with the territory for the job you have.

"I made a personal choice to not have any account, so I don't know what's out there, and in many ways that's helpful for me," she continued. "I have a lot of concerns for people that have become obsessed with it. And it is so much a part of our daily culture for so many people that it's an addiction like many others. There are very few things in this world where you call the person who is engaging with it a user."

It took several years, but Meghan is also now back on Instagram, which offers her the venue for a one-way conversation with her fans. She regularly shares details of her family's life, including photos and videos of her children, but she doesn't allow comments on her posts. A source close to Meghan noted that the social media platform is still a "scary place" for the duchess, hence the guardrails.

It was a slow start, with most early posts promoting her Netflix entertaining series *With Love, Meghan*, Harry's Invictus Games, or her new line of products, As Ever. But eventually she started sharing more openly about her life. Over the course of just one week in June 2025, for example, she posted multiple never-before-seen photos of her daughter, Lilibet, in honor of her fourth birthday, as well as a candid montage of a family trip to Disneyland, imagery that immediately evoked a trip Harry had taken with his mother to Disney World more than three decades prior.

But the most newsworthy upload by far that week was a video

from inside the delivery room, seemingly taken the day Lilibet was born. It shows Meghan and Harry dancing, twerking even, to "The Baby Mama Dance" by Starrkeisha. It quickly went viral, prompting a flood of opinion pieces. Headlines ranged from the harsh—"Did They Think Twerking like Trailer-Trash Teens Would Endear Them to the Masses?" in the *Daily Mail*, and "After the Pregnant Twerking, Can Meghan and Harry Sink Any Lower?" in the *Evening Standard*—to the straightforward: "Meghan Markle and Prince Harry Channeled MomTok with Hospital Dance Before She Gave Birth to Lilibet" in *Us Weekly*.

The Sussexes want to control the narrative, to tell their side of the story to those willing to hear it, without a journalistic intermediary, and they've found the vehicles to do that, whether it's a documentary made by their production company, an update on their foundation's website, a social media account for Meghan, or a memoir, in the case of Prince Harry's *Spare*. But it's a highly curated, sometimes performative version of authenticity. After all, in her cooking and crafting series *With Love, Meghan*, she wants to take viewers into her kitchen, but it's not actually *her* kitchen; rather, it's her neighbors' where she just so happens to be cooking.

Meghan isn't coming into content creation blindly; she's well-versed in the lifestyle space, given her experience with her blog, *The Tig*. A Goop-esque site, but at a smaller scale, *The Tig* was inspired by Tignanello wine, which Meghan used as a sort of metaphor for an aha moment. "Tignanello is a full-bodied red wine that I tried about seven years ago. In wine circles, it is nicknamed 'Tig.' It was my first moment of getting it—I finally understood what people meant by the body, structure, finish, legs of wine," she told designer Tory Burch's blog *Tory Daily* not long after the launch. "The TIG is my nickname for me getting it. Not just wine, but everything." Indeed, it was a wide-ranging lifestyle site with product recommendations, outfit inspiration, travel guides, recipes and entertaining tips, personal essays, and a peek behind the scenes at her life as a working actress. She shut it down in 2017 as her relationship with Prince Harry became more serious, and more public.

"Well, I loved The Tig, but I certainly love my husband more," Meghan told *People* before the 2025 launch of *With Love, Meghan* of the choice she'd made at the time. "I wouldn't change that for a second." But Harry, she says, has enjoyed seeing her back in her element. "My husband met me when I had The Tig, and I see this spark in his eye when he sees me doing the thing that I was doing when he first met me." Meghan feels comfortable sharing pieces of her life in this particular way, and she's good at it. You could imagine in a world in which she never met Harry, *The Tig* might have yielded a TV show (or at least a robust YouTube channel) similar to *With Love, Meghan*.

Unlike Harry and Meghan, working members of the royal family have an obligation to the British papers, given that duties of the monarchy are funded by its people. But they go above and beyond that obligation, regularly collaborating with the press on features and putting forth social media posts about themselves and the causes they support. It's a symbiotic relationship because the royals need to maintain public relations. Rarely do they give interviews with no holds barred; instead they opt to write essays themselves, so the text is fully in their control, or they grant access to friendly interviewers with a singular focus (think Kate speaking candidly about parenthood on the podcast *Happy Mum, Happy Baby* in support of one of her initiatives surrounding the early years of childhood). They know that managing public opinion is critical to their success, the continuation of a centuries' old institution, and the legacy of the family.

In the twenty-first century, it's not enough for the royals to appear at building openings, smile at ship christenings, and wave occasionally from the Buckingham Palace balcony. They are no longer scarred by the 1969 BBC documentary *Royal Family*, which featured authentic footage of life inside the palace but was quickly hidden away after criticism suggested it offered too intimate a perspective on the should-be-mysterious institution of the monarchy. In order to stay relevant today, the royals have an incentive to create media that give the public a more personal look at their lives. After the exodus of Harry and Meghan and the death of Queen Elizabeth, Prince William and Kate have upped their social media game significantly—producing clips of their engagements and compilations of the work they do every month, summaries that showcase (their perspective on) the impact of their duties to their most receptive fans. King Charles, too, is set to appear in multiple documentaries about his work and passions.

These forays have not always been without controversy. Following a 2024 snafu in which Kate manipulated an image of herself alongside her children, picture agencies including the Associated Press, Agence France-Presse, Reuters, and Getty made the image unavailable, citing an "editorial issue." The incident became a mini scandal, for which Kate later issued a personal apology, noting, "Like many amateur photographers, I do occasionally experiment with editing. I wanted to express my apologies for any confusion the family photograph we shared yesterday caused." Since then, the Waleses have generally opted to post such personal family photos on their social media accounts rather than releasing them through formal news channels, so they're no longer required to adhere to the news agencies' editorial standards. Today, they're still sharing with the public, but on their own terms. They're essentially utilizing Instagram to become their own news channel of sorts.

That idea was at the heart of a video announcing Kate's cancer diagnosis in March 2024. The princess delivered the news alone, straight to the camera, in an unprecedented display of openness and vulnerability. She has since used videos posted on X and Instagram not only to share candid updates about her treatment journey but also to remain in the news cycle even when she didn't want to make, or feel capable of making, public appearances. The highly produced footage released when Kate announced she had finished chemotherapy was described as "astonishing in its intimacy." It gave a rare peek at Will and Kate's personal life, of their relationship with their children, with each other, and with Kate's family, the Middletons, who were also featured in the video . . . but the royals were decidedly in control of the narrative.

This strategy of creating media to speak directly to an interested audience is one the Kennedys have been employing for decades. During Jack's presidential campaign, Jackie was pregnant with John. At a certain point during the fall, her doctor advised her that it was no longer healthy to stay on the road. So, relying on her previous experience and skills honed as a reporter at the *Washington Times-Herald* (like Meghan, she gave up a career in media when she married into a dynastic family), she picked up her pen and began communicating with the public via a new column called Campaign Wife, which was distributed by the Democratic National Committee and syndicated in papers nationwide. It was both a way for her to stay present in the campaign and a strategic use of Jackie's editorial skills in appealing to the women of America during the pivotal weeks leading up to the election.

"For the first time since Jack and I have been married, I have not been able to be with him while he is campaigning. You can imagine how frustrating it is to be in Hyannis Port reading all that he's doing and not participating in any way. This week I decided one way to keep from feeling left out was to talk through this column to the friendly people all over the country I would have met while campaigning," she wrote on September 16. "The worst part was not being in Los Angeles for the nomination. To me it seemed it would be surely better to be there than sitting anxiously by the television in Hyannis Port but my obstetrician firmly disagreed."

In the columns, which were published from September 17 to November 1, 1960, Jackie wrote about everything from policy to picking out maternity clothes to child rearing. She used these dispatches to communicate the "Kennedy brand" to voters (even though that concept probably wouldn't mean anything to people at that time), to remind them that she was a stylish young mother, and also to comment on the broader press narrative about her in a casual, nonconfrontational way.

When her son launched *George* magazine thirty-five years later, it seemed ironic. He was becoming part of the media ecosystem that made his life difficult. But he was also creating a vehicle through which he could make his opinion known. *George* was a collaboration with writers, editors, designers, and photographers; it was not *just* John F. Kennedy Jr.'s magazine, as it was sometimes called. And yet, every month, John had an editor's letter, a dedicated space in which he could share his thoughts on whatever was on his mind.

The magazine made a point of not covering John's family more than necessary. "If you are going to write about politics, every now and then there is going to be a Kennedy who is going to be doing something and we should write about it," John told Larry King in a

1995 interview. "We're not going to go out of our way. Certainly, there are enough people that write about the Kennedys without us joining in."

But on rare occasion, John used his magazine to make his feelings known about family members in the headlines. Such was the case in his September 1997 editor's letter.

"I've learned a lot about temptation recently," he wrote, alluding to two of his cousins who were in the news at that time, Representative Joseph P. Kennedy II and Michael Kennedy, calling them the "poster boys for bad behavior." Representative Joseph P. Kennedy II's first wife, Sheila Rauch Kennedy, had recently published a book detailing how the congressman had pressured her into an annulment of their marriage; Michael Kennedy had been accused of having an extramarital relationship with his teenage babysitter.

"Two members of my family chased an idealized alternative to their life. One left behind an embittered wife, and another, in what looked to be a hedge against mortality, fell in love with youth and surrendered his judgment in the process," John wrote. "Perhaps they should have known better. To whom much is given, much is expected, right? The interesting thing was the ferocious condemnation of their excursions beyond the bounds of acceptable behavior. Since when does someone need to apologize on television for getting divorced?"

The letter was accompanied by a nude photo of John, the Adam to Kate Moss's Eve, who posed for the issue wearing only a snake, and holding an apple.

At the time, the picture of John received most of the attention; although the rare criticism of a Kennedy by a fellow family member was also of note. But as Kennedy biographer Kate Storey wrote in a 2019 retrospective on *George* for *Esquire* magazine, "Today, it reads like a tone-deaf defense of the men, ignoring their privilege and power while being disturbingly dismissive of the women, especially the teenage girl who was the victim of an alleged statutory rape." (Norfolk County District Attorney Jeffrey Locke eventually dropped the investigation due to a lack of cooperation from the teenager; hours after Michael shared an apology. "I intend to do all I can to make up for the serious mistakes I have made and to continue the help I need," he said. He died later that year in a skiing accident.)

When John was asked about the letter and its accompanying photo, he said he wouldn't do anything differently. "I did that because that was something I wanted to say and something that I had felt strongly about, which is, we judge harshly people in the public eye for being human," he said in an interview with *Brill's Content* in 1999. "The picture had to accompany the letter, because otherwise the letter would have looked like I was being judgmental. And the picture had to accompany the letter because the picture exposed me to judgment."

More recently, Jackie's grandson, Jack Kennedy Schlossberg, has embraced media, primarily through his fervent posting on Instagram and TikTok; he's become a spokesperson of sorts for his generation of the family. His increased social presence garnered a number of profiles by traditional publications; more than one had a headline playing on the phrase "You don't know Jack." During the 2024 election, he served as *Vogue*'s political correspondent. "Jack Schlossberg is unmistakably a Kennedy," wrote fashion journalist Hannah Jackson in a feature announcing Jack's new role with the magazine. "With his towering frame, dark hair, and strong jawline, the 31-year-old is the spitting image of his uncle John F. Kennedy Jr. To a younger generation, however, he is more notably the man behind a series of outré TikToks filled with colorful characters, playful ditties, and lots (and lots) of props." (To be clear, his social media presence is often more eccentric, crude, and controversial than this sanitized description suggests.) The piece was accompanied by a flashy photo shoot featuring the smiling, handsome Kennedy heir. Schlossberg went on to write six opinion pieces for the publication on topics including a preview of the now-consequential presidential debate between Joe Biden and Donald Trump, a recap of the Republican National Convention, and a deep dive into Kamala Harris's social media strategy.

Post-election, though, the relationship with *Vogue* apparently soured. In April 2025, Schlossberg called for a boycott of the Met Gala, seemingly in response to the ongoing conflict in Gaza. In a video message, he spoke directly to Anna Wintour, the longtime editor in chief of *Vogue* and cochair of the event, explaining his reasoning. "Hey Anna Wintour! I am boycotting the Met Gala this year. With so much happening at home and around the world, it's not the time, it's not the time for a party like that—at least for me . . ."

Even without the backing of a traditional media publication, Jack continued to make content, sharing his perspective directly with his followers and the larger algorithmic audience. He sees social media as the battleground where young voters are won or lost, and much of his content is designed to provoke, particularly regarding his ongoing feud with his cousin RFK Jr.: "It's difficult to break through, especially if you're not saying something that's controversial, or at least, somehow unexpected," he told former White House press secretary and current MSNBC host Jen Psaki on her podcast, *The Blueprint with Jen Psaki*. "And I think that I see that Democrats play that game not as well as we could." He added, "That's kind of the game that the other side's been playing really well, which is flipping people out—and getting a reaction is almost half the battle."

During the summer of 2025, Schlossberg launched his own

YouTube series called *Test Drive.* In the clips, he commented on the political news of the day and pop culture, but in contrast to the royals' performed authenticity, Jack says his persona online is not true to life. "It's not me," he told *New York Magazine.* "It's a character based on an algorithm controlled by giant companies. I can talk all I want about something super-serious, and I'll show you the numbers—it doesn't work."

He views his work as a continuation of his family's legacy.

"I see my grandfather and my uncle as people who understood the media moment of their time. My grandfather was the first televised presidency, and he understood TV. He understood instead of how to use TV to work people's minds and brainwash them, he used celebrity and media to bring people into the political process. My uncle John did the same thing," Schlossberg said on his show. "When I think about my uncle and when I think about my grandfather, I think about privileged young men who, instead of being happy with that for themselves, devoted their lives to figuring out how other people could have the same thing, how other people could get an education, how other people could have health care and to care about their country and what happened to it. To be engaged in their politics and to inspire young people to believe that they can make a difference. And that's exactly what I'm trying to do now." In 2026, Jack is hoping to parlay his social media acumen into a political career. In November 2025, he announced his run for Congress in New York's twelfth district. Naturally, he shared the news in a video on Instagram.

Unlike her son or her grandson, Jackie rarely engaged with any sort of media following her husband's death. She didn't give many interviews; instead, she pursued a career as a book editor, first at Viking and then at Doubleday. Over the course of a nineteen-year career, she edited roughly one hundred titles, both fiction and nonfiction. Her projects ranged from translations of the novels by Egyptian writer and Nobel Prize–winner Naguib Mahfouz to *Dancing on My Grave*, a controversial autobiography from American prima ballerina Gelsey Kirkland. One of her most commercially successful collaborations was with Michael Jackson on his 1988 memoir *Moonwalk*, which sold roughly a half million copies. "She was the only person in America who could get him on the phone," Stephen Davis, the ghostwriter of the book, said many years later. But despite the encouraging sales numbers, the project was a frustrating one for Jackie. "It wasn't a great experience for her," Davis said, detailing how Jackson required a level of control that Jackie wasn't willing to easily give.

Demanding authors weren't the only challenging thing about her career; the media also regularly speculated about her work. In his book *Jackie as Editor*, a biography focused on the literary life of the former First Lady, Greg Lawrence reveals that in 1979, NBC News reported that Jackie was pursuing a tell-all from the recently divorced Earl of Snowdon, Princess Margaret's former husband. In reality, she was vacationing in Jamaica at the time with her son. Rumors also flew about potential books from both Princess Diana and Camilla Parker Bowles. As Lawrence wrote, "According to her Doubleday colleagues, while Diana may have been pursued with a letter of interest, the offer to Bowles never happened and she was never considered by Jackie for a book."

Annoyances aside, Jackie loved working. A 1979 issue of *Ms.* magazine featured Jackie on the cover with the headline "Why Does This Woman Work?" The answer was obvious, at least to Jackie. She wanted to. "What has been sad for many women of my generation is that they weren't supposed to work if they had families. There they were, with the highest education, and what were they to do when the children were grown—watch the raindrops coming down the window pane? Leave their fine minds unexercised? Of course women should work if they want to," she told the publication. "You have to do something you enjoy. That is the definition of happiness: 'complete use of one's faculties along the lines leading to excellence in a life affording them scope.'" But despite her long-standing role in the publishing industry, Jackie never wrote a memoir of her own. After crafting the modern American myth about her family, she felt content to help tell other people's stories.

Family Feuds

Shortly before the 2024 Super Bowl halftime show, the game cut to an ad break, and a chorus of voices began to chant: "Kennedy, Kennedy, Kennedy, Kennedy, Kennedy, Kennedy, Kenn-e-dy for me."

The repetitive jingle had been an earworm when it was used during John F. Kennedy's presidential run. But this wasn't the ad from 1960; rather, JFK's original campaign message had been refashioned in support of his nephew Robert F. Kennedy Jr.'s political ambitions.

The late Robert F. Kennedy's son was following in his father's and his uncle's footsteps by running for president—but not as a member of the party his family members once led. While RFK Jr. had started the 2024 presidential race as a Democrat, he later dropped his primary bid against Joe Biden and instead opted to run as an Independent; hence why the new advertisement asked voters to "Vote Independent," as opposed to "Democratic" like the original did.

The clip swapped pictures of JFK for his nephew but otherwise kept the vintage feel and the iconic Kennedy imagery, set to a shortened version of the jingle. The lyrics "Do you want a man for president who's seasoned through and through, a man who's old enough to know and young enough to do? Well it's up to you" also took on new meaning, given that the age of the candidates—Joe Biden was eighty-one at the time this ad ran and Trump was seventy-seven, while RFK Jr. was seventy—was a central issue in the election.

Roughly 124 million people tuned in to watch the San Francisco 49ers face off against the Kansas City Chiefs—and presumably, most of them would have seen the video, given its coveted placement near Usher's halftime performance. The price of those eyeballs? Seven million dollars.

But as soon as the ad aired, multiple members of the Kennedy family shared their displeasure on social media.

"My cousin's Super Bowl ad used our uncle's faces—and my Mother's. She would be appalled by his deadly health care views. Respect for science, vaccines, & health care equity were in her DNA," Bobby Shriver, the son of Sargent and Eunice Kennedy Shriver, wrote on X, referencing RFK Jr.'s long-standing skepticism about vaccines and promotion of conspiracy theories. Mark Shriver then reposted the message, adding: "I agree with my brother @bobbyshriver simple as that."

RFK Jr. then shared an apology on X, writing, "I'm so sorry if the Super Bowl advertisement caused anyone in my family pain." He also clarified that the ad was purchased by a super PAC, and not his campaign directly. "The ad was created and aired by the American Values Super PAC without any involvement or approval from my campaign. FEC rules prohibit Super PACs from consulting with me or my staff," he wrote, ending with: "I love you all. God bless you." Despite the apology, he left the ad pinned to his profile for at least a day after it aired.

Throughout the 2024 presidential race, RFK Jr. leaned into the political cachet of the Kennedy name. He launched his campaign with a video that positioned him as the successor to his father's legacy; his "Viva Kennedy!" effort to engage Latino voters was modeled directly on his uncle JFK's platform of the same name. He also frequently shared archival family images on social media, and when Biden dropped out of the race, he gave a press conference outside the Kennedy compound in Hyannis Port.

While politics is certainly the Kennedy family business, some of RFK Jr.'s relatives were less than thrilled with his ambitions, and from the start, there was "robust intra-family dialogue" about his bid for the presidency. The public discourse about his Super Bowl advertisement was just one early example of a feud that would go on to leave the dining room to instead be battled out in the public forum.

Many of Bobby's relatives opposed individual policies he proposed, but they also took issue with the way he used Kennedy nostalgia for his own political gain—specifically, how he invoked his father's and his uncle's legacies, seemingly suggesting that he was their political successor (and that had they lived, they would have supported both him and his agenda).

When he first announced his run for the White House in April 2023, his sisters Kerry and Rory spoke out, making it clear that they did not support his candidacy. "I love my brother Bobby, but I do not share or endorse his opinions on many issues, including the COVID pandemic, vaccinations, and the role of social media platforms in policing false information," Kerry said in a statement. For her part, Rory told CNN: "This is a difficult situation for me. I love my older brother Bobby. He has extraordinary charisma and is a very gifted speaker . . . But due to a wide range of Bobby's positions, I'm supporting President Biden."

As RFK Jr.'s rhetoric intensified, so did the Kennedy family's public disavowal. After he made bigoted remarks about COVID-19, specifically that the virus was "ethnically targeted" to spare Jews and Chinese people, Kerry released another statement, which read in part, "I strongly condemn my brother's deplorable and untruthful remarks last week about Covid being engineered for ethnic targeting."

Similarly, their brother Joseph Kennedy II shared his thoughts with *The Boston Globe*: "Bobby's comments are morally and factually wrong. They play on antisemitic myths and stoke mistrust of the Chinese. His remarks in no way reflect the words and actions of our father, Robert F. Kennedy." His nephew Joseph Kennedy III wrote, "My uncle's comments were hurtful and wrong. I unequivocally condemn what he said."

A few days later, Jack Schlossberg entered the conversation with a video posted on social media. In the clip, he called RFK Jr.'s candidacy an "embarrassment" and a "vanity project." "I have no idea why anyone thinks he should be president," he said, offering an endorsement of Joe Biden and accusing his cousin of "trading in on Camelot, celebrity, conspiracy theories, and conflict for personal gain and fame."

Behind the scenes, RFK Jr. complained about his relatives' public comments and spoke with his family members about their negative statements, engaging in "tense discussions." But publicly, he said, "I bear them no ill will. Families can disagree and still love each other," and he emphasized, "Our family was raised in a milieu where we debated. We came home every night at dinner and we were encouraged to debate each other and to debate each other on important issues and still love each other."

Certainly, there were Kennedys who supported RFK Jr.'s run, helping with fundraising and other campaign efforts. And even among those who disagreed with him, not everyone was as full-throated in their opposition as some of his siblings. For example, his sister Courtney Kennedy Hill said, "I love my brother deeply, and while I don't agree with him on a number of issues, theories, I do not want to knock him." She also cited his work as an environmental lawyer and with those suffering from addiction. "I just don't want all that to get lost in the maelstrom around his more controversial statements and views." Others kept quiet about their opinions altogether. Notably Ethel, ever the matriarch, remained neutral in conversations about her son Bobby. Ethel "is unequivocally supportive of her children," her son Chris said, before adding, "But she does have a photo of President Biden on her mantel."

After he dropped out of the race, RFK Jr.'s decision to endorse Trump continued to draw ire from five of his siblings, who called his endorsement "a betrayal of the values that our father and our family hold most dear. It is a sad ending to a sad story."

In the end, it was politics that tore the family—and perhaps even more significantly, the family brand—apart. The feud, which had been simmering for months, seemingly boiled over after Trump nominated RFK Jr. to serve as secretary of the Department of Health and Human Services in his administration. No longer did the family name align wholly with Democratic values. In fact, now the only Kennedy with significant political power was aligned wholly with the MAGA movement or, to use his parlance, MAHA—Make America Healthy Again.

While Bobby's direct relatives—his siblings and their children— were quieter online, Jack Schlossberg aggressively spoke out against his first cousin once removed on social media. His posts, which were eccentric, often profane, and sometimes offensive, accused his cousin of being a liar, corrupt, and a "guru shaman figure" unfit to hold the HHS position.

Jack also called out his cousins who explicitly supported Bobby or were silent, both of which he saw as complicit behavior.

"I'm asking the media to ask my cousins—I have a lot of 'em— what they think and why they don't say anything, and what they know about Bobby Kennedy and why they aren't talking and all the stories they have. The guy's about to be in charge of public health for the United States of America," he said in a video posted on social media. "How about you ask my cousins some real questions? How come I'm the only one who's talking out? Wake up. This is not a fucking drill. These guys are taking over. If they don't want to talk, then you know what side they're on. Later." (Schlossberg would go on to delete his personal social media accounts after a series of erratic, offensive posts, leaving many to speculate about his mental health. RFK Jr.'s daughter Kathleen "Kick" Kennedy commented to the *New York Post*: "I hope he gets the help he needs." When Schlossberg returned to the internet less than two weeks later, he mocked her on Instagram.)

Weeks after the election, Caroline Kennedy was asked if Bobby's views on vaccines and his association with the incoming Trump administration were "tarnishing the family reputation" during an address to the National Press Club of Australia.

"Well, I'm a sitting ambassador and I'm not supposed to comment on politics, and now you're asking me to also comment on family, so it's really a lot," she replied sheepishly before making her views explicitly clear.

"I think Bobby Kennedy's views on vaccines are dangerous, but I don't think that most Americans share them," she said, emphasizing that her family "is united in terms of our support for the public health sector and infrastructure and has the greatest admiration for the medical profession in our country."

"Bobby Kennedy has got a different set of views," she said.

On the eve of Bobby's confirmation hearings, Caroline made another statement, calling for senators to reject her cousin's nomination. She called RFK Jr. a "predator" and shared the disturbing story of how her cousin put live chickens and mice in a blender to feed to a snake in what she described as "a perverse scene of despair and violence." She also detailed how Bobby encouraged their relatives' substance addictions, and she criticized his use of family tragedy as a campaign tactic.

The video was striking not just for its content but also because Caroline almost never publicly criticizes her family. She rarely speaks to the press at all. Even as her cousins were sharing their discontent with Bobby's campaign, Caroline remained quiet. "We just don't hear from her," a source told *People*. "I think it's unprecedented because both she and her mother were known for just not speaking to the press, ever." Her mentality was one akin to that of the royals'. The same source said both Caroline and her mother shared a "never complain, never explain" attitude, much like that of the Windsors.

"I did not comment not only because I was serving in a government position as United States Ambassador to Australia, but because I have never wanted to speak publicly about my family members and their challenges," Caroline said, again underscoring how unusual this kind of a statement was from her. How scathing her message was only emphasized the fervor of her opinion.

"We are a close family. None of that is easy to say. It also wasn't easy to remain silent last year when Bobby expropriated my father's image and distorted President Kennedy's legacy to advance his own failed campaign and then groveled to Donald Trump for a job. Bobby continues to grandstand off my father's assassination and that of his own father."

An essay published by Caroline's daughter Tatiana in November 2025 revealing a terminal cancer diagnosis offers additional insight into why Caroline and Jack chose to be vocal in their criticism of RFK Jr. and his policies.

"As I spent more and more of my life under the care of doctors, nurses, and researchers striving to improve the lives of others, I watched as Bobby cut nearly half a billion dollars for research into mRNA vaccines, technology that could be used against certain cancers; slashed billions in funding from the National Institutes of Health, the world's largest sponsor of medical research; and threatened to oust the panel of medical experts charged with recommending preventive cancer screenings," Tatiana wrote in *The New Yorker*. "Hundreds of N.I.H. grants and clinical trials were cancelled, affecting thousands of patients. I worried about funding for leukemia and bone-marrow research at Memorial Sloan Kettering. I worried about the trials that were my only shot at remission." She passed away a month later. She was just thirty-five years old.

But during RFK Jr.'s confirmation hearings, Caroline didn't share her daughter's diagnosis publicly; instead, she cited both personal reasons (RFK Jr.'s continued use of President Kennedy's legacy and specifically her father's tragic death) and political ones (her cousin's lack of experience necessary to do the job at hand) as reasons why she finally felt compelled to speak, when she hadn't during his campaign.

"It's incomprehensible to me that someone who is willing to exploit their own painful family tragedies for publicity would be put in charge of America's life-and-death situations," Caroline said. "Unlike Bobby, I try not to speak for my father, but I am certain that he and my uncle Bobby, who gave their lives in public service to our country, and my uncle Teddy, who devoted his long Senate career to the cause of improving healthcare, would be disgusted." She finished her statement by simply asking the Senate to reject Trump's nomination.

While the Democrats heeded her word, a plea from the standard-bearer of an aging political dynasty was not enough to stop Trump's power in selecting his cabinet. RFK Jr. was confirmed with only a single Republican, Mitch McConnell, who is a polio survivor, voting against his nomination.

"One reason the Kennedy family was able to command such influence over American politics for so long was that everyone stuck together," summarized *New York Magazine* writer Reeves Wiedeman in his August 2025 feature, "Hijacking the Kennedys." Presenting a unified front in order to protect the family name and its legacy is something the Kennedys have done many, many times over the years. In moments of scandal—whether that be accusations of infidelity, womanizing, rape, or any number of revelations about excessive drinking or drug use—they were loyal to one another and to the myth of Camelot, if not in private, in public.

No scandal better exemplifies the old Kennedy ethos quite like Chappaquiddick. In July 1969, Ted Kennedy's black Oldsmobile crashed off the Dike Bridge on Massachusetts's Chappaquiddick Island and into the water below. While Ted survived the crash, his passenger, Mary Jo Kopechne—a young woman who had worked on Ted's brother Bobby's presidential campaign before he was assassinated—drowned. Her body was found submerged in the vehicle the next morning, prompting myriad questions by the public, the papers, and law enforcement. Chief among them: What happened on that bridge? Had Ted been drinking and driving? Why hadn't he immediately called the police? And what had Mary Jo been doing in his car in the first place, while Ted's pregnant wife rested at home? About a week later Ted pleaded guilty to a charge of leaving the scene of an accident after causing personal injury. That same night, he delivered a nationally broadcast statement in which he explained that he had not been drinking and indeed had tried to save Mary Jo but "was overcome, I'm frank to say, by a jumble of emotions: grief, fear, doubt, exhaustion, panic, confusion and shock." However, details of the evening remain murky. But the Kennedy family didn't question their own. Ted's relatives continued to support his political career. While he was never elected president, his long career in Congress earned him the title of the "Lion of the Senate," and following his father Joe Sr.'s death, he took on the responsibility of the family patriarch. In March 2009, he even received an honorary knighthood from Queen Elizabeth, a recognition for his work on US-UK relations and for his long-standing commitment to peace in Northern Ireland.

Ted has been dead now for more than fifteen years. The secrets of Chappaquiddick died with him, and the Kennedy family of today is much, much larger than that of the 1960s. "Just to state the obvious though it seems often underweighted these days—there are now more than 100 adults in our family so it's pretty different than in the past," Caroline said in a statement given to *New York Magazine*. Her son, Jack, more theatrically described the current state of his family tree. "There is no 'family'—it's not *The Godfather*," Jack told the publication. "We don't all meet every year and have a discussion about what to do. It's just a bunch of individual people."

A FEUD MAKES FOR A GOOD HEADLINE, AND THE ONE BETWEEN RFK Jr. and those Kennedys who disagree with him is rich and layered with history, but there's another reason people continue to be fascinated by the family's discord: It makes the Kennedys seem more relatable. Especially in today's charged, extremely partisan political landscape, many people have a cousin with views different from their own—someone who stirs the pot at Thanksgiving dinner, whom they avoid talking politics with at all costs.

In a similar vein, the royals' recent infighting—namely the "royal rift" between Princes William and Harry—humanizes them. An ongoing public standoff between brothers who grew up together and faced unspeakable tragedy in the public eye cuts harsher than a political dispute between cousins who might not have ever been that close, but it offers the same voyeuristic feeling. These are people who have every luxury afforded to them. They are rich and powerful and even they can't avoid family drama. As longtime royal reporter Richard Palmer put it, "It's a national soap opera." He also confirmed that controversy not only helps sell papers but also drives clicks online.

Sibling rivalry is hardly a new concept for the royals. Shakespeare had it right: It's practically a family tradition. Think Prince John and King Richard, Elizabeth I and her half sister Mary, King Edward VIII and King George VI, or even King Charles and the former Prince Andrew. But in recent history, these have mostly been private squabbles, whispered about by anonymous sources in the tabloid press until a fuller picture is revealed. Closing ranks to protect the institution of the monarchy has always been of utmost importance, and the status and health of the family brand takes precedence over personal disagreement.

Such was the case in 2019 following Prince Andrew's bombshell interview with Emily Maitlis, in which he discussed his friendship with convicted sex offender Jeffrey Epstein. The interview was a disaster for the man widely believed to be the Queen's favorite son. Not only did he stumble answering questions about his association with Epstein, but he also neglected to explicitly denounce Epstein's crimes or to express sympathy for his victims. Eventually, public outcry was so significant that Andrew was forced to step back from public duties and to cease representing the Crown. At the time, the move was described as for the "foreseeable future" but it's practically impossible to imagine a world in which he is invited back into the royal fold in a significant way.

In mid-October 2025, after additional details came to light about his association with Epstein, Andrew gave up the use of royal titles, including "Duke of York."

"In discussion with The King, and my immediate and wider family, we have concluded the continued accusations about me distract from the work of His Majesty and the Royal Family. I have decided, as I always have, to put my duty to my family and country first. I stand by my decision five years ago to stand back from public life," he said in a statement. "With His Majesty's agreement, we feel I must now go a step further. I will therefore no longer use my title or the honours which have been conferred upon me. As I have said previously, I vigorously deny the accusations against me." Later that month, on October 30, 2025, Buckingham Palace announced that King Charles would be removing all of his brother's royal titles, including "prince." "His Majesty has today initiated a formal process to remove the Style, Titles and Honours of Prince Andrew," the palace said in the statement, clarifying that moving forward, Prince Andrew will be known as Andrew Mountbatten-Windsor and he will move out of Royal Lodge in the near future. The statement concluded: "Their Majesties wish to make clear that their thoughts and utmost sympathies have been, and will remain with, the victims and survivors of any and all forms of abuse." This wasn't a case of a sibling squabble, however. Andrew's behavior had so tarnished the reputation of the monarchy that the institution had to come first.

In contrast, Prince Harry broke the mold when he spoke publicly about his falling-out with his brother.

During an interview at the Royal Foundation Forum in early 2018, before Harry and Meghan had wed, the "Fab Four" (William, Kate, Harry, and Meghan) were asked if they ever have family disagreements. William, Kate, and Meghan chuckled awkwardly, but Harry scowled and swiveled his chair to look at his brother, who simply said, "Oh, yes."

"Healthy disagreements," Harry added, as Meghan placed her hand on his arm, seemingly trying to steady him. When asked to elaborate on the disputes, Harry dodged the question by making a joke. "I can't remember, they come so thick and fast," he said.

"Is it resolved? We don't know," William added, before the interviewer joked rather tellingly, "You're putting on a great show if it's not."

But Prince Harry had the final word. "I think it's really good that we've got four different personalities and we've all got the same passion to want to make a difference, but different opinions. I think those opinions work really, really well. Working as family does have its challenges, of course it does, and the fact that everyone is laughing shows they know exactly what it's like," he said. "But look, we're stuck together for the rest of our lives." In retrospect, it's a conversation with so much significance, and one indicative of how quickly things really fell apart.

Harry has never publicly revealed the origins of his fight with William (and certainly William hasn't either). Many have speculated that Harry's relationship with Meghan is what initially broke up the brothers. And certainly, there's a grain of truth to that misogynistic line of thinking. But reporting by *The Times* suggests that tensions were simmering even before Harry started dating Meghan—and that they stemmed from the brothers' differing perspectives on wildlife conservation, of all things.

"They are both very passionate about saving protected species but didn't always share the same view about how to run projects in Africa," a source told *The Times*. "William believes you should focus on community-led schemes where local people over time feel empowered to protect the land. Harry, on the other hand, was more interventionist. He felt that you need a more hands-on approach to ensure wildlife habitats were securely protected to enact change quickly."

Harry referenced this disagreement in his memoir, *Spare*, indeed confirming that it dates back prior to the end of 2015. He suggests that Prince William felt a sort of ownership over Africa as a philanthropic category. "Africa and Invictus, these had long been the causes closest to my heart. But now I wanted to dive in deeper," Prince Harry wrote. "One small problem: Willy. Africa was *his* thing, he said. And he had the right to say this, or felt he did, because he was the Heir. It was ever in his power to veto *my* thing, and he had every intention of exercising, even flexing that veto power."

Per Harry, they'd even had a fight about it in front of childhood friends. "Why can't you both work on Africa?" they'd asked. "Because rhinos, elephants, that's mine!" Prince William reportedly replied. (Notably, Harry neglects to point out the problematic, colonialist undertones of this kind of language.)

Yes, on the surface, it was an argument about conservation, but it was also fueled by the clear anger and resentment Prince Harry feels about his position of "spare" in the royal family and how the institution of the monarchy is inherently hierarchical, a system that, per Harry, both prioritizes and protects his brother as the heir to the throne—sometimes to the explicit detriment of Harry and his immediate family. Of course, adhering to the royals' long-standing unofficial motto of "Never Complain, Never Explain," Prince William has yet to share his side of the story. But regardless of how the rift started, Harry's relationship with Meghan certainly deepened the chasm.

From the beginning, Prince William was hesitant about Harry's relationship with Meghan, cautioning his brother that he thought things were moving too quickly and discouraging him from proposing too early. Understandably, Harry wasn't pleased with this reaction to the woman he hoped to marry.

"It's too fast, he'd told me. Too soon [to propose]," Harry wrote in *Spare*. "In fact, he'd actually been pretty discouraging about my even dating Meg. One day, sitting together in his garden, he'd predicted a host of difficulties I could expect if I hooked up with an 'American actress,' a phrase he always managed to make sound like a 'convicted felon.'"

But when Meghan walked down the aisle in May 2018, any sense of discord between the brothers was kept tightly under wraps. To everyone watching, it appeared to be a real-life fairy tale—a happy ending for the little boy who had suffered so much. By his side was his older brother.

But the honeymoon didn't last long. Rumors that the two brothers weren't getting along started to surface in earnest just a few months after Harry and Meghan tied the knot. In November 2018, a source told reporter Katie Nicholl that Harry was upset his brother wasn't making enough of an effort to welcome Meghan into the family. "Harry felt William wasn't rolling out the red carpet for Meghan and told him so," the source said. "They had a bit of a fall out which was only resolved when Charles stepped in."

Not long after Harry and Meghan got back from their honeymoon to the Mediterranean, they visited Will and Kate for tea "to clear the air." After all, Meghan was part of the family now. But this airing of grievances did little to repair the relationships, as petty disagreements on both sides were raised. According to Harry, the Cambridges (the last name used by William and Kate before the Queen's death and William's appointment as Prince of Wales) were upset over a lack of Easter gifts between the families and the overly familiar way Meghan referenced Kate's hormones. For their part, the Sussexes were miffed that Will and Kate had swapped place cards at their wedding. (Will and Kate denied they had altered the seating arrangements.)

"Was this really happening? Had it actually come to this? Shouting at each other about place cards and hormones?" Harry questioned in his memoir. "Meg said she'd never intentionally do anything to hurt Kate, and if she ever did, she asked Kate to please just let her know so it wouldn't happen again. We all hugged. Kind of. And then I said we'd better be going."

The press was only beginning to sniff out the beginnings of a rift, but behind the scenes, things continued escalating. Meghan and Kate were hardly the best friends some royal-watchers had hoped. Meghan struggled with William and Kate's formality. "I was a hugger, always been a hugger," she said in the Netflix series *Harry & Meghan*. "I didn't realize that that is really jarring for a lot of Brits."

"I guess I'd start to understand very quickly that the formality on the outside, carried through on the inside," she continued. "There is a forward-facing way of being, and then you close the door and you relax now. But that formality carries over on both sides, and that was surprising to me."

As their husbands' relationship deteriorated, so, too, did any closeness that might have existed between the two women, as ex-emplified by the drama over who made who cry about a brides-maid dress.

For those unfamiliar with the saga, following the royal wedding, reports surfaced that Meghan had made Kate cry over the tailoring of Princess Charlotte's bridesmaid dress. During her interview with Oprah, Meghan refuted that story, saying that "the reverse hap-pened," meaning that Kate had made *Meghan* cry. Further reporting, including in the biography by Tom Quinn, *Yes, Ma'am: The Secret Life of Royal Servants*, suggests that both women cried. "I can tell you that all the papers and commentators got this wrong, the truth is that as with many of these spats between sisters, brothers or even sisters-in-law, both sides were really upset," one anonymous royal staffer said. "Both women were crying their eyes out!" Neither side has been in-clined to speak further about the incident, with Meghan revealing only that Kate "apologized, and she brought me flowers and a note apologizing," in her interview with Oprah. Meghan continued, "I don't think it's fair to her to get into the details of that because she apologized, and I've forgiven her."

In the spring of 2019, the rift deepened yet again. Prince Harry alleges that's when Prince William pushed him to the floor during an argument about Meghan, in which William called her "difficult," "rude," and "abrasive." Harry and Meghan began to separate their working lives from William and Kate's, and in June 2019, they launched their own charitable organization, the Archewell Foundation. In October of that year, Harry addressed the suggestion of a family feud publicly for the first time.

"Inevitably, you know, stuff happens. But look, we're brothers, we'll always be brothers. And we're certainly on different paths at the moment, but I'll always be there for him, as I know he'll always be there for me," he said during ITV's documentary *Harry & Meghan: An African Journey* when asked how much of the media's speculation about a "rift" between him and William was true.

"We don't see each other as much as we used to because we're so busy, but you know, I love him dearly. And the majority of this stuff [in the press] is created out of nothing, but you know, as brothers, you know, you have good days, you have bad days."

In the same program, Meghan opened up to journalist Tom Bradby about how difficult her experience in the royal family had been. The conversation primarily focuses on her relationship with the tabloid press and the stresses of being a new mother, but one comment in particular is clearly a statement about the royal family. When Bradby asks her if she's okay, she thanks him, and says simply, "Not many people have asked if I'm okay," not so subtly implying that her in-laws had not.

Things came to a head in January 2020, with Harry and Meghan's decision to step back from their royal roles and to move to Canada. At the time, the brothers issued a joint statement denying a report that Harry and Meghan had been "bullied" out of the royal family. In the Netflix documentary *Harry & Meghan*, Harry revealed that he hadn't been consulted. "I was told about a joint statement that had been put out in mine and my brother's name squashing the story about him bullying us out of the family," Harry says. "I couldn't believe it. No one had asked me," he continued. "No one had asked me permission to put my name to a statement like that."

In the years that have followed, Meghan has reunited with the rest of the royal family just twice: for Queen Elizabeth's Platinum Jubilee celebrations in June 2022 and then again for the Queen's funeral that September. The former Fab Four put any disagreements aside to pay tribute to the late monarch by visiting a flower memorial to the Queen in Windsor on September 10, two days after her death. The appearance sparked international headlines. At her funeral, William and Harry stood side by side as they walked behind the Queen's coffin as it left Buckingham Palace, a poignant echo of an image seared into history from when their mother died. At least as of this writing, Meghan hasn't been back.

In May 2025, Harry told the BBC that he "would love reconciliation with my family. There's no point in continuing to fight anymore—life is precious." But he also illustrated just how disconnected he is from the royals by saying, "I don't know how much longer my father has. He won't speak to me . . . but it would be nice to reconcile." A little more than a year prior, in February 2024, Buckingham Palace announced that King Charles had been diagnosed with cancer and he began receiving treatment, which has continued into 2025. Medical details regarding what type of cancer he has and the specific treatments he is receiving have been kept out of the press, and clearly, the royals are also limiting the information shared with Prince Harry about his father's condition. Trust between the two parties has broken down, with Harry scarred by anonymous leaks to the press from inside the Palace, and William and Charles rightfully cautious to speak candidly with Harry considering his track record of sharing his truth publicly—whether that be via a highly publicized sit-down interview, an intimate Netflix docuseries, or a revealing memoir.

However, a meeting between Charles and Harry—their first in nineteen months—at Clarence House in September 2025 suggests that tensions could be thawing, at least between father and son, if not between brothers. But given Charles's ongoing health struggles, it does raise the question: Will Harry be able to reconcile with his father and brother before King Charles passes away, thrusting William onto the throne? And if they don't, will it be too late to make peace with his family?

Man Becomes Myth

On the day Queen Elizabeth died, Imelda Staunton and Lesley Manville were on the set of *The Crown*. The two esteemed British actresses were filming an emotional scene from the final season of the series, in which the Queen (played by Staunton) goes to visit Princess Margaret (played by Manville) in the hospital.

The episode, titled "Ritz," is told across two timelines. The first shows the sisters breaking out of Buckingham Palace to celebrate Victory in Europe Day. The young girls then go on an adventure—with the future Queen drinking and dancing with American soldiers, a brief moment of spontaneity and freedom in a life of consistency and responsibility. But the second plot focuses on the two women in the early 2000s, as Princess Margaret's health deteriorates following a series of strokes. In the particular scene Manville and Staunton were filming, the Queen sits at her sister's sickbed.

"I'm afraid it's serious this time. I can feel it—or can't feel it, more like. I can't feel anything, or see anything," Manville-as-Margaret says, slurring her words. "My body's deserting me, one limb at a time." The princess, once glamorous and vibrant, is barefaced, in a frumpy pink cardigan. As she holds her sister's hand, a tear runs down her face.

"It's a very beautiful examination of the sisters and their relationship and their huge love for each other," Manville said of the episode. "I mean, they were probably the biggest loves of each other's lives."

When the production went on a break for lunch, Staunton and Manville were told that they might hear some sad news about the real-life British monarch that day. Just after 12:30 p.m. on September 8, 2022, Buckingham Palace had issued a statement about the Queen's well-being. "Following further evaluation this morning, the Queen's doctors are concerned for Her Majesty's health and have recommended she remain under medical supervision," it read, adding that she is "comfortable" and would remain at Balmoral. She had been in poor health for months, but ever committed to duty, she was still making appearances when able. Just two days prior, she had met with Liz Truss and formally appointed her as prime minister. In her memoir, Truss recalled the Queen standing as she greeted her in the drawing room.

"I was told she'd made a special effort to do so but she gave no hint of discomfort throughout our discussion," Truss said. But as members of the royal family flocked to Scotland to be by their matriarch's side later that week, many saw the vague announcement for what it was: a sign that the end of the second Elizabeth age was about to abruptly come to an end.

Despite the apprehension, the actresses told the crew they'd like to carry on with filming. "It was a very strange day," Manville later said. "We were doing a scene together, just the two of us all day." They wrapped around 4 p.m. and headed home, and at 6:30 p.m. local time the royals confirmed that the family's matriarch had passed away: "The Queen died peacefully at Balmoral this afternoon," the statement read, noting that the new King and his Queen Consort would remain at the family's Scottish estate for the evening, with plans to return to London the following day.

Immediately, news outlets both in the UK and around the world began a carefully crafted slate of memorial programming, most of it positive, with segments that had been in the works for years, if not decades.

"I felt a loss, I really did. It was fascinating because the television, the BBC especially, was wall-to-wall coverage of her life, and it was a privilege to see those images, to see how beautiful she was," said Jonathan Pryce, who played Prince Philip in the final seasons of the series. "You think, oh yeah, *of course* they describe a queen as radiant, and then you go, oh my god, but she *was*."

Even before it was announced that Queen Elizabeth had passed away, the media started a meticulously orchestrated plan of coverage—and once Buckingham Palace confirmed the news that she had died, the hagiography was instant. Tributes telling a carefully crafted version of the Queen's reign started to roll, and they didn't stop for days.

Despite her offering glimpses into her life—whether by being the first monarch to broadcast her coronation or by bringing cameras into her home for a documentary—the public never had a full understanding of the British monarch, and the number of people who knew the *real* Elizabeth (not the icon depicted on stamps who stood every summer on the Buckingham Palace balcony, but the woman, friend, mother, and wife) grows smaller by the day. All that remains is a perception, one that was curated by both the royal family and the press for decades and cemented with the hours of commentary that accompanied her televised funeral.

She was more than a woman. She had become an emblem, a tangible representation of duty, of service, of constancy, and of Britain itself—for good and for bad. In her death, the Queen's story has become myth.

Staunton was "inconsolable" the night Elizabeth II died. And, strangely enough, she had ten days off from filming, the exact time allotted for official court mourning of the monarch, and was grateful for the time to regroup. Even if she hadn't, *The Crown* suspended production on September 9 as well as the day of the Queen's funeral, September 19, out of respect for the late monarch and her family. But when Stanton returned to filming after the royal funeral, people on set had a hard time seeing her fully transformed into Elizabeth. "I got my head around it, got dressed, but then we had a lot of supporting artists in that day, and then 'the shape' walked on. And I think, for them, it was quite hard."

Over the course of its six-season run, *The Crown* earned praise from critics and fans alike—winning awards and drawing in viewers to Peter Morgan's dramatization of Queen Elizabeth's life and reign. But as the story sped toward the modern day, those close to the royal family became more vocal in their criticism of the program and the liberties it took with history.

Fact-checking episodes also became an entire genre of content online, with outlets ranging from *The Washington Post* and *The New York Times* to *Town & Country* and *Vanity Fair* publishing articles analyzing the veracity of each storyline and the accuracy of minute details. Viewers of the show began pausing the action to Google: "Did that actually happen?" Often, the answer was yes, kind of, but not exactly how it was shown on-screen.

The Crown never presented itself as a documentary. "We're not pretending this is a chronological record of those years," Robert Lacey, the British biographer who served as a historical consultant on the Netflix series, said. Conversations, glances, and sometimes whole plot points were invented to tell a compelling story in the medium of television. (Such was certainly the case when the series re-created the Kennedys' 1961 visit to Buckingham Palace.) But even when what's on-screen deviates from fact, Lacey said, there is still a veracity to the show. "There are two sorts of truth. There's historical truth and then there's the larger truth about the past."

It's difficult to deny that the show introduced an entirely new audience of viewers to the royal story, many of whom were unfamiliar with the real events the drama is based on. In the latter seasons, as the series prodded at still-painful wounds in the royal family's more recent history—Charles's infidelity, Diana's death—a campaign to educate the public and ensure they knew *The Crown* was not entirely accurate took root.

Just a few weeks after the Queen's funeral and a few weeks before the season five premiere of the series, Dame Judi Dench joined the crowd of voices calling for Netflix to add a disclaimer clarifying that the show is a fictionalized version of history. The actress, who is known both for her long-standing friendship with Charles and Camilla and for her impressive career (which has seen her play multiple members of the royal family in dramatizations), even accused the show of "crude sensationalism," saying "Given some of the wounding suggestions apparently contained in the new series—that King Charles plotted for his mother to abdicate, for example, or once suggested his mother's parenting was so deficient that she might have deserved a jail sentence—this is both cruelly unjust to the individuals and damaging to the institution they represent."

She went on: "No one is a greater believer in artistic freedom than I, but this cannot go unchallenged."

The royal family itself never commented publicly on the requests to Netflix, though a few members of the House of Windsor are said to have watched the program. In 2021, Prince Harry spoke about the series on James Corden's late-night show—and suggested that seeing his family portrayed on the Netflix drama was preferable to the kind of coverage the royals had previously received in the tabloids.

(Though, an ongoing business relationship with Netflix could have influenced his perspective.)

"It's fictional, but it's loosely based on the truth," Harry said of the show when asked how he felt about it. "Of course, it's not strictly accurate, but loosely . . . it gives you a rough idea about what that lifestyle—what the pressures of putting duty and service above family and everything else—what can come from that. I'm way more comfortable with *The Crown* than I am seeing the stories written about my family, or my wife, or myself."

Ultimately, Netflix did add a note to the season five trailer, but the show largely remains disclaimer-free (as do many other period dramas focused on the Windsors and their ancestors). But the concern by monarchists is understandable, even if a disclaimer isn't justifiable. History is a perception of fact and can certainly be influenced by popular culture, even when it's dramatized. For the royals, what people *believe* about their history—their legacy—is arguably more important than what really happened.

"ALL HISTORY IS GOSSIP." JOHN F. KENNEDY ONCE SAID THAT— or, well, he *might* have said it. It's an apt phrase for a man whose life and accomplishments have become equal parts myth and fact, but it's difficult, perhaps fittingly so, to find the original source of the quote.

As much as Kennedy is remembered for the man that he was—a politician, father, naval officer, loving husband, philanderer—there are few people alive today whose memories of him remain uncolored by the carefully crafted narratives that have been curated over the more than sixty years since his death. Much like the Queen, he has become a symbol at this point. He represents what could have been, lost potential, a life taken too soon. It remains the ultimate what-if in modern American history: What if Kennedy hadn't died? In a way, he didn't.

Kennedy lives on in popular culture, in movies and television, fictionalized and historical versions of his life and death—serious biopics and time-travel superhero shows, and so many documentaries—that it can be difficult to parse the truth from a good story. JFK was elected thanks to the screen, and he has come to be immortalized by it.

It's almost become a rite of passage for actors to try their hand at that *very specific* Boston accent (to, let's be honest, varying degrees of success) and to step into the Oval Office of the early 1960s. These on-screen depictions of Kennedy started even before that fatal day in Dallas. In *PT 109*, a film released just a few months before Kennedy's death, Cliff Robertson portrays a young Jack, then a naval officer during World War II fighting to save his crew after a Japanese destroyer struck their boat, the PT-109. It marked the first time a major movie studio made a film about a sitting president, and the White House was even given casting approval for what one trailer described as "the most-talked-about part of the year." Jack himself chose Robertson for the role, picking him over Peter Fonda and Jeffrey Hunter after watching his audition. (Warren Beatty notably turned down the role.) Undoubtedly, Jack would have thought of this film as a way to keep his heroics in the Pacific top of mind for voters.

As politicians tend to, he told his own story throughout his career, nimbly utilizing the press's fascination with his family to craft a version of the truth to suit a broader narrative, to be sure. But in the end, when he became a martyr, Jackie became his mythmaker. Even before she buried her husband, she began to spin the Kennedy legacy through his funeral, using visuals to solidify his position in history: the riderless horse, the eternal flame, the ties to Abraham Lincoln's own memorial.

Days after the funeral, Jackie linked Kennedy forever to the legend of King Arthur and his court, with a little help from *Life* magazine and journalist Theodore H. White. "For one brief shining moment there was Camelot," White wrote of the time when Jackie and JFK served as representatives of America's loftiest ideals: progress, prosperity, excellence, charisma, and youth.

But following President Kennedy's death, Jackie saw the power in the imagery and the language of monarchy and used it to shape her late husband's story. Queen Elizabeth helped cement that comparison when she dedicated the Kennedy memorial at Runnymede, the site where King John had signed the Magna Carta, marking the blending of monarchy and democracy in Britain. Sixty years on, the idea of a Kennedy Camelot, and of the Kennedys as the closest thing America has to a royal family, persists.

Though some have argued that the myth is fraying—amid a MAGA political conversion, an eccentric social media–loving scion (who himself rejects any association with an American version of royalty), and a twenty-first-century family feud—the Camelot narrative is kept alive, by both biopics and biographies, but also the small references in popular culture. Taylor Swift, Olivia Rodrigo, Billy Joel, the Postal Service, Bob Dylan, Pitbull, the Spice Girls, Stephen Sondheim, and My Chemical Romance have all written songs mentioning the Kennedys; Jackie continues to be a pervasive fashion muse, as does her daughter-in-law Carolyn Bessette-Kennedy. On any given day, a reference to the family—be it a lyric on the radio, a plot point in a sci-fi show, or a model with a headscarf and oversize shades walking down the runway—isn't difficult to find. A controversial new television series about John and Carolyn's love story, which is opposed by many closest to the couple—prior to its debut, Jack Schlossberg called it "grotesque"—is only further igniting discourse, and keeping them part of the modern media conversation.

A quarter of a century after her death, Princess Diana, too, is omnipresent in the media. There are musicals, movies, TV shows, documentaries, and museum exhibitions. The Princess Diana Beanie Baby is shorthand for a specific type of millennial-tinged nostalgia. But the woman who is remembered, revered even, is not the woman who lived. Like President Kennedy and his son, she was gone too soon and quickly canonized. She became something of a saint, a symbol yet again of the loss of what could have been.

Unlike today, when everyone has a camera in their pocket, offering a seemingly endless stream of content about anything, there is a finite limit to what we can see of these figures—how many images, letters, and mementos are out there.

The Kennedys and the Windsors continue to be romanticized by both the media and the public, and so the dynasties live on. And through their legacies, it becomes increasingly clear how these two families didn't just coexist; they drew inspiration from each other to craft a narrative so convincing it could alter the record of history. It's why Diana wore a pillbox hat that looked just like Jackie's and Meghan Markle sees Carolyn Bessette as the ultimate style icon; it's why JFK Jr. wanted the Princess of Wales for the cover of his magazine and Prince William named his largest campaign after President Kennedy's Moonshot. These two families know the power of a symbol, and by tying themselves to a global history, they ensure they will have a place in the future as well.

The Future Generations

WHEN ETHEL KENNEDY DIED IN OCTOBER 2024 AT AGE NINETY-six from complications related to a stroke, her obituary ran on the front page of *The New York Times*. She was memorialized in what can only be described as a semi-state funeral at the Cathedral of St. Matthew the Apostle in Washington, DC, the same church where JFK's own funeral Mass was held more than a half century prior. President Joe Biden gave the eulogy.

"For over 50 years, with Ethel's own iron will and moral courage, she gave it everything she had," Biden said. "We're a better nation and a better world because of Ethel Kennedy." Former Presidents Barack Obama and Bill Clinton also paid their respects, as did Martin Luther King III. Stevie Wonder, Sting, and Kenny Chesney all performed.

Ethel was one of the last remaining vestiges of the Camelot era. She'd outlived not only her husband but also each of his brothers and sisters, and most of their spouses. Referred to by many as the Kennedy family matriarch, Ethel was, as the *Times* put it, a "vital force in the Kennedy political dynasty"—while she herself wasn't a politician, she was both an advocate in her own right and a witness to history. Her death, and more specifically the way it was commemorated, serves as an example of the place the Kennedy family holds in American culture—and also how their legacy is being shaped for the future.

"These things don't happen by themselves. These moments in history, these moments that become headlines, it is orchestrated. It has to be done by a phalanx of teams of people," said gossip columnist and PR professional R. Couri Hay, who has known the Kennedy family for years.

"The presidents don't line up to speak at Ethel Kennedy's funeral, and the church isn't lined up, and this and that. It's done, it's created, it's orchestrated. And I'm not saying it's wrong. In fact, I'm saying it's right. The point is the Kennedy machine hasn't stopped."

In the United States, few families have multigenerational prominence to the same degree as the Kennedys. The Bushes are one other example that comes to mind. The family has produced two presidents, and Jenna Bush Hager's position as an anchor on the *Today* show gives her both broad popularity and influence.

But typically speaking, families don't remain prominent in society and politics for more than two or three generations without significant effort. The drive, and frankly the social strategy, that originally brought the family prominence and power seems to be an inherited trait—though now, it's being used to ensure that the Kennedy name continues to be part of America's present and not just the country's past.

"They're very adept at staying in the news and being part of the news cycle," Hay said of the Kennedys. "Whether it's Kerry deciding to honor and give an award to Meghan and Harry or it's arranging for a major semi-state funeral, really, with presidents and so forth, they're very adept at thinking ahead."

However, in a world where "nepo baby" isn't a compliment and dynasties—particularly American ones—are increasingly viewed as a relic of another age, what does it mean to grow up in one?

At the John F. Kennedy Hyannis Museum on Cape Cod, a family tree takes up an entire wall of the permanent exhibit. At the top are Joe and Rose; below them are their nine children: Joseph Jr., John, Rosemary, Kathleen, Eunice, Patricia, Robert, Jean, and Edward. The tree continues on from there, and even though Joe Jr., Rosemary, and Kick did not have children, the list of Kennedy descendants continues to expand, with the grandchildren and great-grandchildren of Joe and Rose filling the space. Bobby and Ethel alone had more than thirty grandkids.

While they inherited the names of Kennedys who came before them—Kick, Rose, John, Joe, Teddy, Bobby—many of the younger people on that wall try to stay *out* of the public eye, making headlines only when there's a scandal, a death, or, more cheerfully, a wedding.

But some have sought the spotlight by dating celebrities, connections that reinforce the Kennedy family's long-standing association with Hollywood and its nostalgic glamour.

Patrick Schwarzenegger, the son of Maria Shriver and grandson of Eunice Kennedy and Sargent Shriver, is an actor and model himself, who once dated Miley Cyrus; his sister Katherine married Chris Pratt in 2019. They may be more familiar with the industry, given that their father is actor and politician Arnold Schwarzenegger, but they're not the only modern Kennedys to be linked romantically to famous people. Robert F. Kennedy Jr.'s son Conor Kennedy had a brief relationship with Taylor Swift in 2012. (Around this time, the pop icon wrote "Starlight" about Ethel and Bobby's marriage.) He's currently engaged to Brazilian pop star Giulia Be.

RFK's granddaughter Michaela Kennedy-Cuomo was even linked to Alex Ogilvy, the grandson of Queen Elizabeth's cousin Princess Alexandra, when they were both attending Brown University. While the relationship didn't last, it was, perhaps, the closest America's royal family has been to being related by marriage to the British one.

Regardless of whether the bride and groom are big names in the movie or music industry, a reception under a big white tent on the lawn of the Kennedy compound in Hyannis Port is still a surefire way to garner a story in a national magazine.

"We chose to host our wedding weekend events at the Kennedy Compound and surrounding family homes because of how special it is to us as a backdrop to our lives," Sarah Kennedy, the daughter of Christopher Kennedy and granddaughter of Bobby and Ethel, told *People* after her 2023 nuptials, the quotes accompanied by a gorgeous spread of photos. "It is where we have celebrated the great times and come together in heartbreaking times. It truly feels like coming home."

Just as the media highlights these love stories, that family heartbreak Sarah referenced is equally as enticing to the press—and frankly, to the public, who are drawn to tragedy. Whether they believe in the so-called Kennedy curse—or are more simply reacting with empathy and an immediate thought of "Hasn't this family suffered enough?"—there's still a ready audience eager to read about this family's worst days as well as its best.

In every generation, the Kennedys have endured great loss, and the great-grandchildren of Rose and Joe are no exception. Saoirse Kennedy Hill, the daughter of Courtney Kennedy Hill and granddaughter of Ethel and Bobby, died of an accidental overdose in 2019. She was only twenty-two years old. Less than a year later, another of Bobby's granddaughters, Maeve Kennedy Townsend McKean, and her eight-year-old son, Gideon, drowned in Chesapeake Bay after a canoeing accident. In both instances, the family was required to grieve in public, releasing statements as numerous outlets breathlessly covered every update.

Tatiana Schlossberg opted to take control of the narrative surrounding her terminal cancer diagnosis, writing a beautiful, devastating essay sharing her experience with acute myeloid leukemia with the world. She published her writing on the anniversary of her grandfather's death, using his legacy and the attention that day brings to pen a love letter to her family while also speaking out against her cousin Robert F. Kennedy Jr. and his policy decisions. After she died, the Kennedys gathered once again at the Church of St. Ignatius of Loyola on the Upper East Side, where Jackie's funeral had been held, to say goodbye. Photos of Tatiana's relatives arriving at the service ran in *People* magazine.

The youngest members of the Kennedy family live with the knowledge that their darkest moments could be splashed across front pages and the internet. That is a price that comes with the privilege of the Kennedy family name. But while being a member of America's most-recognized political dynasty undoubtedly grants them access and connections, it doesn't necessarily still come with a bank account that can support a life of leisure.

Certainly Joe Sr. was forward-thinking in setting up trusts that ensured his children and grandchildren would be comfortable, allowing them to pursue public service as opposed to working for financial gain alone. But because the modern family tree has many branches—and given that those coffers continue to be divided among the descendants—most fourth-generation Kennedys are pursuing careers of their own. As Maeve succinctly told *Glamour* in 2008, "By the time you get to the fourth generation, the money's run out," revealing that she took out student loans for law school and worked at Dunkin' Donuts while in college.

Some, of course, have entered the family business of politics.

Joe Kennedy III is the most prominent political name in this generation. He served as the US representative for Massachusetts's fourth congressional district from 2013 to 2021, championing health care and giving the Democratic response to President Donald Trump's state of the union speech in 2018.

But in 2020, Joe's ambitions for the Senate were crushed when he lost in the primary to incumbent Ed Markey, even after his grandmother Ethel appeared in an ad directly tying him to his family's legacy. "I hope with all my heart you vote for Joe," she said. "He reminds me of Bobby and Jack and Teddy." It wasn't enough to secure the votes. With the loss, *Politico* declared, "The Kennedy dynasty is dead."

And in a way, it was. It marked the first time a Kennedy had ever lost an election in Massachusetts, and it led to a rare moment with no Kennedy in Congress. (Kennedys held elected office in Washington for sixty-three consecutive years, a run that was first broken when Patrick Kennedy of Rhode Island vacated his House seat in 2011.) But Joe III wasn't finished with his pursuit of public service; under the Biden administration, he served as special envoy to Northern Ireland. Back in the States during the second Trump administration, he spent the summer of 2025 retracing his grandfather Bobby's steps in the Mississippi Delta with his organization, Groundwork Project, which supports pro-democracy and social justice community organizers and activists in the American Deep South, Appalachia, and the Plains. When asked by *The New York Times* if he'd pursue elected office again, he left the question unanswered. "I'm 44," he said. "And at some point down the road, I wouldn't necessarily rule anything out." In a subsequent interview with *New York Magazine*, one of his advisers suggested that Joe thinks he's "the only Kennedy who could run for office and still win, and air-quotations Camelot needs someone to keep that door open."

Notably, that quote was given before Jack Schlossberg launched his congressional campaign. In a natural progression from advocating for politicians and various democratic causes on social media, in

November 2025, he announced his run for office in New York. "This district should have a representative who can harness the creativity, energy, and drive of this district and translate that into political power in Washington. I'm not running because I have all the answers to our problems. I'm running because the people of New York 12 do," he said in his announcement video.

In his early interviews and promotional materials, Jack walks a fine line between leaning on his family legacy and wanting to stand on his own two feet. A vintage "Our Man Jack" poster from JFK's 1960 presidential run features prominently in one campaign image; another of Jack on a bike is a clear reference to his late uncle. However, in an interview with Maureen Dowd for *The New York Times*, he rejected his family's long-standing "American royalty" nickname. "I always shudder when I hear royalty associated with our family," he said. And when asked "if he felt more like a Bouvier or a Kennedy," he said, "I feel like Jack Schlossberg."

He wants the name recognition, and his family's multigenerational association with public service, but he knows a political dynasty won't play well with the kinds of voters he's courting. That said, his thoughts on the Kennedy legacy and his place in it go beyond political strategy.

On one Instagram live stream in summer 2025, Jack's father asked him why he likes surfing. "If you catch a wave, it's not because you're a Kennedy," Jack replied rather poetically. "It's objective feedback, and it's hard to get that from the world."

Public service is a common pursuit among the young Kennedys—and it comes in many forms.

Several members of the Shriver branch of the Kennedy family tree, for example, are still very involved in the Special Olympics, an organization Eunice Kennedy Shriver started, inspired by her sister Rosemary. Notably, her grandson Teddy Shriver, who works as a firefighter, is on the founder's council of the nonprofit, alongside many of the younger members of the Shriver family.

Matthew Maxwell Taylor Kennedy Jr., the son of Bobby and Ethel's son Max, is perhaps best known as a whistleblower. He filed an anonymous complaint about Jared Kushner's COVID-19 task force, detailing the dysfunction and revealing that the Trump administration's response to the pandemic "was like a family office meets organized crime, melded with *Lord of the Flies*."

In October 2022, the aforementioned Conor Kennedy shared on Instagram that he had traveled to Ukraine to enlist in their fight against Russia. He says his time in the country "wasn't long" but that he "liked being a soldier."

Other great-grandchildren of Rose and Joe are pursuing careers in the private sector. There are entrepreneurs and business owners, a yoga instructor, writers, actors, a dancer, filmmakers, and influencers.

While the Kennedy administration and its tragic end undeniably play a pivotal part in this country's history, there's no guarantee that the Kennedys, particularly this younger generation, will continue to be a part of the American story, especially as the accomplishments of icons like Jack and Jackie and Bobby and Ethel begin to fade from living memory. The family's position is far from codified, so they will continue to have to work to stay part of the conversation, lest they simply become a nice wealthy family, related to a dead president, and a poignant symbol of nostalgia with little power, influence, or relevancy in the modern world.

In contrast, the role of the monarchy is enshrined in British culture, but that doesn't mean the royals don't have to be strategic to ensure that it remains that way. An anonymous source once told biographer Craig Brown that members of the royal family "live in a constant state of fear."

"It's all to do with the precarious nature of the monarchy," Brown said, explaining that the anxiety has deep roots, stemming at least in part from the Russian revolution of 1918, in which the entire imperial family, including children, was executed. In the years that followed, virtually every other monarch in Europe disappeared, or saw their role diminished. "I think they are very, very aware that they have to remain popular, and that their position sort of depends on it." Or, as Prince Harry described in *Spare*, fear dictated so much of royal decision-making. "Fear of the public," he wrote. "Fear of the future. Fear of the day the nation would say: OK, shut it down."

Republicans in the UK vehemently oppose King Charles's role as head of state, and the government's funding of the royal family and its work, and campaign for a democratic alternative. Additionally, for anti-monarchists in the fourteen other Commonwealth realms, those last relics of a British Empire of which Charles remains king and head of state, the Queen's death offered a symbolic break, and an opportunity for governments to sever ties with the British monarchy altogether. Jamaica, for example, is poised to begin the process.

Maintaining public relations was a core concern throughout Queen Elizabeth's reign, and now it's a pressing priority for King Charles. But it's a difficult needle to thread. The royals have to be likable and cost-conscious, providing value for money while at the same time giving the public moments of pomp and circumstance—and glamour. They must be relatable, but not so relatable that they seem ordinary. Is a princess still a princess in Zara jeans? Seeing a banquet with tiara-wearing royals on the front page of newspapers is to some a whimsical escape from the drudgery of a cost-of-living crisis. To others, it's a mockery and in poor taste.

In the weeks following Queen Elizabeth's funeral, the phrase "slimmed-down monarchy" was oft repeated. No longer would all the King's cousins, nieces, and nephews be on the payroll, deployed to open hospitals or unveil plaques on a regular basis; instead, there would be a select few senior working royals, only those most closely related to Charles. Reducing the figures even more, Harry and Meghan had stepped away from their senior royal roles and charted their own path in the US, while Andrew Mountbatten-Windsor was stripped of his titles, removed from his duties following the significant public backlash to his association with convicted sex offender Jeffery Epstein, and effectively hidden away—albeit in a home privately owned by the King.

Some of those who remain, like Princess Anne, are known for their work ethic. The optics are good. There's no longer a bloated crowd on the Buckingham Palace balcony, and it's easier to keep a small, tight-knit group on message. But reducing the number of working royals also has several more complicated consequences. Fewer people (and fewer young people) are left to do the same amount of work, and there hasn't been a reduction in pay from the government— the opposite, in fact; meaning, to a certain extent, the royals are less value for money. And it leaves a great number of relatives without official roles, and therefore without a clear path forward.

To be a real-life princess (or even simply a distant relative of the British monarch) is both a blessing and a curse. No one would deny it's a position that comes with enormous privilege—but a last name like Windsor (or Mountbatten-Windsor, the surname authorized specifically for use by descendants of Queen Elizabeth and Prince Philip, for that matter) also comes with pressure and intense media scrutiny. And if you aren't officially representing the Crown (and effectively on the government payroll), what are you supposed to do exactly? For someone like Princess Beatrice, the granddaughter of a monarch and the niece of the King, succeeding in a regular nine-to-five is harder than it might sound. You're still expected to be an unofficial royal representative and to deal with the press and publicity that has followed you since you were born. That kind of life doesn't always square itself with a typical career. Furthermore, some kinds of employment—of shady business deals with foreign investors courting political access or trading on the family name to hawk Windsor-related products, for example—have historically been considered distasteful and out of the question if one wants to keep in good standing with the Firm. But that said, the royal association can offer a helpful leg up in certain career paths.

Charles's more distant relatives face a similar dilemma. As Princess Margaret is often quoted as having said, "My children are not royal; they just happen to have the Queen for their aunt." But Margaret's grandchildren, and other less prominent royals, are still shackled—with a golden handcuff—to their family association.

Many of them pursue the arts. Flora Ogilvy, the granddaughter of Queen Elizabeth's cousin Princess Alexandra, for example, is an art historian; Princess Margaret's grandson Samuel Chatto is a skilled ceramicist; his cousin Lady Margarita Armstrong-Jones is a jewelry designer. Some have parlayed good looks and a notable last name into modeling careers. Lady Amelia Windsor, the granddaughter of Prince Edward, Duke of Kent, and a second cousin once removed of King Charles III, for example, has worked as a model, boasts one hundred thousand Instagram followers, and was named the "most beautiful member of the royal family" by *Tatler* in 2016. Others still hew more closely to royal tradition and go into the military, like Samuel Chatto's brother, Arthur, who is a member of the Royal Marines, and the aforementioned Alex Ogilvy, who graduated from the Royal Military Academy Sandhurst in 2025.

But like the young Kennedys, they know that their triumphs and their trials will be chronicled in equal measure both in papers and online. When Thomas Kingston, the son-in-law of the Queen's cousin, Prince Michael of Kent, died by suicide in February 2024, for example, his wife faced a barrage of unfounded internet conspiracy theories about his death.

Any misstep by a Windsor could be used to criticize not only them but also the centuries-old institution they're only tangentially a part of. Generally speaking, they are keen to remain in good graces with the family—because they are just that, family. A slimmed-down monarchy is a smaller workforce, but the Windsor family tree has no fewer branches. And while certainly there is money to be made for a royal-adjacent tell-all or by flaunting ties to the King on a reality-TV show, most want to maintain their relationships with their relatives—and for that matter, their invitations to brunch at the palace—so they tread lightly.

Even if lesser-known royals never step out of line, the monarchy must still change to survive. And eschewing official help from those further down the line of succession places the future vitality of the monarchy firmly on the shoulders of Prince William and Kate Middleton, a burden that becomes heavier in a health crisis like the one Kate faced in 2024.

The PR-related unease is not entirely unwarranted. But the Windsors' survival depends on how they adapt; the Kennedys maintain status in the public eye today because Jackie drew on the imagery of the monarchy, shaping a legacy; but now, in order to not fade away, the royals must look to the Kennedys of the 1960s to inject some youth and vitality to a centuries-old aging institution, to modernize and propel into the future.

ACKNOWLEDGMENTS

I signed the contract for this book when I was just a few months pregnant with my first child, a decision that felt ambitious at the time, but in retrospect was bordering on delusional. But you have this book in your hands, and that's thanks to many, many people.

"If you bungle raising your children, I don't think whatever else you do well matters very much," Jackie once said to a reporter. Years later, when she was working as an editor, she told one of her authors, "If you produce one book, you will have done something wonderful in your life." It is such a privilege that I have been able to both write my first book and raise my son at the same time—but I could not do either without villages, both personal and professional.

Thank you to the entire team at Putnam, especially Michelle Howry and Ashley Di Dio for your support and keen editorial judgment in shaping this story. To all the designers, editors, proofreaders, and members of the publicity and marketing teams, including Maija Baldauf, Almudena Rincón, Erin Byrne, Brittany Bergman, Lorie Pagnozzi, Maureen Klier, Vi-An Nguyen, Shina Patel, and Katie Grinch: *The Kennedys and the Windsors* is better because of you all, and I'm so appreciative of your hard work.

This book wouldn't be possible without the enthusiasm and critical eye of my wonderful literary agent, Susan Canavan, who has been with me since day one of this project.

The expertise of archivists at the John F. Kennedy Library and Museum, the Duke Library, the Royal Archives, the Lyndon Baines

Johnson Presidential Library, the National Archives, the Virginia Museum of History & Culture, and the Library of Congress was invaluable to me, as was the assistance of researchers Ryan Donaldson and Sydney Marshall and the librarians and staffers at the Green Hills branch of the Nashville Public Library.

Throughout the writing process, I relied on the reporting of the many, many writers, biographers, and journalists who have chronicled the lives and actions of various members of these two families over the twentieth and twenty-first centuries. In particular, Susan Ronald's *The Ambassador* was valuable in shaping my perspective of Joe Kennedy Sr. and his time working in the UK. And Carl Sferrazza Anthony's interviews with those close to Jackie, as well as his biography *Camera Girl*, revealed rich details about the early career of the future first lady. Craig Brown's biographies of both Princess Margaret and Queen Elizabeth were essential in my understanding of the lives of these two women. Similarly, Sarah Bradford's biography of Jackie, *America's Queen*, served as a key resource, as did Andrew Morton's collaboration with Princess Diana, *Diana: Her True Story*.

Also hugely helpful were the numerous accounts written of John F. Kennedy Jr.'s life, and in particular his time at the helm of *George* magazine, including but not limited to *JFK Jr.: An Intimate Oral Biography* by Liz McNeil and RoseMarie Terenzio; *What Remains* by Carole Radziwill; *JFK Jr., George, & Me: A Memoir* by Matt Berman; and *American Son* by Richard Bradley.

Thank you also to those who were willing to share their time and memories, including Dickie Arbiter, Tony Badger, Harry Benson, Matt Berman, Richard Bradley, Sasha Chermayeff, Alejandra Cicognani, Rachel Clarke, Lady Anne Glenconner, Johnny Grimond, R. Couri Hay, Clint Hill, Patrick Jephson, Platon, Selima Salaun, James Sherwin, and RoseMarie Terenzio, as well as those who have chosen to remain anonymous.

I've had the experience of working with amazing writers and editors over the course of my career, but the team at *Town & Country* is truly the best in the business. Thank you to Elizabeth Angell for taking a chance on me, and for teaching me how to cover this beat responsibly and with a point of view.

To my fantastic colleagues past and present, you know who you are, but a special shout-out to Roxanne, Sophie, Emily, Rachel, Ana, Maggie, Lucia, Chloe, Sam, Lauren, Michael, Adam, Norman, Lindsay, Annie, and everyone who has been a part of this journey in big and small ways. Thank you. If I had to be at Hearst Tower at three in the morning to cover a royal wedding or funeral, I'm glad I was there with you. And of course, thank you to our fearless leader, Stellene Volandes, for her invaluable insight and for championing my work.

I am enormously grateful to Victoria Murphy, my colleague across the pond, for her unparalleled perspective on the royal family, and to journalist Richard Palmer for sharing his thoughts on the modern monarchy. I also very much appreciate Elizabeth Holmes, Diana Pearl, and Christine Ross, and our conversations about fashion and the significance of style.

Adrienne Westenfeld and Carly Ledbetter deserve a special thank-you for serving as much-needed fresh sets of eyes at various times during this writing process, as does Kate Storey, who showed me that writing a book like this was possible, and for being incredibly patient with my questions, whether they be about the Kennedy family or the publishing industry. Thank you also to my fantastic fact-checker, Hilary McClellan, for double-checking my work.

I could not have written this book without the support of my amazing friends. To my Harpeth Hall girls—Cari, Emily, Kaitlin, Mary Lindsay, Reed, Sally Anne, Sarah, and Sophie—what a gift to meet once-in-a-lifetime friends in high school. To Emily, Liz, Madelyn, and Molly, thank you for your text messages, dinner dates, and unyielding enthusiasm about this project. Will Collins, your love of history is always appreciated.

This is a book about many things—legacy, power, fashion, the press—but first it's a story about family. I must thank my brother, Jack; my sister, Lauren; and my parents for always loving and encouraging me. Thank you to the Farnos for cheering me on throughout this process.

And finally, Patrick, thank you for being my partner in every sense of the word, my first editor, and my biggest fan; for taking care of Tommy while I spent days in libraries and archives, and hunkered down in the office, thumbing through books; and for believing in me more than I ever believed in myself.

Tommy, you are my whole world. Mama loves you so very much.

NOTES

Introduction: "Two Households, Both Alike in Dignity"

3 **"probably put Jack":** Rose Fitzgerald Kennedy, *Times to Remember* (Doubleday, 1995), 197.

Chapter 1: The Kennedys at Court

5 **"With the advantages":** Rose Fitzgerald Kennedy, *Times to Remember* (Doubleday, 1995), 45.

6 **colorful "pixielike" man:** Robert Dallek, *John F. Kennedy: An Unfinished Life, 1917–1963* (Penguin, 2004), 9.

6 **"One cannot prove a negative":** Daniel Okrent, *Last Call: The Rise and Fall of Prohibition* (Scribner, 2010), 371.

7 **"from such acorns":** Okrent, *Last Call*, 367–68.

7 **"Father was not going to remove":** James Roosevelt with Bill Libby, *My Parents: A Differing View* (Playboy Press, 1976), 208.

7 **"We've got to do something for old Joe":** Roosevelt, *My Parents*, 208.

7 **"I'd like to be ambassador to England":** Roosevelt, *My Parents*, 208.

7 **"He wanted to build as high a platform":** Kirk LeMoyne "Lem" Billings, recorded interview by Walter D. Sohier, June 24, 1964, transcript, 169, John F. Kennedy Library Oral History Program, https://www .jfklibrary.org/asset-viewer/archives/jfkoh-klb-03.

8 **"laughed so hard he almost toppled":** Roosevelt, *My Parents*, 208–9.

8 **"appealed to Roosevelt's mischievous sense of humor":** Susan Ronald, *The Ambassador: Joseph P. Kennedy at the Court of St. James's, 1938–1940* (St. Martin's Press, 2021), 49.

9 **"full fledged" ambassador:** Joseph P. Kennedy, diary, March 8, 1938, quoted in Amanda Smith, ed., *Hostage to Fortune: The Letters of Joseph P. Kennedy* (Viking, 2001), 239.

9 **"The coaches, with their scarlet-coated drivers"**: Joseph P. Kennedy, diary, March 8, 1938, quoted in Smith, *Hostage to Fortune*, 239.

9 **"Nothing like the Kennedy family"**: Deborah Devonshire, *Wait for Me! Memoirs of the Youngest Mitford Sister* (Farrar, Straus and Giroux, 2010), 85.

9 **"eleven Ambassadors for the price of one"**: "The Nine Kennedy Kids Delight Great Britain," *Life*, April 11, 1938, 17.

9 **"passed around (before"**: C. L. Sulzberger, *The Last of the Giants* (Macmillan, 1970), 629.

10 **"Those first months passed in a whirl"**: Rose Fitzgerald Kennedy, *Times to Remember*, 203.

10 **"at ease" with the royal**: Rose Fitzgerald Kennedy, *Times to Remember*, 204.

10 **"It was a period during which I would guess"**: Billings, interview.

11 **"Rose, this is a helluva long way"**: Rose Fitzgerald Kennedy, *Times to Remember*, 204.

11 **"She impressed me"**: Joseph P. Kennedy, diary, April 9, 1938, quoted in Smith, *Hostage to Fortune*, 251.

11 **"She has a very pleasing voice"**: Rose Fitzgerald Kennedy, *Times to Remember*, 206.

11 **"I must be dreaming"**: Rose Fitzgerald Kennedy, *Times to Remember*, 206.

12 **"I insisted they would help"**: Joseph P. Kennedy, diary, April 9, 1938, quoted in Smith, *Hostage to Fortune*, 251.

12 **"I suppose this was a pattern"**: Rose Fitzgerald Kennedy, *Times to Remember*, 207.

12 **"the best thing that ever"**: Kathleen Kennedy to Nancy Astor, April 19, 1938, University of Reading Special Collections, quoted in Barbara Leaming, *Kick Kennedy: The Charmed Life and Tragic Death of the Favorite Kennedy Daughter* (Thomas Dunne Books, 2016), 14.

12 **"one of the most utterly simple"**: Rose Fitzgerald Kennedy, *Times to Remember*, 208.

13 **"Mr. Kennedy, who had planned"**: Robert P. Post, "Queen Curbs 'Social Racket,'" *New York Times*, April 17, 1938, https://www.nytimes.com/1938/04/17/archives/queen-curbs-social-racket-kennedys-ban-on-court-presentations-is-a.html.

13 **"The girls and I had decided"**: Rose Fitzgerald Kennedy, *Times to Remember*, 210.

13 **"a little like Cinderella"**: Rose Fitzgerald Kennedy, *Times to Remember*, 211.

13   **"Debutante of 1938":** "Kathleen 'Kick' Kennedy, Lady Hartington (née Kennedy, 1920–1948)," Chatsworth, accessed September 19, 2025, https://www.chatsworth.org/visit-chatsworth/chatsworth-estate /history-of-chatsworth/meet-the-devonshire-family/extended-family /kathleen-kick-kennedy.

13   **"Walked by very quickly":** Kathleen Kennedy, diary, May 11, 1938, 1938–1939, Rose Fitzgerald Kennedy Personal Papers, John F. Kennedy Presidential Library and Museum, Boston, https://www.jfklibrary .org/asset-viewer/archives/rofkpp-128-015.

14   **"While all the pomp and circumstance":** Rose Fitzgerald Kennedy, *Times to Remember*, 212.

14   **"Vital, intelligent and outgoing":** Devonshire, *Wait for Me!*, 85.

14   **"Well, if that's not just like Hollywood!":** Rose Fitzgerald Kennedy, *Times to Remember*, 214.

14   **"very hot and very dull procedure":** Kathleen Kennedy, diary, July 18, 1938, 1938–1939, Rose Fitzgerald Kennedy Personal Papers.

15   **"Queen came without King":** Rose Fitzgerald Kennedy, *Times to Remember*, 220.

15   **"In the end it was":** Rose Fitzgerald Kennedy, *Times to Remember*, 221.

15   **"having a great time":** John F. Kennedy to Kirk LeMoyne "Lem" Billings, March 1939, Nigel Hamilton Papers at the Massachusetts Historical Society, as quoted in Robert Dallek, *John F. Kennedy: An Unfinished Life, 1917–1963* (Penguin, 2004), 56.

15   **"It takes place in the morning":** Kennedy to Billings, Nigel Hamilton Papers.

16   **"It was quite sad":** Rose Fitzgerald Kennedy, *Times to Remember*, 230.

16   **"As I entered the Palace":** Eunice Kennedy, "My Court Presentation," n.d., in John F. Kennedy Personal Papers, John F. Kennedy Presidential Library and Museum, https://www.jfklibrary.org/asset-viewer /archives/jfkpp-004-023#?image_identifier=JFKPP-004-023-p0006.

17   **"This country is at war":** Neville Chamberlain, "Address by Neville Chamberlain," London, September 3, 1939, transcript, Avalon Project, Yale Law School, https://avalon.law.yale.edu/wwii/gb2.asp.

17   **"What an ironic way":** Rose Fitzgerald Kennedy, *Times to Remember*, 233.

17   **"He looked at the War very much":** George VI, diary, September 9, 1939, quoted in Ronald, *The Ambassador*, 184.

18   **"On thinking over what you said":** George VI to Joseph P. Kennedy, September 11, 1939, quoted in Ronald, *The Ambassador*, 184.

18   **"The King's words":** Ronald, *The Ambassador*, 184.

18 **"Democracy is finished in England":** Louis M. Lyons, "Kennedy Says Democracy All Done," *Boston Sunday Globe*, November 10, 1940, quoted in "The Kennedys: Is Democracy Finished?," *American Experience*, PBS, accessed September 6, 2025, https://www.pbs.org/wgbh/americanexperience/features/kennedys-democracy-finished.

19 **"Only Rose Kennedy came into the room":** Brian Mulroney, *Memoirs* (McClelland & Stewart, 2008), 326.

19 **"So deeply shocked":** Elizabeth, the Queen Mother, telegram to Rose Kennedy, June 6, 1938, quoted in *Counting One's Blessings: The Selected Letters of Queen Elizabeth the Queen Mother*, ed. William Shawcross (Farrar, Straus and Giroux, 2012), 538.

19 **"I could not believe":** William Cavendish, Marquess of Hartington, to Rose Fitzgerald Kennedy, April 30, 1944, quoted in Smith, *Hostage to Fortune*, 584.

20 **"I am very glad that you":** George VI to Edward Cavendish, 10th Duke of Devonshire, May 5, 1944, Devonshire Collection Archives (Chatsworth, UK), quoted in Paula Byrne, *Kick: The True Story of JFK's Sister and the Heir to Chatsworth* (Harper, 2016), 223.

20 **"There were very great difficulties":** Rose Fitzgerald Kennedy, *Times to Remember*, 268.

20 **"were very fond of Billy":** Rose Fitzgerald Kennedy, *Times to Remember*, 273.

21 **"her father received condolences":** "Rich Peer Victim of French Crash," *New York Times*, May 15, 1948, https://timesmachine.nytimes.com/timesmachine/1948/05/15/88119994.pdf.

Chapter 2: Two Unlikely Leaders

23 **"This child is the future president":** J. Randy Taraborrelli, *JFK: Public, Private, Secret* (St. Martin's, 2025), 54.

23 **about the "excellent impression":** Rose Fitzgerald Kennedy, *Times to Remember* (Doubleday, 1995), 246.

23 **"With your stand on the war":** Arthur M. Schlesinger Jr., *Robert Kennedy and His Times* (Ballantine Books, 1979), 43.

24 **"In their long brotherly, friendly rivalry":** Rose Fitzgerald Kennedy, *Times to Remember*, 262–63.

24 **"It may be felt":** "Joseph P. Kennedy Jr.," John F. Kennedy Presidential Library and Museum, Boston, accessed September 11, 2025, https://www.jfklibrary.org/learn/about-jfk/the-kennedy-family/joseph-p-kennedy-jr.

24 **"to stay with it until"**: "Joseph P. Kennedy Jr.," John F. Kennedy Presidential Library and Museum.

25 **"I am going to do something different"**: Doris Kearns Goodwin, "Joe Jr.'s Deadly Last Mission May Have Been Cry of a Rebel," *The Tennessean*, April 9, 1987.

25 **"One of the greatest evils of war"**: As quoted in Michael E. Ruane, "Joseph P. Kennedy Jr. Was a Family Star Until Tragedy Struck in 1944," *Washington Post*, August 10, 2024, https://www.washingtonpost.com/history/2024/08/10/kennedy-bomber-explosion-joseph-john-world-war-ii.

25 **"Now the burden falls to me"**: Cari Beauchamp, "Two Sons, One Destiny," *Vanity Fair*, December 2004.

25 **"Just as I went into politics because Joe died"**: "Death of Brother in War Thrust Kennedy into Career of Politics," *New York Times*, November 23, 1963.

25 **"I got Jack into politics"**: "Death of Brother in War," *New York Times*.

26 **"We all liked politics"**: "Death of Brother in War," *New York Times*.

26 **"I have found it impossible"**: Edward VIII, "Edward VIII Abdication speech," radio address, London, December 11, 1936, BBC, https://www.bbc.com/historyofthebbc/anniversaries/december/edward-viii-abdication-speech.

27 **"My whole life whether it be long or short"**: Princess Elizabeth, "A Speech by the Queen on Her 21st Birthday, 1947," radio address, Cape Town, April 21, 1947, Royal Household, https://www.royal.uk/21st-birthday-speech-21-april-1947.

Chapter 3: A Royal Debut

29 **"rain never falls"**: Nancy Davis and Barbara Donahue, *Miss Porter's School: A History* (Northeast Graphics, 1992), 55.

29 **"It happened gradually"**: Jacqueline Bouvier Kennedy Onassis Personal Papers, John F. Kennedy Presidential Library and Museum, Boston, accessed December 1, 2025, https://www.jfklibrary.org/asset-viewer/archives/jbkopp-sf042-004#?image_identifier=JBKOPP-SF042-004-p0009.

30 **"By nature, she was a loner"**: Nancy Tuckerman, *The Estate of Jacqueline Kennedy Onassis* (Sotheby's, 1996), 18.

31 **"If you were a 'Farmington' girl"**: Carl Sferrazza Anthony, *As We

Remember Her: Jacqueline Kennedy Onassis, in the Words of Her Family and Friends (Perennial, 1997), 32.

32 **"Miss Bouvier's coming out party"**: "Christening at Trinity and Debut at Home Mark Day in Hugh Auchincloss Family," *Newport Mercury and Weekly News*, August 8, 1947.

32 **"No, I cannot explain it"**: Randy J. Taraborrelli, *Jackie: Public, Private, Secret* (St. Martin's Press, 2023), 40.

32 **as simply "nice"**: Mary Van Rensselaer Thayer, *Jacqueline Bouvier Kennedy* (Doubleday, 1961), 70.

32 **"the way all coming-out parties"**: Thayer, *Jacqueline Bouvier Kennedy*, 70.

33 **"a cheap strapless number"**: Diana Dubois, *In Her Sister's Shadow* (St. Martin's Press, 1995), 23.

34 **"Queen Deb of the Year is Jacqueline Bouvier"**: Cholly Knickerbocker, "Cholly Knickerbocker Observes," *Pittsburgh Sun-Telegraph*, January 15, 1948, 12.

34 **"I felt something very special in her"**: Sarah Bradford, *America's Queen* (Penguin, 2000), 39.

34 **"fell irrevocably in love"**: Thayer, *Jacqueline Bouvier Kennedy*, 76.

34 **and their "heavenly"**: Bradford, *America's Queen*, 40.

35 **"THEIR MAJESTIES' AFTERNOON PARTY"**: Royal Archives, Windsor Castle.

35 **"most festive garden party since the war's end"**: "Royal Garden Party Is Attended by 6,000," *New York Times*, July 23, 1948.

35 **"the requisite dressy afternoon gowns"**: Thayer, *Jacqueline Bouvier Kennedy*, 76.

35 **"The afternoon splendid, & not too hot"**: "The Garden Party at Buckingham Palace, 20 June 1887," Royal Collection Trust, https://www.rct.uk/collection/stories/royal-gardens/the-garden-party-at-buckingham-palace-20-june-1887.

35 **"from all walks of life"**: "Garden Parties," Royal Household, accessed September 12, 2025, https://www.royal.uk/garden-parties.

36 **"shared hospitality and sunshine"**: "Royal Garden Party Is Attended by 6,000," *New York Times*.

36 **as a "mob scene"**: Thayer, *Jacqueline Bouvier Kennedy*, 76.

36 **"the most exciting moment of [her] life"**: Carl Sferrazza Anthony, *Camera Girl: The Coming of Age of Jackie Bouvier Kennedy* (Gallery Books, 2023), 4.

36 **"Although not a monarchist"**: Hugh D. Auchincloss III, "Growing

Up with Jackie: My Memories, 1941–1953," 1997, Hugh D. Auchincloss Personal Papers, HDAPP-001-031, John F. Kennedy Presidential Library and Museum.

37 **"They had spotted Winston Churchill"**: Thayer, *Jacqueline Bouvier Kennedy*, 76.

37 **"We could all see that they hadn't built"**: Anthony, *As We Remember Her*, 37.

37 **"I wonder if she ever told the General"**: Hugh D. Auchincloss III, "Growing Up with Jackie: My Memories, 1941–1953," *Groton School Quarterly* 60, no. 2 (May 1998).

Chapter 4: Inquiring Camera Girl

40 **"under his bed throughout the trip"**: *The Queen: Elizabeth II and the Monarchy* (HarperCollins, 2002), 170.

40 **"I want you all to know how deeply"**: George Kennedy, "Press Reception for Princess Is Spectacular Affair," *Evening Star* (Washington, DC), November 1, 1951, A-6.

41 **"I know everyone in town"**: Carl Sferrazza Anthony, *Camera Girl: The Coming of Age of Jackie Bouvier Kennedy* (Gallery Books, 2023), 144.

41 **"She was shocked"**: Anthony, *Camera Girl*, 144.

41 **"Is Princess Elizabeth as pretty as her picture?"**: Jacqueline Bouvier, Inquiring Photographer, *Washington Times-Herald*, November 2, 1951, Library of Congress.

42 **"What would you talk about if you"**: Anthony, *Camera Girl*, 171.

42 **"What's it like observing"**: Jacqueline Bouvier, Inquiring Camera Girl, *Washington Times-Herald*, April 21, 1953, 24, reprinted at https:// blogs.loc.gov/headlinesandheroes/2018/05/jackie-kennedy-inquiring -camera-girl.

42 **"He began taking her out all the time"**: Kirk LeMoyne "Lem" Billings, recorded interview by Walter D. Sohier, July 7, 1964, John F. Kennedy Library Oral History Program, https://www.jfklibrary.org /asset-viewer/archives/jfkoh-klb-05.

43 **"If you're so much in love with Jack Kennedy"**: Janet Lee Bouvier Auchincloss, recorded interview by Joan Braden, September 5, 1964, John F. Kennedy Library Oral History Program, https://static.jfkli brary.org/fpdcu827y1y8lf8w3as35416ho2lswkc.pdf?odc=202311 15182822-0500.

43 **"I should think":** Janet Lee Bouvier Auchincloss, interview.

44 **"saved every receipt":** Anthony, *Camera Girl*, 259.

44 **the "coronation crossing":** Jacqueline Bouvier, "Liner Heading to Coronation a Happy Ship," *Washington Times-Herald*, May 31, 1953.

44 **"tingling excitement" and sartorial choices:** Bouvier, "Liner Heading to Coronation."

44 **"like all great literature":** Bouvier, "Liner Heading to Coronation."

44 **"Passengers stare at the Duke":** Bouvier, "Liner Heading to Coronation."

45 **"If you're a really big stockholder":** Jacqueline Bouvier, "Dog's Life Not So Bad on Ship to Coronation," *Washington Times-Herald*, June 1, 1953.

45 **"It was a very impressive ceremony":** "Windsor Sees Royal Rites on Television," *Washington Times-Herald*, June 3, 1953.

46 **"Wait 'til you see the old place":** Jacqueline Bouvier, "Crowds of Americans Fill 'Bright and Pretty' London," *Washington Times-Herald*, June 2, 1953.

46 **"how the English rent their flats":** Bouvier, "Liner Heading to Coronation."

46 **the traffic was "unbelievably congested":** Bouvier, "Crowds of Americans."

46 **"Are you people in America":** Bouvier, "Crowds of Americans."

47 **"We wear tiaras":** Bouvier, "Crowds of Americans."

47 **"secret" mark on the crown:** Bouvier, "Crowds of Americans."

47 **"pale blue balconets":** Bouvier, "Crowds of Americans."

48 **"That's where all":** Bouvier, "Crowds of Americans."

48 **"like the inside of a jewel box":** Bouvier, "Crowds of Americans."

48 **"Articles excellent—but you are missed":** Carl Sferrazza Anthony, *As We Remember Her: Jacqueline Kennedy Onassis, in the Words of Her Family and Friends* (Perennial, 1997), 76.

48 **"many transatlantic calls":** Billings, interview.

48 **"She had a number of urgent calls":** Anthony, *Camera Girl*, 267.

49 **"never been so cold":** Patricia Kennedy Lawford to Rose Kennedy and Joseph Patrick Kennedy, June 4, 1953, Rose Fitzgerald Kennedy Personal Papers, John F. Kennedy Presidential Library and Museum, Boston.

49 **bumpy coach as "horrible":** "It's Not Meant for Travelling in at All," *The Coronation*, BBC, January 12, 2018, https://www.bbc.co.uk/programmes/p05tk7mj.

49 **"I've noticed how the English":** Jacqueline Bouvier, "Miss Bou-

vier Gets Views of Man-on-Street," *Washington Times-Herald*, June 3, 1953.

50 **"the most lavish party"**: Perle Mesta, with Robert Cahn, *Perle—My Story* (McGraw-Hill, 1960), 186.

50 **"One hears a lot on the promenade deck"**: Bouvier, "Liner Heading to Coronation."

50 **"A striking young girl"**: Perle Mesta, "First Ladies I Have Known," *McCall's*, March 1963, 164–65.

51 **"I'm here on assignment"**: Mesta, "First Ladies I Have Known."

51 **"I did not know, of course"**: Mesta, "First Ladies I Have Known."

51 **townhome "practically bulged"**: Mesta, *Perle*, 186.

51 **"the belle of the ball"**: Jacqueline Bouvier, "Nobility and Film Folk Strut at Perle Mesta's Clambake," *Washington Times-Herald*, June 9, 1953.

51 **"The guests circulated between the huge ballroom"**: Mesta, *Perle*, 187.

52 **"full of everybody"**: Patricia Kennedy Lawford to Rose Kennedy and Joseph Patrick Kennedy, June 4, 1953.

52 **"Young Jacqueline Bouvier"**: Meryl Gordon, *The Woman Who Knew Everyone: The Power of Perle Mesta, Washington's Most Famous Hostess* (Grand Central, 2025), 207.

52 **"While these impromptu performances were going on"**: Mesta, *Perle*, 187.

52 **"We started serving scrambled eggs"**: Mesta, *Perle*, 188.

52 **"the show to see in London last week"**: Gordon, *The Woman Who Knew Everyone*, 207.

53 **"It was the first time"**: Janet Lee Bouvier Auchincloss, interview.

53 **"ready to kill"**: Anthony, *Camera Girl*, 268.

53 **"I just want you to know that I'm engaged"**: Mary Van Rensselaer Thayer, *Jacqueline Bouvier Kennedy* (Doubleday, 1961), 92.

53 **"Jack Kennedy—the Senate's Gay Young Bachelor"**: Paul F. Healy, "The Senate's Gay Young Bachelor," *Saturday Evening Post*, June 13, 1953, reprinted at https://www.saturdayeveningpost.com/reprints/the -senates-gay-young-bachelor.

53 **"What is your candid opinion of marriage?"**: Bouvier, Inquiring Camera Girl, *Washington Times-Herald*, June 4, 1953, 23; reprinted at https://blogs.loc.gov/headlinesandheroes/2018/05/jackie-kennedy -inquiring-camera-girl.

Chapter 5: Royal Weddings

55 **"Senator Kennedy Goes a-Courting":** *Life*, July 20, 1953, https:// books.google.com/books?id=XkIEAAAAMBAJ.

56 **"Now you know how it feels":** "Senator, Fiancee Jackie Enjoying Cape Week-End," *Boston Globe*, June 28, 1953, 17.

56 **"honeymoon pictures of her posed":** "A Portrait of Mrs. Kennedy: Spirited, Shy and Chic," *New York Times*, November 10, 1960, https:// www.nytimes.com/1960/11/10/archives/a-portrait-of-mrs-kennedy-spir ited-shy-and-chic.html.

56 **"Jackie should have been posing for color pictures":** "Senator, Fiancee Jackie Enjoying Cape Week-End."

56 **"planning a small wedding":** Elizabeth Watts, "Senator Kennedy's Fiancee Quits Job to Plan Their Fall Wedding," *Boston Globe*, June 25, 1953.

56 **"Joe Kennedy not only condoned":** Sarah Bradford, *America's Queen* (Penguin, 2001), 65.

57 **"Jackie didn't want to have reporters":** Carl Sferrazza Anthony, *As We Remember Her: Jacqueline Kennedy Onassis in the Words of Her Family and Friends* (Perennial, 1997), 80.

57 **"broke through police lines":** "Notables Attend Senator's Wedding; Senator Kennedy Weds in Newport," *New York Times*, September 13, 1953, https://www.nytimes.com/1953/09/13/archives/notables-attend -senators-wedding-senator-kennedy-weds-in-newport.html.

57 **"The crowds were unbelievable":** Anthony, *As We Remember Her*, 80.

57 **"The wedding will be just awful":** Thurston Clarke, *Ask Not: The Inauguration of John F. Kennedy and the Speech That Changed America* (Henry Holt, 2004), 250.

59 **looked like a "lampshade":** Jennifer Latson, "Jackie Kennedy's Wedding Dress Almost Didn't Make It to the Ceremony," *Time*, September 12, 2014, https://time.com/3274116/jfk-wedding-1953.

59 **"[Jackie] told me that at the beginning":** Bradford, *America's Queen*, 88.

59 **"I never saw my father out of it or drunk":** Bradford, *America's Queen*, 72.

60 **"just like the coronation":** "The Senator Weds," *Life*, September 28, 1953, 45, https://books.google.com/books?id=7UcEAAAAMBAJ& pg=PA45.

60 **"The marriage of Washington's best-looking":** "The Senator Weds," *Life*, 45.

60 **"Notables Attend Senator's Wedding"**: "Notables Attend Senator's Wedding," *New York Times*.

62 **"a flash of colour on the hard road"**: Winston S. Churchill, remarks in UK House of Commons debate, "Marriage of Princess Elizabeth," October 22, 1947, https://hansard.parliament.uk/Commons/1947-10-22/debates/6e27b272-4a1d-486b-b2e8-f3e9409077d2/MarriageOfPrincess Elizabeth.

63 **"Charles said that people could see"**: Andrew Morton. *Diana: Her True Story—in Her Own Words* (Michael O'Mara Books, 1997), 62.

63 married **"tradition and modernity"**: "The Wedding Dress, Brides-maids' Dresses and Pages' Uniforms," Royal Household, April 29, 2011, https://www.royal.uk/wedding-dress-bridesmaids-dresses-and-pages-uniforms.

63 **"This is a first for us"**: Rory Cellan-Jones, "Digital Royal Wedding: Or #rw2011," BBC, April 19, 2011, https://www.bbc.co.uk/blogs/thereporters/rorycellanjones/2011/04/digital_wedding_or_rw2011.html.

64 **"I always say that the high watermark"**: Richard Palmer, interview with author, April 2025.

65 **"the stuff of which fairy tales are made"**: "Text of Archbishop's Wedding Address," UPI, July 29, 1981, https://www.upi.com/Archives/1981/07/29/Text-of-archbishops-wedding-address/4072230254562.

65 **"I knew she was there, of course"**: Morton, *Diana*, 65.

65 **"I refuse to be the only"**: Jack Royston, "Diana: Her True Voice; We Publish the Full Transcript of the Bombshell Diana Tapes as Her Former Private Secretary Backs Channel 4 Documentary," *The Sun*, August 1, 2017, https://www.thesun.co.uk/news/4141886/publish-full-transcript-diana-tapes-channel-4-documentary.

66 had a **"passionate friendship"**: Gordon Rayner and Beth Hale, "Prince Philip's 'Passion' for Duchess," *London Evening Standard*, April 12, 2012, https://www.standard.co.uk/hp/front/prince-philips-passion-for-duchess-6956344.html.

66 **"A lady is not normally expected"**: Michael Thornton, "Prince Philip and the Angry 'Showgirl'," *The Telegraph*, September 24, 2012, https://www.telegraph.co.uk/news/uknews/theroyalfamily/9562833/Prince-Philip-and-the-angry-showgirl.html.

66 **"Have you ever stopped to think"**: Adam Lusher, "Prince Philip: The Royal Who Has Made the Nation Laugh, Though More at Him Than with Him," *The Independent*, May 5, 2017, https://www.independent.co.uk/news/uk/home-news/prince-philip-gaffes-duke-of-edinburgh-retires

-from-public-life-stands-down-no-longer-carrying-out-public-engage
ments-aged-95-affairs-unfaithful-racist-royal-family-queen-husband-re
publican-criticism-arguments-a7718501.html.

66 **"The rumors are completely false":** Maria Noyen, "Rumors Prince William Is Having an Affair with Rose Hanbury Are Flooding Social Media Again After Stephen Colbert Waded into 'Katespiracy,'" *Business Insider*, March 16, 2024, https://www.businessinsider.com/prince -william-rose-hanbury-rumor-kate-middleton-explained-2024-3.

67 **"I made sure to warn them in advance":** Rose Fitzgerald Kennedy, *Times to Remember* (Doubleday, 1995), 41.

67 **"I'd known Jack a long time":** Kirk LeMoyne "Lem" Billings, re-corded interview by Walter D. Sohier, July 7, 1964, John F. Kennedy Library Oral History Program, https://www.jfklibrary.org/asset-viewer /archives/jfkoh-klb-05.

Chapter 6: Dinner at Buckingham Palace

69 **"The fact that Tina had survived":** Lee Radziwill, *Happy Times* (Assouline, 2000), 72–75.

70 **"The very fact that he would like to stay":** Sir Harold Caccia, tele-gram from Washington to the Foreign Office, for Mr. Philip de Zulu-eta, April 15, 1961, UK National Archives, Kew.

70 **"I had no particular reason":** Alistair Horne, *Macmillan 1957–1986*, vol. 2 (Macmillan, 1988), 280.

70 **"Within twenty-four hours":** Christopher Sandford, *Harold and Jack: The Remarkable Friendship of Prime Minister Macmillan and President Kennedy* (Prometheus Books, 2014), 37.

71 **"You have had a long journey":** "Arrival in London," *New York Times*, June 5, 1961, https://www.nytimes.com/1961/06/05/archives/arrival -in-london.html.

71 **"I hope I may say":** John F. Kennedy, "Remarks upon Arrival at the London Airport," June 4, 1961, American Presidency Project, https:// www.presidency.ucsb.edu/documents/remarks-upon-arrival-the-london -airport.

72 **"The Queen would really be very glad":** Philip de Zulueta (Foreign Office) to Washington, telegram, delivered 1:24 p.m., April 24, 1961, UK National Archives, Kew.

72 **"divine house on Buckingham Place":** Nicky Haslam, "The Real Lee Radziwill," *T: The New York Times Style Magazine*, February 7, 2013,

https://archive.nytimes.com/tmagazine.blogs.nytimes.com/2013/02/07/the-real-lee-radziwill.

72 **"had turned the house inside out":** Lee Radziwill, *Happy Times*, 71.

72 **"completely overwhelmed by the ruthlessness":** Harold Macmillan to Queen Elizabeth II, as quoted in Alistair Horne, *Macmillan 1957–1986*, 303–304.

72 **"It was a very sober two days":** "Kennedy's Address to the Nation on His Talks in Europe," *New York Times*, June 7, 1961, https://www.nytimes.com/1961/06/07/archives/kennedys-address-to-the-nation-on-his-talks-in-europe.html.

73 **day was "unbelievable":** Kirk LeMoyne "Lem" Billings, recorded interview by Walter D. Sohier, January 9, 1966, John F. Kennedy Library Oral History Program, https://www.jfklibrary.org/asset-viewer/archives/jfkoh-klb-11.

73 **"I am the man who":** John F. Kennedy, "News Conference 12," Palais Chaillot, Paris, June 2, 1961, 1:15 p.m., John F. Kennedy Presidential Library and Museum, https://www.jfklibrary.org/archives/other-resources/john-f-kennedy-press-conferences/news-conference-12.

73 **"was a lovely woman":** Lee Radziwill, *Lee* (Assouline, 2015), 67.

74 **"It was a most extraordinary scene":** Joseph W. Alsop, recorded interview by Elspeth Rostow, June 18, 1964, John F. Kennedy Library Oral History Program, https://www.jfklibrary.org/asset-viewer/archives/jfkoh-jwa-01.

74 **"I have much pleasure in sending to you":** Queen Elizabeth to John F. Kennedy, message, May 29, 1961, London, 0100, Papers of John F. Kennedy, Presidential Papers, President's Office Files, Countries, United Kingdom: General, 1961: June 1–December 31, John F. Kennedy Presidential Library and Museum, Boston, https://www.jfklibrary.org/asset-viewer/archives/jfkpof-127-006#?image_identifier=JFKPOF-127-006-p0036.

75 **"This caused a little commotion":** Billings, interview.

75 **"not to bother about us":** Gore Vidal, *Palimpsest: A Memoir* (Random House, 1995), 372.

75 **Chez Ninon "freehand interpretation":** "Blue Evening Gown," John F. Kennedy Presidential Library and Museum, accessed September 13, 2025, https://jfk.artifacts.archives.gov/objects/5185/blue-evening-gown.

75 **"The geometric cut":** Oleg Cassini, *A Thousand Days of Magic: Dressing Jacqueline Kennedy for the White House* (Rizzoli, 2015), 76.

76 **"subliminally reinforcing the Kennedy administration's":** Hamish Bowles, *Jacqueline Kennedy: The White House Years; Selections from the*

John F. Kennedy Library and Museum (Bulfinch Press/Little, Brown, 2001), 135.

76 **"The First Lady silently and smilingly"**: Bowles, *Jacqueline Kennedy*, 135.

76 **"London's fashion industry today"**: "First Lady Spurs British Sales Boom," *New York Times*, June 7, 1961, 34, https://timesmachine.nytimes.com/timesmachine/1961/06/07/97240630.html?pageNumber=34.

77 **"No Margaret, no Marina"**: Vidal, *Palimpsest*, 372.

77 **"The Queen very kindly invited"**: Macmillan and Catterall, *The Macmillan Diaries*, 391.

77 **Princess Margaret "nodded thoughtfully"**: Gore Vidal, "Dinner with the Princess," *New Yorker*, June 24, 1996, https://www.newyorker.com/magazine/1996/06/24/dinner-with-the-princess.

78 **"heartiest congratulations" to the princess**: John F. Kennedy and Jacqueline Kennedy to the Right Honourable the Earl of Snowdon and Her Royal Highness the Princess Margaret, message, November 3, 1961, Papers of John F. Kennedy, Presidential Papers, https://www.jfklibrary.org/asset-viewer/archives/jfkpof-127-006#?image_identifier=JFKPOF-127-006-p0050.

78 **"nice but nervous"**: Vidal, *Palimpsest*, 372.

78 **"But that's what she's *there for*"**: Vidal, *Palimpsest*, 372.

78 **"One felt absolutely no relationship"**: Vidal, *Palimpsest*, 372.

78 **"The queen was human only once"**: Vidal, *Palimpsest*, 372.

78 **described as "strangely quaint"**: Lee Radziwill, *Happy Times*, 75.

78 **"depressed about Vienna"**: Henry Ehrlich, "Lord Harlech Talks About the Kennedys," *Look* 32, no. 20 (October 1, 1968): 31.

78 **"the roughest thing in my life"**: Nathan Thrall and Jesse James Wilkins, "Kennedy Talked, Khrushchev Triumphed," *New York Times*, May 22, 2008, https://www.nytimes.com/2008/05/22/opinion/22thrall.html.

79 **"As the meal progressed"**: Ehrlich, "Lord Harlech Talks About the Kennedys," 31.

79 **"He was very concerned about preparing"**: Lord Harlech (William David Ormsby-Gore), recorded interview by Richard E. Neustadt, March 12, 1965, John F. Kennedy Library Oral History Program, https://www.jfklibrary.org/asset-viewer/archives/jfkoh-lwh-01.

79 **"That was almost an amusing experience"**: Angier Biddle Duke, recorded interview by Frank Sieverts, July 10, 1964, John F. Kennedy Library Oral History Program, https://www.jfklibrary.org/asset-viewer/archives/jfkoh-abd-03.

79 **"I was quite impressed":** Lee Radziwill, *Lee*, 67.

79 **"You're just like me":** Lee Radziwill, *Lee*, 67.

80 **"That's a good horse":** Vidal, *Palimpsest*, 372.

80 **"said they were all tremendously kind":** Cecil Beaton, diary, June 11, 1961, in *The Restless Years: Diaries, 1955–63* (Weidenfeld and Nicolson, 1976), 182.

80 **dinner as "very pleasant":** Macmillan and Catterall, *The Macmillan Diaries*, 391.

80 **"It was a delightful evening":** Duke, interview.

80 **"The Queen and the Duke of Edinburgh":** David K. E. Bruce, diary, June 5, 1961, Virginia Museum of History & Culture, Richmond, VA.

80 **"Our day in London, capped by a meeting":** "Kennedy's Address to the Nation on His Talks in Europe," *New York Times*, June 7, 1961.

81 **"May I also at the same time say":** John F. Kennedy to Queen Elizabeth II, letter, June 9, 1961, Papers of John F. Kennedy, Presidential Papers, https://www.jfklibrary.org/asset-viewer/archives/jfkpof-127-006#?image_identifier=JFKPOF-127-006-p0034.

81 **"I have received with":** Queen Elizabeth II to John F. Kennedy, message, June 13, 1961, 11:02 a.m., Papers of John F. Kennedy, Presidential Papers, https://www.jfklibrary.org/asset-viewer/archives/jfkpof-127-0 06#?image_identifier=JFKPOF-127-006-p0038.

Chapter 7: A Pair of Queens

83 **it was later upgraded to a "semi-official" visit:** "Trip to East Upgraded," *New York Times*, January 25, 1962, https://timesmachine.nytimes.com/timesmachine/1962/01/25/89494232.html?pageNumber=3.

83 **"Ken [Galbraith, the US ambassador to India]":** Joan Braden, "An Exclusive Chat with Jackie Kennedy," *Saturday Evening Post*, May 12, 1962, https://www.saturdayeveningpost.com/reprints/an-exclusive-chat-with-jackie-kennedy.

83 **"The sheer number":** Clint Hill and Lisa McCubbin Hill, *My Travels with Mrs. Kennedy* (Gallery Books, 2022), 59.

84 **described the trip as a "benign competition":** "Foreign Relations: Benign Competition," *Time*, March 30, 1962, https://time.com/archive/6830950/foreign-relations-benign-competition.

84 **"trying to outdo the other":** "Foreign Relations," *Time*.

84 **"was not slavishly given over":** "A First-Rate Junket for a First Lady,"

Life, March 23, 1962, https://books.google.com/books?id=SlUEAAAA MBAJ.

84 **"Jackie *ki jai!*" and "Ameriki Rani!":** Anne Chamberlin, "Jackie Leaves Her Mark on India and Vice Versa," *Life*, March 30, 1962, https://books .google.com/books?id=21QEAAAAMBAJ.

84 **"Part of the time she had":** Braden, "An Exclusive Chat with Jackie Kennedy."

85 **"Nothing else happened in India":** Oleg Cassini, *A Thousand Days of Magic: Dressing Jacqueline Kennedy for the White House* (Rizzoli, 2015), 121.

85 **"tremendous" crowds that greeted them:** Lee Radziwill, *Happy Times* (Assouline, 2000), 110.

85 **"The press was nearly out of control":** Lee Radziwill, *Happy Times*, 110.

85 **"It was a fascinating experience":** Peter Hunt, "Diana Taj Mahal Photo Captured Disintegrating Marriage," BBC News, April 16, 2016, https://www.bbc.com/news/uk-36058295.

86 **"All my life I've dreamed of coming":** "Foreign Relations," *Time*.

86 **"never take a trip like this again without Jack":** Braden, "An Exclusive Chat with Jackie Kennedy."

86 **"Jack's always so proud of me":** Braden, "An Exclusive Chat with Jackie Kennedy."

86 **"would not turn into a fashion show":** Chamberlin, "Jackie Leaves Her Mark."

86 **"She has worn only two things a second time":** Chamberlin, "Jackie Leaves Her Mark."

86 **if it was accurate to call her hair a "bouffant":** Braden, "An Exclusive Chat with Jackie Kennedy."

87 **They were "earth-shaking":** Chamberlin, "Jackie Leaves Her Mark."

87 **"the best-dressed woman in the world":** Chamberlin, "Jackie Leaves Her Mark."

87 **"I wanted Jackie to stand out":** Cassini, *A Thousand Days of Magic*, 118.

87 **"These colors would make an impact":** Cassini, *A Thousand Days of Magic*, 118.

87 **"complete state of exhaustion":** Cassini, *A Thousand Days of Magic*, 140.

87 **the trip "a dream":** Chamberlin, "Jackie Leaves Her Mark."

87 **"The President had a large map":** Maud Shaw, recorded interview by Pamela Turnure, April 27, 1965, John F. Kennedy Oral History Collection, https://static.jfklibrary.org/8ha1j22afjb232u6m07hgy158r0j1u 0o.pdf.

88 **"plagued with all sorts of details":** David K. E. Bruce, diary, March 23, 1962, Virginia Museum of History & Culture, Richmond, VA.

88 **"girlish, ice-cream pink suit":** "Jackie Brings Touch of Spring," *Northern Wig*, March 27, 1962, https://www.britishnewspaperarchive.co.uk /viewer/bl/0001542/19620327/015/0001.

89 **wearing a "makeshift turban":** Cassini, *A Thousand Days of Magic*, 144.

89 **"This was the kind of gathering Jackie preferred":** Cassini, *A Thousand Days of Magic*, 142.

89 **"We gather Mrs. Kennedy":** "It's All Quiet for Jackie . . . ," *Daily Mirror*, March 26, 1962, 9, https://www.britishnewspaperarchive.co .uk/viewer/bl/0000560/19620326/086/0009.

90 **"How do you feel about having lunch":** Hill and McCubbin Hill, *My Travels with Mrs. Kennedy*, 115.

90 **"It's a great honor":** "Jackie Lunches with the Queen," *Evening News*, March 28, 1962, https://www.britishnewspaperarchive.co.uk/viewer /bl/0005764/19620328/014/0001.

90 **"I'm feeling full of beans":** Hamish Bowles, *Jacqueline Kennedy: The White House Years* (Metropolitan Museum of Art, 2001), 136.

90 **"Why should I wave?":** Hill and McCubbin Hill, *My Travels with Mrs. Kennedy*, 115.

90 **"She was very agreeable":** Harold Macmillan and Peter Catterall, *The Macmillan Diaries: Prime Minister and After, 1957–1966*, vol. 2 (Macmillan, 2003), 462.

91 **"I think it's the Queen's only private hobby":** "How Peggy the Shetland Pony Sparked the Queen's Passion for Horses," ITV News, September 10, 2022, https://www.itv.com/news/meridian/2022-09-10 /how-peggy-the-shetland-pony-sparked-the-queens-passion-for-horses.

91 **"When the Queen was with horses":** Jenny Gross, "The Cowboy and the Queen," *New York Times*, September 12, 2022, https://www .nytimes.com/2022/09/12/world/europe/monty-roberts-queen.html.

92 **"He liked to see me ride":** Jacqueline Kennedy, *Jacqueline Kennedy: Historic Conversations on Life with John F. Kennedy* (Hyperion, 2011), 185.

92 **"I did not realize it at the time":** John H. Davis, *Jacqueline Bouvier: An Intimate Memoir* (John Wiley and Sons, 2009), 39.

92 **"They had a good relationship":** Clint Hill, interview with author, September 2022.

92 **"It is my hope that every time you ride":** Clint Hill and Lisa McCubbin, *Mrs. Kennedy and Me: An Intimate Memoir* (Gallery Books, 2014), 138.

92 **"He is magnificent":** Hill and McCubbin, *Mrs. Kennedy and Me*, 138.

92 **"How the hell am I going to":** Hill and McCubbin Hill, *My Travels with Mrs. Kennedy*, 93.

92   **"It was a great pleasure to meet Mrs. Kennedy again":** Queen Elizabeth to John F. Kennedy, May 14, 1962, JFKL, https://www.jfklibrary.org/asset-viewer/archives/jfkpof-127-007#?image_identifier=JFKPOF-127-007-p0042.

93   **"we were just two mothers":** Hill and McCubbin Hill, *My Travels with Mrs. Kennedy,* 115.

93   **"Her Majesty was so kind to have me there":** Hill and McCubbin Hill, *My Travels with Mrs. Kennedy,* 116.

93   **"Tell me everything":** Hill and McCubbin Hill, *My Travels with Mrs. Kennedy,* 116.

Chapter 8: Nobody's Kid Sister

95   **"She was marvelous":** Joan Braden, "An Exclusive Chat with Jackie Kennedy," *Saturday Evening Post,* May 2, 1962, https://www.saturdayeveningpost.com/reprints/an-exclusive-chat-with-jackie-kennedy.

96   **less-than-kind publications:** Ewan Fletcher, "Kate's 'Wisteria Sister' Pippa Reaches Top of the Social Tree," *Daily Mail,* November 1, 2008, https://www.dailymail.co.uk/femail/article-1082350/Kates-wisteria-sister-Pippa-reaches-Tatlers-social-tree.html.

96   **Pippa has been described:** Sarah Lyall, "A Star Turn for a Lady-in-Waiting," *New York Times,* May 2011, https://www.nytimes.com/2011/05/08/fashion/08Pippa.html.

96   ***Tatler*'s Little Black Book:** Richard Dennen, "The Little Black Book," *Tatler,* December 2008.

96   **"Catherine's li'l sis":** Dennen, "The Little Black Book."

97   **"Her Royal Hotness":** Catherine Ostler, "Her Royal Hotness: How Kate's Foxy Sister Pippa Stole the Show (Leaving Naughty Uncle Gary to Languish in the Shadows)," *Mail on Sunday,* April 29, 2011, https://www.dailymail.co.uk/femail/article-1381873/Royal-wedding-2011-Kate-Middletons-sister-Pippa-stole-show.html.

97   **"It is a bit startling":** Pippa Middleton, *Celebrate: A Year of Festivities for Families and Friends* (Michael Joseph, 2012), 8.

97   **"No year is complete":** Pippa Middleton, "Pippa Middleton on Wine, Fishing and Kim Kardashian," *The Spectator,* December 13, 2014, https://www.spectator.co.uk/article/pippa-middleton-on-wine-fishing-and-kim-kardashian.

97   **"Pippa's Book a Bum-mer":** Carla Spartos, "Pippa's Book a Bum-

mer," *New York Post*, October 23, 2012, https://nypost.com/2012/10/23 /pippas-book-a-bum-mer.

97 **"Pippa Middleton's Getting":** Victoria Coren, "Pippa Middleton's Getting a Bum Deal Here," *The Guardian*, December 3, 2011, https://www .theguardian.com/commentisfree/2011/dec/04/victoria-coren-pippa-mid dleton-parties.

97 **"I'm Not Saying It's Basic":** Jan Moir, "I'm Not Saying It's Basic, but It's Perfect for Anyone Who Needs a Recipe for Making Ice: Jan Moir Reviews Pippa's New Book," *Daily Mail*, October 21, 2012, https:// www.dailymail.co.uk/debate/article-2221194/Pippa-Middletons-book -reviewed-Jan-Moir-Its-perfect-needs-recipe-making-ice.html.

98 **"Kate married William":** Victoria Murphy, interview with author, April 2025.

98 **"By all accounts":** Victoria Murphy, interview with author, April 2025.

98 **"Does Pippa Dress in the Dark?":** Liz Jones, "Does Pippa Dress in the Dark? A Fabulous Figure, Fashion Freebies Galore, and Endless Parties to Show Off at . . . but Kate's Sister Can Never Get Her Outfit Right," *Daily Mail*, June 28, 2013, https://www.dailymail.co.uk/femail /article-2351312/Pippa-Middleton-Kates-sister-outfit-right.html.

98 **"I have felt publicly bullied":** Eun Kyung Kim, "9 Things We Learned About Pippa Middleton in Her First TV Interview," Today.com, June 30, 2014, https://www.today.com/news/pippa-middleton-speaks-heres -9-things-we-learned-1D79862019.

99 **"Obviously she has pressures":** "Matt Lauer Interviews Pippa Middleton," *Today*, YouTube, July 8, 2014, https://www.youtube.com/watch ?v=Po8lPZorODk.

99 **"You have to think about":** Murphy, interview with author, April 2025.

99 **"My ambition is to":** Mark Peikert, "The Shocking True Story of Lee Radziwill's Doomed Dreams of Movie Stardom," *Town & Country*, January 28, 2022, https://www.townandcountrymag.com/society /money-and-power/a38665742/lee-radziwill-actress-laura-movie-truman -capote.

100 **"A new star is not born":** William Leonard, "A Flawed but Poised Play," *Chicago Tribune*, June 21, 1967, https://chicagotribune.newspapers .com/image/376634213.

100 **"She is just not an actress":** Quoted in Robert D. McFadden, "Lee Radziwill, Ex-Princess and Sister of Jacqueline Kennedy Onassis, Dies at 85," *New York Times*, February 16, 2019, https://www.nytimes.com /2019/02/16/obituaries/lee-radziwill-dead.html.

100 **she filmed sit-downs with her famous friends:** Judy Klemesrud, "For Lee Radziwill, Budding Careers and New Life in New York," *New York Times*, September 1, 1974, https://www.nytimes.com/1974/09/01/ar chives/for-lee-radziwill-budding-careers-and-newlife-in-new-york-6.html.

100 **"would hurt people":** Lee Wohlfert, "The Society Kid Who Was 'Always Moving Furniture' at Home Becomes Lee Radziwill, Decorator," *People*, November 1, 1976.

100 **"It's the subject":** Sam Kashner, "The Complicated Sisterhood of Jackie Kennedy and Lee Radziwill," *Vanity Fair*, May 2016, https://www .vanityfair.com/style/2016/04/jackie-kennedy-lee-radziwill-sisterhood.

100 **"I'm nobody's kid sister":** Wohlfert, "The Society Kid."

101 **"Lee Radziwill, Ex-Princess and Sister":** McFadden, "Lee Radziwill."

101 **"didn't care about the princess thing":** Alejandra Cicognani, interview with author, February 2025.

102 **"Being the younger sister":** Tina Brown, "Tina Brown on the Final Two Episodes of 'The Crown': Love and Duty," *New York Times*, November 23, 2016, https://www.nytimes.com/2016/11/23/arts/television /the-crown-netflix-episodes-9-10-recap.html.

102 **"When my sister and I were growing up":** Andrew Duncan, "'The Press Tried to Say I Was Wicked': Behind the Real Princess Margaret," *Radio Times*, September 11, 2018, https://www.radiotimes.com/tv/doc umentaries/behind-the-real-princess-margaret-press-branded-wicked.

102 **She "always said, 'I was never educated'":** "Princess Margaret's Childhood," *Princess Margaret: The Rebel Royal*, series 1, *"Pleasure v Duty,"* BBC Two, September 11, 2018, https://www.bbc.co.uk/programmes /p06kwz6w.

102 **"'was the first time'":** *Margaret: The Rebel Princess*, PBS, 2018, streaming video, Amazon Prime Video, https://www.amazon.com/Margaret -Rebel-Princess-Season-1/dp/B07N31YXRD.

103 **"I think she was afraid of being belittled":** *Margaret: The Rebel Princess*, PBS.

103 **"I would like it to be known":** Charles Nevin, "Obituary: Princess Margaret," *The Guardian*, February 9, 2002, https://www.theguardian .com/uk/2002/feb/09/monarchy.princessmargaret1.

103 **"strength and stay":** Queen Elizabeth II, "A Speech by the Queen on Her Golden Wedding Anniversary," Royal Household, November 20, 1997, https://www.royal.uk/golden-wedding-speech.

104 **A phone with a direct line:** Reinaldo Herrera, "A Royal Family Friend Recalls the Bond Between Queen Elizabeth and Her Sister,"

Vanity Fair, May 2016, https://www.vanityfair.com/style/2016/04/queen-elizabeth-princess-margaret-sisters-bond.

104 **"subconsciously jealous" of her sister:** Sarah Bradford, "The Woman Who Wasn't Quite Queen," *The Telegraph*, February 10, 2002, https://www.telegraph.co.uk/comment/personal-view/3572852/The-woman-who-wasnt-quite-Queen.html.

104 **"Had lunch one day":** Sarah Bradford, *America's Queen: The Life of Jacqueline Kennedy Onassis* (Viking, 2000), 219.

104 **her father "favored Jackie":** Lee Radziwill, *Happy Times* (Assouline, 2012), 134.

104 **"I am very happy to have been":** "Jackie to Wed on Island in Few Hours," *The Sun-Herald*, October 20, 1968, https://news.google.com/newspapers?nid=1301&dat=19681020&id=UJwpAAAAIBAJ&sjid=0uYDAAAAIBAJ&pg=7052,3812549&hl=en.

104 **"How could she do this to me!":** Diana Dubois, *In Her Sister's Shadow: An Intimate Biography of Lee Radziwill* (St. Martin's Press, 1995), 209.

104 **described as "magnetic":** Lee Radziwill, *Happy Times*, 120.

104 **quipped, "Who didn't?":** Kashner, "The Complicated Sisterhood."

105 **"I have made no provision":** Jacqueline Kennedy Onassis, *The Last Will and Testament of Jacqueline Kennedy Onassis* (Carroll & Graf, 1997), 3.

105 **"I love you so much":** J. Randy Taraborrelli, *Jackie, Janet & Lee: The Secret Lives of Janet Auchincloss and Her Daughters Jacqueline Kennedy Onassis and Lee Radziwill* (St. Martin's Press, 2018), 457.

105 **"Lee Radziwill was always painted":** Lady Anne Glenconner, interview with author, February 2023.

105 **"In my own humble way":** Duncan, "'The Press Tried to Say I Was Wicked.'"

106 **"Oh, it's so much easier":** Sarah Bradford, *Elizabeth: A Biography of Britain's Queen* (Penguin Books, 2002), 101.

106 **"My sister has an aura":** Duncan, "'The Press Tried to Say I Was Wicked.'"

106 **"Pippa has been something":** Sarah Robertson, "Inside Princess Kate's Unbreakable Bond with Her 'Backbone' Sister Pippa Middleton," *Daily Express*, July 18, 2024, https://www.express.co.uk/news/royal/1924774/princess-kate-pippa-middleton-relationship.

106 **"It's just the most ludicrous":** Lee Wohlfert, "The Society Kid Who Was 'Always Moving Furniture' at Home Becomes Lee Radziwill, Decorator," *People*, November 1, 1976.

106 **"My impression of Lee's relationship":** Cicognani, interview with author, February 2025.

107 **"It was in the evening, in London":** Nicky Haslam, "The Real Life Radziwill," *T: The New York Times Style Magazine*, February 7, 2013, https://archive.nytimes.com/tmagazine.blogs.nytimes.com/2013/02/07/the-real-lee-radziwill.

107 **"everything she could to support her sister":** Joelle Goldstein and Liz McNeil, "Jackie O.'s Secret Service Agent Reveals How Sister Lee Radziwill Comforted Her After JFK's Death," *People*, February 18, 2019, https://people.com/politics/lee-radziwill-comforted-sister-jackie-onassis-after-john-f-kennedy-assassination.

107 **"had gone through hell":** Kashner, "The Complicated Sisterhood."

107 **"She came to Washington":** Goldstein and McNeil, "Jackie O.'s Secret Service Agent."

107 **"Good night my darling Jacks":** Kashner, "The Complicated Sisterhood."

Chapter 9: The Death of a President

109 **"I am so deeply distressed":** Queen Elizabeth II to Jacqueline Kennedy, telegram, November 22, 1963, in Jay Mulvaney and Paul De Angelis, eds., *Dear Mrs. Kennedy: The World Shares Its Grief, Letters November 1963* (St. Martin's Press, 2010), 169.

110 **"My deepest sympathy goes out":** Harry S. Truman, "Statement by the President on the Death of King George VI," February 6, 1952, American Presidency Project, ed. Gerhard Peters and John T. Woolley (University of California, Santa Barbara), https://www.presidency.ucsb.edu/documents/statement-the-president-the-death-king-george-vi.

110 **"barely taken charge of the Government":** Alec Douglas-Home, *The Way the Wind Blows: An Autobiography* (Collins, 1976), 197.

110 **"just distraught, openly crying in the streets":** William Manchester, *The Death of a President: November 20–November 25, 1963* (Harper & Row, 1967), 557.

111 **"Things became flat":** Lee Radziwill, *Happy Times* (Assouline, 2000), 7.

111 **"was ready and gay in conversation":** David K. E. Bruce, diary, November 12, 1963, Virginia Museum of History & Culture, Richmond, VA.

111 **"In respect and admiration of a great statesman":** *Condolence Book:*

United Kingdom; American Embassy in London (MS-1964-254), *John F. Kennedy Tributes*, JFKTRIB-040-001 and JFKTRIB-040-002, John F. Kennedy Presidential Library and Museum, Boston.

112   **"it in mind to attend":** Foreign Office to Washington, telegram, November 23, 1963, 12:43 a.m., in Prime Minister's Office: Correspondence and Papers, 1951–1964, UK National Archives, Kew.

112   **"definitely decided to come himself":** Foreign Office to Washington, telegram, November 23, 1963, 1:15 p.m., in Prime Minister's Office: Correspondence and Papers, 1951–1964, UK National Archives, Kew.

112   **"it would take at least two weeks to plan":** Robert Keith Guntler, "Piping at the Funeral of President John F. Kennedy," *Piping Press*, accessed September 13, 2025, https://pipingpress.com/the-last-happy -day-the-great-highland-bagpipe-in-jfks-camelot/piping-at-the-funeral -of-president-john-f-kennedy.

113   **"Salinger, Mr. West, Clifton, Queen":** Manchester, *The Death of a President*, 483.

113   **"hogging space"** in the church: Manchester, *The Death of a President*, 557.

113   **"a staggering blow":** Harold Macmillan and Peter Catterall, *The Macmillan Diaries: Prime Minister and After, 1957–1966*, vol. 2 (Macmillan, 2003), 617.

113   **"one of the strangest dinners of my life":** Deborah Devonshire to Patrick Leigh Fermor, December 6, 1963, in *In Tearing Haste: Letters Between Deborah Devonshire and Patrick Leigh Fermor*, ed. Charlotte Mosley (John Murray, 2008), 98.

114   **"started talking about aeroplanes":** Deborah Devonshire, *Wait for Me! Memoirs of the Youngest Mitford Sister* (Farrar, Straus and Giroux, 2010), 321.

114   **"If it hadn't been for such a sad sad reason":** Devonshire to Fermor, December 6, 1963, *In Tearing Haste*, 98.

114   **"chaotic"** the funeral planning had been: Deborah Devonshire, *Wait for Me!*, 321.

115   **"I'll never forget coming out of the Capitol":** Clint Hill, interview with author, September 2022.

115   **"in a fat black Cadillac":** Manchester, *The Death of a President*, 485.

115   **"walked with a poise and grace":** Manchester, *The Death of a President*, 580.

116   **"given the American people from this day":** Manchester, *The Death of a President*, 580.

116   **"most anxious" for them to be a part:** Sir David Ormsby-Gore, telegram from Washington to the Foreign Office, November 24, 1963, 4:27 p.m., UK National Archives.

116   **"I hope that this is in accordance":** Ormsby-Gore, telegram from Washington to the Foreign Office.

117   **"had their eyes and rifles firmly fixed upwards":** Douglas-Home, *The Way the Wind Blows*, 198.

117   **"I think it's too small":** Manchester, *The Death of a President*, 485.

117   **"Prince Philip, it is true":** Douglas-Home, *The Way the Wind Blows*, 198.

117   **"They were jammed in like sardines":** Manchester, *The Death of a President*, 583.

118   **"Oh it was strange":** Devonshire to Fermor, December 6, 1963, *In Tearing Haste*, 98.

118   **"stern blue look":** Deborah Devonshire, *Wait for Me!*, 324.

119   **"just came into my head":** Manchester, *The Death of a President*, 550.

119   **"They decided on Sunday they wanted":** "Vignette 060—Pres. Kennedy's Eternal Flame at Arlington Cemetery," US Army Corps of Engineers, Historical Vignettes: Parks and Monuments, accessed September 13, 2025, https://www.usace.army.mil/About/History/Historical-Vignettes/Parks-and-Monuments/060-Eternal-Flame.

119   **"Jackie looked tragic, with tears glistening":** Devonshire, *Wait for Me!*, 322.

120   **"There was a great sense of sorry and emptiness":** Devonshire, *Wait for Me!*, 323.

120   **"It would be most ungracious of me":** Dora Jane Hamblin, "Mrs. Kennedy's Decisions Shaped All the Solemn Pageantry," *Life*, December 6, 1963, 49.

120   **"I have to comb my hair for all these dignitaries":** Manchester, *The Death of a President*, 606.

120   **"She'd decided to receive certain heads of state":** "Jackie, Remembered," *Town & Country*, July 1994.

121   **"I've got one like that":** Maud Shaw, *White House Nannie: My Years with Caroline and John Kennedy, Jr.* (New American Library, 1966), 199.

121   **"John, did you make your bow":** Manchester, *The Death of a President*, 609.

122   **"I'm no longer the wife of a chief of state":** Manchester, *The Death of a President*, 611.

122   **"I'd advise you, you know, to have the line":** Manchester, *The Death of a President*, 606.

123 **"I feel sorry for poor Mrs. Roosevelt":** Sarah Bradford, *America's Queen* (Penguin, 2000), 31.

Chapter 10: Runnymede

125 **"It's very important to us":** Lyndon B. Johnson and Jacqueline Kennedy, telephone conversation #7158, sound recording, March 25, 1965, 4:56 p.m., White House Telephone Recordings and Transcripts, Recordings and Transcripts of Telephone Conversations and Meetings, Lyndon B. Johnson Presidential Library, Austin, Texas, accessed September 13, 2025, https://discoverlbj.org/item/tel-07158.

126 **"Please do not let it be Air Force One":** Jacqueline Kennedy, letter to President Lyndon B. Johnson, March 28, 1965, Lyndon B. Johnson Presidential Library.

126 **"The same Air Force sergeant":** Maud Shaw, *White House Nannie: My Years with Caroline and John Kennedy, Jr.* (New American Library, 1966), 195.

126 **"Miss Shaw will know":** Shaw, *White House Nannie*, 194.

127 **"quite entranced" by the cavalrymen:** Shaw, *White House Nannie*, 200.

128 **"The next thing we knew":** Shaw, *White House Nannie*, 201.

128 **"You don't have to put your arm":** Steven M. Gillon, *America's Reluctant Prince* (Dutton, 2020), 80.

128 **"I just thought it was such":** Sarah Bradford, *America's Queen* (Penguin, 2000), 306.

128 **"an appropriate British memorial":** Alec Douglas-Home, "President Kennedy (National Memorial)," House of Commons Debate, December 5, 1963, Hansard, https://hansard.parliament.uk/Commons/1963-12-05/debates/2cc172ba-b7ea-4dd2-aee2-3e15686f2f77/PresidentKennedy(NationalMemorial).

129 **as the most ambitious of all the memorials:** "Kennedy Scholarship Program to Expand," *Harvard University Gazette*, April 13, 2007, https://web.archive.org/web/20070717173530/http://www.news.harvard.edu/gazette/2007/04.19/99-kennedy.html.

129 **"would have valued very, very highly":** "Why Is There a British Memorial to President Kennedy?," Kennedy Memorial Trust, accessed September 21, 2025, https://web.archive.org/web/20240721091131/https://www.kennedytrust.org.uk.

129 **"deeply touched" by the idea:** "Notes of a Meeting: The President

Kennedy Memorial," 10 Downing Street, London, March 4, 1964, 3:30 p.m., UK National Archives, Kew.

129 **"deep and direct interest in the memorial":** "Minutes of a Meeting of the President Kennedy Memorial Committee, Conference Room 'A,' Cabinet Office, Whitehall, 28 February 1964, 2:30 p.m.," UK National Archives.

130 **"Good afternoon, My Majesty":** Shaw, *White House Nannie*, 194.

131 **"The idea that you walked up":** "The Kennedy Memorial at Runnymede," London and South East National Trust, YouTube, January 2, 2024, https://www.youtube.com/watch?v=ySuQ01T5wqA.

132 **"None of us will ever forget":** Lord Harlech (William David Ormsby-Gore), "Introductory Remarks," speech, Inauguration of the John F. Kennedy Memorial, Runnymede, Surrey, UK, May 14, 1965.

132 **"Bonds like these cannot be broken":** Queen Elizabeth II, "Address at the Inauguration of the John F. Kennedy Memorial," speech, Runnymede, Surrey, UK, May 14, 1965.

133 **"I do so with the joy":** Dean Rusk, "Address at the Inauguration of the John F. Kennedy Memorial," speech, Runnymede, Surrey, UK, May 14, 1965.

133 **"No spectacle could have been better":** David K. E. Bruce, diary, May 14, 1965, Virginia Museum of History & Culture, Richmond, VA.

133 **"It was such an emotional and difficult day":** Jacqueline Kennedy, letter to President Lyndon B. Johnson, May 16, 1965, Lyndon B. Johnson Presidential Library.

133 **"My husband loved history":** Anthony Lewis, "British Shrine Honors Kennedy; Kennedy Memorial at Runnymede Dedicated by Queen Elizabeth," *New York Times*, May 15, 1965, https://www.nytimes.com /1965/05/15/archives/british-shrine-honors-kennedy-kennedy-memorial -at-runnymede.html.

134 **"It was good to see them":** Harold Macmillan and Peter Catterall, *The Macmillan Diaries: Prime Minister and After, 1957–1966*, vol. 2 (Macmillan, 2003), 662.

134 **"All that family, and all the confusion":** Jacqueline Kennedy, letter to Harold Macmillan, as quoted in Christopher Sandford, *Union Jack* (ForeEdge, 2017), 254.

134 **"brought new hope and vitality":** Jacqueline Kennedy, letter to Prime Minister Harold Wilson, May 14, 1965, UK National Archives.

134 **"The sense of loss in this country":** Prime Minister Harold Wilson, letter to Jackie Kennedy, May 19, 1965, UK National Archives.

135 **"For everyone else Jack has receded":** Jacqueline Kennedy, letter to Harold Macmillan, as quoted in Bradford, *America's Queen*, 307.

136 **Carolyn called to ask:** Carole Radziwill, *What Remains: A Memoir of Fate, Friendship, and Love* (Scribner, 2005), 218.

136 **"was more excited about a private tour":** Elizabeth Beller, *Once upon a Time: The Captivating Life of Carolyn Bessette-Kennedy* (Gallery Books, 2024), 277.

136 **"lightly managed by the National Trust":** "The Kennedy Memorial at Runnymede," Kennedy Memorial Trust, accessed September 21, 2025, https://apply.kennedytrust.org.uk/display.aspx?id=1871&pid=0&tabId=230.

137 **"We have come here today to honor his memory":** "John F Kennedy Remembered at Runnymede Memorial," BBC News, November 22, 2013, https://www.bbc.com/news/uk-england-surrey-25049235.

137 **"I'm just deeply moved by the fact":** "John F Kennedy Remembered at Runnymede Memorial," BBC News.

138 **"In the end she didn't come":** Johnny Grimond, interview with author, July 2024.

138 **"true whirlwind" of a tour:** Prince Harry, *Spare* (Random House, 2023), 281.

138 **"I'd laid dozens of wreaths before":** Prince Harry, *Spare*, 87.

138 **"My grandmother would very much":** Erin Hill, "Prince William Honors JFK, 'a Man Whom My Family Continues to Hold in the Highest Esteem,'" *People*, October 13, 2016, https://people.com/royals/prince-william-honors-jfk-a-man-whom-my-family-continues-to-hold-in-the-highest-esteem.

Chapter 11: Eligible Royalty

141 **"to the long-range interests":** John F. Kennedy, "Acceptance Speech," Hyannis Armory, Hyannis, Massachusetts, November 9, 1960, John F. Kennedy Presidential Library and Museum, Boston, accessed September 21, 2025, https://www.jfklibrary.org/archives/other-resources/john-f-kennedy-speeches/hyannis-ma-acceptance-speech-19601109.

142 **she requested a ban on outlets:** "Virtual Tour—First Children: Caroline and John Jr. in the Kennedy White House," John F. Kennedy Library Foundation, YouTube, March 23, 2022, https://www.youtube.com/watch?v=_ohUjrZiY6k.

142 **"major effort to be made"**: "Virtual Tour," John F. Kennedy Library Foundation, 5:35.

142 **"If press has questions about children"**: "Virtual Tour," John F. Kennedy Library Foundation, 5:16.

142 **"waged a three-year war"**: Helen Thomas, *Front Row at the White House: My Life and Times* (Scribner, 2014), 244.

142 **had been named *People*'s Sexiest Man Alive**: Joyce Wadler, "John F. Kennedy Jr. the Sexiest Man Alive," *People*, September 12, 1988, https://people.com/archive/cover-story-the-sexiest-kennedy-vol-30-no-11.

143 **"I'm clearly not a major legal genius"**: Emily Mitchell, "Pass-Fail," *Time*, May 14, 1990, https://content.time.com/time/subscriber/article/0,33009,970101,00.html.

143 **"change the definition of a political magazine"**: John F. Kennedy Jr., interview with Larry King, *Larry King Live*, September 1995, https://archive.org/details/john-f.-kennedy-jr-larry-king-interview-september-1995.

143 **"The way Americans were accessing information"**: John F. Kennedy Jr., interview with Larry King.

144 **"Not just politics as usual"**: *George*, October/November 1995.

144 **"what *Rolling Stone* was to music"**: Lisa DePaulo, "John F. Kennedy Jr. and *George* Magazine: A Story of Politics, Love and Loss, 20 Years Later," *Hollywood Reporter*, April 9, 2019, https://www.hollywoodreporter.com/movies/movie-features/john-f-kennedy-jr-george-magazine-stars-share-stories-project-1200375.

144 **"psychobiography in semimonthly installments"**: Richard Bradley, *American Son: A Portrait of John F. Kennedy, Jr.* (Henry Holt, 2002), 91.

144 **"I think that my mother would be"**: "John F. Kennedy Jr. Unveils *George* Magazine at 1995 News Conference," Eyewitness News, ABC 7 NY, YouTube, September 27, 2019, https://www.youtube.com/watch?v=6LPv3j786sE.

144 **"John's interviews were really his own research"**: Richard Bradley, interview with author, December 2023.

145 **"Not if it was in the bedroom"**: John F. Kennedy, "SHOWDOWN: Shocking Truth Behind Jkf Jr's Secret Summit with Tabloid Honcho Iain Calder!," *George*, August 1996.

146 **"It seems obvious why"**: Sasha Chermayeff, interview with author, September 2022.

146 **"He was America's equivalent of Diana"**: Platon, interview with author, September 2022.

146 **"keen on the idea"**: RoseMarie Terenzio and Liz McNeil, *JFK Jr.: An Intimate Biography* (Simon & Schuster, 2024), 249.

147 **"We agreed that she would find time"**: Terenzio and McNeil, *JFK Jr.*, 249.

147 **"I always think that people imagine"**: Steven M. Gillon, *America's Reluctant Prince* (Dutton, 2020), 326.

147 **"She has the most unusual upwards glance"**: William Sylvester Noonan, *Forever Young: My Friendship with John F. Kennedy, Jr.* (Viking, 2006), 97.

147 **"annoyed about everybody hinting"**: Chermayeff, interview with author, September 2022.

147 **"When you're talking about people"**: Richard Johnson, interview with author, December 2023.

148 **"We were laughing and carrying on"**: DePaulo, "John F. Kennedy Jr. and *George* Magazine."

148 **"Nothing extravagant, not full-tilt-boogie"**: Terenzio and McNeil, *JFK Jr.*, 248.

148 **"Rosie, come with me"**: Terenzio and McNeil, *JFK Jr.*, 248.

148 **hotel's discretion as "extraordinary"**: James Sherwin, interview with author, September 2023.

149 **"I had remembered"**: Liz McNeil, "What Really Happened the Day JFK Jr. Met Princess Diana—and What He Said About Her After," *People*, June 29, 2017, https://people.com/royals/what-really-happened-the-day-jfk-jr-met-princess-diana-and-what-he-said-about-her-after.

149 **"He was very, very polite"**: Patrick D. Jephson, interview with author, October 2022.

149 **"It was a working meeting"**: Terenzio and McNeil, *JFK Jr.*, 249.

149 **"He was quite in awe of her"**: Terenzio and McNeil, *JFK Jr.*, 249.

150 **"I suspect that invitation"**: Bradley, interview with author, December 2023.

150 **"I remember sending him over"**: Matt Berman, interview with author, October 2024.

150 **"Why is it OK for everyone else"**: DePaulo, "John F. Kennedy Jr. and *George* Magazine."

150 **"And on our cover, Drew Barrymore reprises"**: John F. Kennedy Jr., editor's letter, *George*, September 1996, 14.

151 **"Well, you know, this is all very nice"**: Terenzio and McNeil, *JFK Jr.*, 250.

151 **"I'm hoping he'll grow up to be"**: Tina Brown, "A Woman in Earnest," *New Yorker*, September 15, 1997, https://www.newyorker.com/magazine/1997/09/15/princess-diana-tina-brown-a-woman-in-earnest.

152 **"very intrigued"**: Nicki Gostin, "Ex-Vanity Fair Editor Graydon Carter Disses Oscars and Dishes on Tom Cruise, Princess Diana and Meghan Markle: 'Adrift on Reality,'" Page Six, *New York Post*, March 23, 2025, https://pagesix.com/2025/03/23/celebrity-news/graydon-carter-disses-oscars-says-meghan-markle-adrift-on-reality.

152 **"The Princess's wish to meet"**: Patrick D. Jephson, *Shadows of a Princess* (HarperCollins, 2000), 137.

152 **"It was brief"**: RoseMarie Terenzio, interview with author, October 2024.

152 **"facility for drug-addled"**: "We the People," *George*, September 1996, 48.

152 **"a pleasant enough"**: Jephson, *Shadows of a Princess*, 137.

152 **"I remember he felt like"**: Chermayeff, interview with author, September 2022.

152 **"moment of pure lust"**: Simone Simmons and Ingrid Seward, *Diana: The Last Word* (Orion Books, 2005), 3.

152 **"I stayed in the room throughout"**: Jephson, interview with author, October 2022.

153 **"We've got to get ready for the next thing"**: Terenzio and McNeil, *JFK Jr.*, 250.

153 **"words to the effect of"**: Terenzio and McNeil, *JFK Jr.*, 250.

153 **"I can't remember the words"**: Terenzio and McNeil, *JFK Jr.*, 250.

153 **Diana wrote him a note:** McNeil, "What Really Happened."

153 **"She's tall, taller than I thought"**: DePaulo, "John F. Kennedy Jr. and *George* Magazine."

153 **"I could tell he was disappointed"**: Terenzio, interview with author, October 2024.

154 **"Well, she said no, but she had a great pair"**: Matt Berman, *JFK Jr., George, & Me: A Memoir* (Gallery Books, 2014), 186.

154 **"At the end of the day"**: DePaulo, "John F. Kennedy Jr. and *George* Magazine."

154 **"She's all-American, a self-made woman"**: Berman, *JFK Jr., George, & Me*, 72.

154 **"Princess Di's peace of mind"**: Marla Maples, "If I Were President," *George*, August 1997.

155 **"regrettably" turn down:** Terenzio and McNeil, *JFK Jr.*, 252.

155 **writing "I hope"—with "hope" underlined:** Terenzio and McNeil, *JFK Jr.*, 252.

155 **"I think she saw in him a fellow victim":** Terenzio and McNeil, *JFK Jr.*, 251.

155 **"graciously met by something that sounded like":** Aileen Mehle, "Suzy," *WWD*, July 8, 1998, https://wwd.com/fashion-news/fashion -features/article-1099591.

Chapter 12: The Vanishing Lady

157 **The French interior minister announced:** "Diana, Princess of Wales, Killed in Car Crash," BBC News, 1997, https://www.bbc.co.uk/news /special/politics97/diana/accident.html.

157 **"We'll talk about it":** Lisa DePaulo, "John F. Kennedy Jr. and *George* Magazine," *Hollywood Reporter*, April 9, 2019, https://www.hollywood reporter.com/movies/movie-features/john-f-kennedy-jr-george-mag azine-stars-share-stories-project-1200375.

158 **"Instead of talking about Diana":** RoseMarie Terenzio and Liz McNeil, *JFK Jr.: An Intimate Biography* (Simon & Schuster, 2024), 249.

158 **"My reaction was, 'Oh my gosh'":** Richard Bradley, interview with author, December 2023.

158 **"hesitated" in planning:** Terenzio and McNeil, *JFK Jr.*, 286.

158 **"I told him you can't":** Terenzio and McNeil, *JFK Jr.*, 286.

158 **was "too central":** Richard Bradley, *American Son: A Portrait of John F. Kennedy, Jr.* (Henry Holt, 2002), 187.

159 **"It was entirely Matt Berman's concept":** RoseMarie Terenzio, interview with author, October 2024.

159 **"It was obviously an enormous story":** Matt Berman, interview with author, October 2024.

159 **described as both "mass hysteria":** Jonathan Freedland, "A Moment of Madness?," *The Guardian*, August 12, 2007, https://web.archive.org/web /20170203172846/https://www.theguardian.com/uk/2007/aug/13/brit ishidentity.monarchy.

159 **shared "nervous breakdown":** *"Diana—Seven Days That Shook the World,"* series 1, episode 1, BBC Worldwide America, YouTube, May 30, 2017, https://www.youtube.com/watch?v=YnaT-7bpghk.

159 **"I just feel disbelief":** "Diana's Body Arrives in Britain," CNN, August 31, 1997, https://www.cnn.com/WORLD/9708/31/diana.11a .update.

160   **"It's completely unprecedented"**: "London Begins Cleanup of Floral Tributes to Diana," CNN, September 11, 1997, https://www.cnn.com /WORLD/9709/11/diana.flowers.

160   **"Where Is Our Queen?"**: Gillian Brockell, "The Moment the Queen Gave Princess Diana Her Due 25 Years Ago," September 10, 2022, https://www.washingtonpost.com/history/2022/09/10/queen-elizabeth -princess-diana-funeral.

160   **"Your People Are Suffering, Speak to Us Ma'am"**: Brockell, "The Moment the Queen."

160   **"Show Us You Care"**: Brockell, "The Moment the Queen."

160   **"as your Queen and as a grandmother"**: "Queen Broadcasts Live to Nation," BBC News, 1997, accessed September 14, 2025, https://www .bbc.co.uk/news/special/politics97/diana/queen.html.

160   **"It was indeed dreadfully sad"**: Andrew Pierce, "'We Have All Been Through a Very Bad Experience': Revealed, the Queen's Anguished Letter That Lays Bare Her Pain over Diana," *Daily Mail*, August 11, 2017, https://www.dailymail.co.uk/news/article-4783554/Queen-s -anguished-letter-lays-bare-pain-Diana.html.

161   **"spirit of the nation"**: Platon, interview with author, September 2022.

161   **"You've got to remember"**: Platon, interview with author, September 2022.

161   **"Englishness" to connect**: Platon, interview with author, September 2022.

161   **resulted was a feature titled:** "The Lady Vanishes: The People's Funeral for Diana, Princess of Wales," *George*, November 1997, 136.

161   **"Exclusive: Diana Photos of the Mourning After"**: *George*, November 1997.

161   **"the loss of their improbable heroine"**: "The Lady Vanishes," *George*, 136.

162   **"It was a very moving experience"**: Platon, interview with author, September 2022.

162   **reaction to Diana's death a "worldwide *depression*"**: "The Lady Vanishes," *George*, 137.

162   **"For a few days, everyone was gentle"**: Platon, interview with author, September 2022.

162   **"It was incredibly moving"**: Terenzio, interview with author, October 2024.

162   **was quite "relaxed"**: "The Lady Vanishes," *George*, 140.

163   **she was a "guaranteed seller"**: "The Lady Vanishes," *George*, 140.

163 **"What I saw was that by sheer force of will"**: John F. Kennedy Jr., editor's letter, *George*, November 1997, 23.

163 **"both a remembrance and a prophecy"**: Bradley, *American Son*, 188–89.

164 **"intolerable, almost unlivable"**: Paul Vitello, "Ron Galella, Celebrity-Hounding Photographer, Dies at 91," *New York Times*, May 2, 2022, https://www.nytimes.com/2022/05/02/business/media/ron-galella-dead.html.

164 **"generally accepted notions of privacy"**: Martin London, "There Oughta Be a Law . . . ," *George*, November 1997, 63.

165 **"I think it scared her"**: Terenzio, interview with author, October 2024.

165 **"I'm not sure what I'm going to do"**: William Sylvester Noonan, *Forever Young: My Friendship with John F. Kennedy, Jr.* (Viking, 2006), 224.

165 **"in a world of her own"**: Terenzio and McNeil, *JFK Jr.*, 286.

165 **"When she was up here"**: Kathy McKeon, *Jackie's Girl: My Life with the Kennedy Family* (Gallery Books, 2018), 295.

166 **"John believed once he got married"**: Liz McNeil, "Inside the Final Days of JFK Jr. and Wife Carolyn: They 'Didn't Know What Was Going to Happen in Their Relationship,'" *People*, July 3, 2019, https://people.com/politics/jfk-jr-wife-carolyn-bessette-final-days-before-crash.

166 **"She just didn't want to leave the apartment"**: Sasha Chermayeff, interview with author, September 2022.

167 **"Like Diana's death"**: Chermayeff, interview with author, September 2022.

167 **"I remember saying to him"**: Platon, interview with author, September 2022.

Chapter 13: The Public Funeral

169 **"And then—I just remember"**: RoseMarie Terenzio and Liz McNeil, *JFK Jr.: An Intimate Portrait* (Simon & Schuster, 2024), 354.

170 **"for the safety of the loved ones"**: Marc Fisher and Pamela Ferdinand, "In Hyannis Port, Wedding Day Turns into Day of Sadness," *Washington Post*, July 18, 1999.

170 **"At the end of the service"**: Mike Allen and Carey Goldberg, "Rescue Search in Kennedy Crash Ends; Coast Guard Tells Family There Is Little Hope," *New York Times*, July 19, 1999.

170 **"There are a lot of people":** Fisher and Ferdinand, "Wedding Day Turns into Day of Sadness."

171 **"What if they hadn't held":** "Irish Priest Tells First-Hand Story of Kennedy Grief," *Irish Independent*, July 31, 1999, https://www.inde pendent.ie/irish-news/irish-priest-tells-first-hand-story-of-kennedy-grief /26260370.html.

171 **"For more than 40 years now":** President Clinton, "Statement by the President on John F. Kennedy, Jr., Carolyn Kennedy, and Lauren Bessette," The White House, Office of the Press Secretary, July 18, 1999, https://clintonwhitehouse3.archives.gov/WH/New/html/19990718 .html.

171 **"I have spent some very painful moments":** Allen and Goldberg, "Rescue Search in Kennedy Crash Ends."

172 **"He was a Kennedy, but that was just a name":** Dale Russakoff, "Grieving Public Seeks Ways to Say Goodbye to the JFK They Knew," *Washington Post*, July 22, 1999.

172 **"the pilot's failure to maintain control":** "Almanac: John Kennedy Jr.," CBS News, July 16, 2017, https://www.cbsnews.com/news/almanac -john-kennedy-jr.

172 **"We are filled with unspeakable grief":** "Ted Kennedy Says Family Is 'Filled with Unspeakable Grief,'" CNN, July 19, 1999, https://www .cnn.com/US/9907/19/kennedy.statement.

172 **"Each of these three young people":** "Statement of Grief by Wife's Family," *New York Times*, July 21, 1999.

173 **"I don't want the girls separated":** Terenzio and McNeil, *JFK Jr.*, 375.

174 **"Caroline said I could pick five":** Terenzio and McNeil, *JFK Jr.*, 375.

174 **As Carole Radziwill put it:** Carole Radziwill, *What Remains: A Memoir of Fate, Friendship, and Love* (Scribner, 2007), 20.

174 **"They're voyeurs. They feed like coffin flies":** Carole Radziwill, *What Remains*, 20.

175 **"The fact that the onlookers":** N. R. Kleinfield, "The Kennedy Memorial: The Service; Doors Closed, Kennedys Offer Their Farewells," *New York Times*, July 24, 1999.

175 **"We're not here to gawk":** Richard Pyle, "Another Somber Memorial for Kennedys," *Cape Cod Times*, July 24, 1999, https://www.capecod times.com/story/news/1999/07/24/another-somber-memorial-for-ken nedys/51037197007.

175 **"From the first day of his life":** "Ted Kennedy Pays Tribute to His Nephew," CNN, July 23, 1999, https://www.cnn.com/US/9907/23 /kennedy.eulogy.

175 **"It was so public"**: RoseMarie Terenzio, interview with author, June 2024.

176 **"My mother had just died"**: Angela Levin, "Exclusive: Prince Harry on Chaos After Diana's Death and Why the World Needs 'the Magic' of the Royal Family," *Newsweek*, June 21, 2017, https://www.newsweek .com/2017/06/30/prince-harry-depression-diana-death-why-world-needs -magic-627833.html.

176 **"I seem to remember him saying"**: Cassidy McDonald, "Princess Anne Walks Behind Casket as the Only Woman in Philip's Funeral Procession," CBS News, April 18, 2021, https://www.cbsnews.com /news/prince-philip-funeral-princess-anne-funeral-procession.

177 **"There was that balance between duty and family"**: *Diana—Seven Days That Shook the World*, series 1, episode 1, BBC Worldwide America, YouTube, May 30, 2017, https://www.youtube.com/watch?v=YnaT -7bpghk.

177 **"Come morning, bright and early"**: Prince Harry, *Spare* (Random House, 2023), 24.

177 **"It was very, very strange after her death"**: *Diana, Our Mother: Her Life and Legacy*, HBO, YouTube, July 24, 2017, https://www.youtube .com/watch?v=zlJmX8K0UZo.

178 **"I remember clearly the shock"**: Julia Samuel, "Prince George's Godmother: Diana's Death Taught Me to Grieve," *Time*, January 17, 2018, https://time.com/5104471/princess-diana-friend-julia-samuel-grief -counselor.

178 **"He was really, really, really taken down"**: Sasha Chermayeff, interview with author, September 2022.

Chapter 14: A Signature Style

181 **"I weigh in on all of Rachel's outfit choices"**: Kate Friedman, "Here's an Exclusive Sneak Peek at *Suits* Star Rachel Zane's Wedding Dress," *Glamour*, March 2, 2016, https://www.glamour.com/story/ suits-wedding-dress-rachel-zane.

182 **"I knew at the onset I wanted a bateau neckline"**: Gregory Katz, "Meghan's Wedding Gown Goes on Display at Windsor Castle," AP News, October 26, 2018, https://apnews.com/article/af771ce0ade14b 699c42778f6d5fa476.

182 **"being absolutely perfect for the occasion"**: Omid Scobie, "The Story of Meghan Markle's Wedding Dress," *Harper's Bazaar*, May 22, 2018,

https://www.harpersbazaar.com/celebrity/latest/a20764293/meghan
-markle-wedding-dress-givenchy-clare-waight-keller-design-details.

183 **"It was wonderful to have no press around":** Kevin Sack, "The Island That Kept a Wedding a Secret," *New York Times*, September 26, 1996, https://www.nytimes.com/1996/09/26/us/the-island-that-kept-a-wedding-a-secret.html.

183 **"In the end, this was a wedding":** Caroline Hallemann, "Royal Wedding Guest Janina Gavankar Shares the Story Behind Her Striking Dress, and Details of the Intimate Evening Reception," *Town & Country*, May 24, 2018, https://www.townandcountrymag.com/style/fashion-trends/a20901371/janina-gavankar-royal-wedding-reception-interview.

183 **"The role that she's taken on is very austere":** "Stella McCartney: Meghan Markle's Evening Dress 'Reflected Her Human Side,'" BBC News, June 12, 2018, https://www.bbc.com/news/av/entertainment-arts-44462424.

186 **"Not being able to meet his mom":** "FULL Interview: Prince Harry and Meghan Markle," BBC News, YouTube, November 27, 2017, https://www.youtube.com/watch?v=LQicq60aJaw.

187 **"I have no idea how to go about describing myself":** Jacqueline Bouvier, "Feature—Question 1" (Prix de Paris submission excerpt), *Vogue*, 1951, JBKOPP-SF042-004, Jacqueline Bouvier Kennedy Onassis Personal Papers, Letitia Baldrige Files, John F. Kennedy Presidential Library and Museum, Boston.

188 **"If her husband is elected":** Marylin Bender, "'The Woman Who' . . . Wins High Fashion's Vote Is Jacqueline Kennedy," *New York Times*, July 15, 1960, https://www.nytimes.com/1960/07/15/archives/-the-woman-who-wins-high-fashions-vote-is-jacqueline-kennedy.html.

188 **"I couldn't spend that much":** "WOMEN: Devil-May-Care Chic," *Time*, September 26, 1960.

188 **"All the talk over what I wear":** Jacqueline Kennedy, Campaign Wife, press release, September 16, 1960, Democratic National Committee Records, John F. Kennedy Presidential Library and Museum.

188 **"I refuse to have Jack's administration":** Jacqueline Kennedy to Oleg Cassini, December 13, 1960, in Oleg Cassini, *A Thousand Days of Magic: Dressing Jacqueline Kennedy for the White House* (Rizzoli, 1995), 220.

188 **"resort to muumuus":** "WOMEN: Devil-May-Care Chic," *Time*, September 26, 1960.

188 **"With great foresight":** Cassini, *A Thousand Days of Magic*, 39.

189 **aesthetics became a "political tool":** Margaret Leslie Davis, "The Two First Ladies," *Vanity Fair*, October 6, 2008, https://www.vanityfair.com/news/2008/11/monalisa_excerpt200811.

189 **"helped to break down a certain Puritanism":** Cassini, *A Thousand Days of Magic*, 43.

189 **"We spoke of how fashion is a mirror of history":** Cassini, *A Thousand Days of Magic*, 20.

190 **"When we look back on the relationship":** Elizabeth Holmes, interview with author, August 2025.

191 **"To sum it up":** Kirk LeMoyne "Lem" Billings, recorded interview by Walter D. Sohier, June 24, 1964, John F. Kennedy Library Oral History Program, https://www.jfklibrary.org/asset-viewer/archives/jfkoh-klb-03.

191 **"setting a national pace":** "You Don't Have to Look Hard . . . to See Another Jackie," *Life*, January 20, 1961, 17, https://books.google.com/books?id=U0kEAAAAMBAJ.

192 **"Jackie's slightest fashion whim triggers":** as quoted in Michael Kilian, "Festival Honors Jackie's Style, Role in History," *Chicago Tribune*, June 20, 2002.

192 **"off like zingo":** Lilly Pulitzer, *Essentially Lilly: A Guide to Colorful Entertaining* (HarperResource, 2004).

192 **"That morning I'd gone to yoga as usual":** Katie Nicholl, "Life After the Kate Effect," *You (Mail on Sunday)*, February 22, 2017, https://www.dailymail.co.uk/home/you/article-4228010/Life-Kate-Effect-Issa-Helayel.html.

193 **"If they wear something, people will buy it":** Christine Ross, interview with author, February 2024.

194 **"The Princess of Wales does not want":** Ross, interview with author, February 2024.

195 **"Fashion is something":** Elizabeth Segran, "How Meghan Built Her Pioneering Partnership with Netflix," *Fast Company*, May 27, 2025, https://www.fastcompany.com/91340227/meghan-markle-duchess-of-sussex-confessions-of-a-female-founder-as-ever-netflix.

195 **"ghost influencers," a phrase coined:** Vanessa Friedman, "Carolyn Bessette Kennedy, Ghost Influencer," *New York Times*, October 24, 2023, https://www.nytimes.com/2023/10/24/style/carolyn-bessette-kennedy-fashion-influencer.html.

195 **"We're in this era of Instagram":** Diana Pearl, interview with author, March 2025.

196 **"Khaite, The Row, these brands are totally":** Selima Salaun, interview with author, May 2024.

196 **"If you look at a photograph of Carolyn":** RoseMarie Terenzio, interview with author, June 2024.

196 **"There wasn't social media":** Terenzio, interview with author, June 2024.

197 **"There are very few interviews":** Pearl, interview with author, March 2025.

Chapter 15: The Dark Side of a Fairy Tale

199 **"three of us in this marriage":** *"Panorama* Interview with Princess Diana," BBC News, November 20, 1995, https://www.bbc.com/history ofthebbc/anniversaries/november/diana-interview.

200 **"about how dark [their son Archie's] skin might be":** Meghan, Duchess of Sussex, and Prince Harry, Duke of Sussex, interview by Oprah Winfrey, *Oprah with Meghan and Harry: A CBS Primetime Special,* CBS, March 7, 2021.

200 **"the difference between racism":** "Prince Harry Denies He and Meghan Said the Royal Family Was Racist," ITV News, January 8, 2023, https://www.itv.com/news/2023-01-08/prince-harry-denies-he -and-meghan-said-the-royal-family-was-racist.

201 **"Were you silent or were you silenced?":** Meghan and Prince Harry, *Oprah with Meghan and Harry.*

201 **"She choked out that she didn't want to do this":** Prince Harry, *Spare* (Random House, 2023), 354.

201 **"These are the thoughts that I'm having":** Meghan and Prince Harry, *Oprah with Meghan and Harry.*

202 **"Everybody who gets married":** Meghan and Prince Harry, *Oprah with Meghan and Harry.*

203 **"I just watched the M&H sit down":** Carole Radziwill (@Carole Radziwill), "I just watched the M&H sit down. Wow. I love how people say Meghan knew what she was getting into . . . people said the same thing about Carolyn Bessette when she married into the Kennedy family. You could never know. Meghan said it right the perception is nothing like the reality," X (formerly Twitter), March 8, 2021, https://x.com/CaroleRadziwill/status/1368795560359133187.

204 **"It's not like they gave me a handbook":** Carole Radziwill, *What Remains: A Memoir of Fate, Friendship, and Love* (Scribner, 2007), 172.

204 **"She tried to tuck herself in neatly"**: Carole Radziwill, *What Remains*, 173.

204 **"I tried so hard"**: *Harry & Meghan*, Netflix, December 8, 2022, https://www.netflix.com/title/81439256.

204 **called the comment "disingenuous"**: Kara Swisher, "Tina Brown on Harry and Meghan's 'Scorched Earth' Exit," *Sway* (podcast), Opinion, *New York Times*, April 25, 2022, https://www.nytimes.com/2022/04/25/opinion/sway-kara-swisher-tina-brown.html.

204 **"As humans, we sit there"**: RoseMarie Terenzio, interview with author, June 2024.

205 **"The popular myth paints a homely picture"**: Andrew Morton, *Diana: Her True Story—in Her Own Words* (Michael O'Mara Books, 1997), 169.

205 **"There was no guidance"**: Meghan and Prince Harry, *Oprah with Meghan and Harry*.

206 **"I went into this incredibly naive"**: Ashitha Nagesh, "Prince Harry Says He Was Bigoted Before He Met Meghan," BBC News, January 6, 2023, https://www.bbc.com/news/uk-64189396.

206 **"John felt that"**: Terenzio, interview with author, June 2024.

206 **"The comparison was obvious"**: Sasha Chermayeff, interview with author, September 2022.

207 **"It's true what Meghan Markle told Oprah"**: Maria Shriver (@MariaShriver), "It's true what Meghan Markle told @Oprah, we don't know what goes on in people's lives behind closed doors. That's something we can all remember," X (formerly Twitter), March 7, 2021, https://x.com/mariashriver/status/1368790202903195651.

207 **"caused me anguish"**: *Galella v. Onassis*, 353 F. Supp. 196 (S.D.N.Y. 1972), https://law.justia.com/cases/federal/district-courts/FSupp/353/196/2344771.

207 **"Galella's unrelenting pursuit of his subjects"**: Andrew Goldman, "Barbarian at the Lens: Ron Galella and the Dawn of the Age of Paparazzi," *Town & Country*, May 10, 2020, https://www.townandcountrymag.com/society/money-and-power/a30171412/ron-galella-paparazzi-photographer-jackie-kennedy.

208 **"The Reaction Here Is Anger"**: Judy Klemesrud, "The Reaction Here Is Anger, Shock and Dismay," *New York Times*, October 19, 1968, https://www.nytimes.com/1968/10/19/archives/the-reaction-here-is-anger-shock-and-dismay-few-interviewed-in.html.

208 **"Prince William is very unhappy"**: "Kate Runs the Paparazzi Gauntlet on Her 25th Birthday," *Evening Standard*, April 12, 2012, https://www

.standard.co.uk/hp/front/kate-runs-the-paparazzi-gauntlet-on-her-25th
-birthday-7275842.html.

208 **her "exotic" DNA:** Rachel Johnson, "Sorry Harry, but Your Beautiful
Bolter Has Failed My Mum Test," *Mail on Sunday*, November 6, 2016,
https://www.dailymail.co.uk/debate/article-3909362/RACHEL-JOHN
SON-Sorry-Harry-beautiful-bolter-failed-Mum-Test.html.

209 **"would pop up every few weeks perhaps":** Victoria Murphy, interview with author, April 2025.

209 **"For the family, they very much have":** Meghan and Prince Harry,
Oprah with Meghan and Harry.

209 **"furious" when he put out a statement:** Prince Harry, *Spare*, 301.

209 **"racial undertones of comment pieces":** "Prince Harry Condemns
Media's 'Abuse and Harassment' of His Girlfriend, Meghan Markle,"
New York Times, November 9, 2016, https://www.nytimes.com/2016
/11/09/world/europe/prince-harry-girlfriend-meghan-markle.html.

209 **"Harry's Girl Is":** Ruth Styles, "Harry's Girl Is (Almost) Straight Outta
Compton," MailOnline (*Daily Mail*), November 2, 2016, https://www
.dailymail.co.uk/news/article-3896180/Prince-Harry-s-girlfriend-actress
-Meghan-Markles.html.

210 **"My statement made":** Prince Harry, *Spare*, 301.

210 **"They felt as though":** Prince Harry interview by Anderson Cooper,
"Prince Harry: The 60 Minutes Interview Transcript," *60 Minutes*, CBS
News, January 8, 2023, https://www.cbsnews.com/news/prince-harry
-interview-transcript-60-minutes-2023-01-08.

210 **"sacrificed [him] on her personal PR altar":** Prince Harry, *Spare*, 100.

210 **"the pain and suffering of women":** "Harry & Meghan | Official
Trailer | Netflix," August 30, 2024, https://www.youtube.com/watch
?v=2rlVhiXlcHU.

210 **"I didn't want history to repeat itself":** *Harry & Meghan*, Netflix.

211 **"someone with a natural nobility":** Charles Spencer, *Eulogy for Princess Diana,"* address delivered at Westminster Abbey, London, BBC
News, September 6, 1997, https://www.bbc.co.uk/news/special/poli
tics97/diana/spencerfull.html.

212 **"It is an undisputed fact":** Sally Bedell Smith, "Diana and the Press,"
Vanity Fair, September 1998, https://archive.vanityfair.com/article
/share/81f2c07a-ece0-4bb7-841f-08baeab9e0c3.

212 **"Well maybe I was the first person":** "Diana's 1995 BBC Interview:
The Princess and the Press," transcript of interview, *Frontline*, WGBH,
accessed October 18, 2025, https://www.pbs.org/wgbh/pages/frontline
/shows/royals/interviews/bbc.html.

212 **She was keenly aware of what the media wanted:** Dickie Arbiter, interview with author, January 2025.

213 **"To see another woman in my life":** *Harry & Meghan*, Netflix.

213 **"The whole family is saddened to learn":** "Meghan and Harry Interview: Palace Taking Race Issues 'Very Seriously,'" BBC News, March 10, 2021, https://www.bbc.com/news/uk-56340451.

214 **"Sir, have you spoken to your brother":** "Royal Rift: Prince William Says 'We Are Very Much Not a Racist Family,'" Sky News, YouTube, March 11, 2021, https://www.youtube.com/watch?v=2-F2bzXdF80.

Chapter 16: An Earthshot

215 **"Where do you really come from?":** Sean Coughlan, "Lady Susan Hussey Quits over Remarks to Charity Boss Ngozi Fulani," BBC News, December 1, 2022, https://www.bbc.com/news/uk-63810468.

215 **to "an interrogation":** Sarah Campbell, "Ngozi Fulani: Dialogue Held over Buckingham Palace Remarks, BBC Told," BBC News, December 4, 2022, https://www.bbc.com/news/uk-63850466.

215 **"denounce [her] British citizenship":** Andre Rhoden-Paul, "Ngozi Fulani: Lady Susan Hussey's Race Comments Were Abuse, Says Charity Boss," BBC News, December 1, 2022, https://www.bbc.com/news/uk-63819482.

216 **"I'm very happy for Ngozi Fulani":** Jessica Kwong, "Prince Harry Interview with Tom Bradby in Full," *Metro*, January 8, 2023, https://metro.co.uk/2023/01/08/prince-harry-interview-with-tom-bradby-in-full-18061892.

216 **"This is a matter for Buckingham Palace":** Author notes, November 30, 2022.

217 **"Earthshot has really almost shifted":** Victoria Murphy, interview with author, April 2025.

218 **"I believe," he said:** Michele Ostovar, "The Decision to Go to the Moon: President John F. Kennedy's May 25, 1961 Speech Before a Joint Session of Congress," NASA, September 22, 1998, https://www.nasa.gov/history/the-decision-to-go-to-the-moon.

218 **"We choose to go to the moon":** John F. Kennedy, "Address at Rice University on the Nation's Space Effort," speech, Rice University Stadium, Houston, Texas, September 12, 1962, https://www.jfklibrary.org/archives/other-resources/john-f-kennedy-speeches/rice-university-19620912.

218 **"John F. Kennedy was handsome":** Douglas Brinkley, *American Moonshot: John F. Kennedy and the Great Space Race* (Harper Perennial, 2020), xiv.

219 **Stanford University's "moonshot effort":** Andrew Myers, "Moonshot Effort Aims to Bioprint a Human Heart and Implant It in a Pig," *Stanford Report*, September 28, 2023, https://news.stanford.edu/stories/2023/09/moonshot-effort-aims-bioprint-human-heart-implant-pig.

219 **"It seemed crazy":** Prince William, "This Decade Calls for Earthshots to Repair Our Planet," TED, October 2020, https://www.ted.com/talks/prince_william_this_decade_calls_for_earthshots_to_repair_our_planet.

220 **"Over the past 60 years":** "John F. Kennedy Library Foundation Announces Partnership with the Earthshot Prize," press release, September 13, 2021, https://www.jfklibrary.org/about-us/news-and-press/press-releases/john-f-kennedy-library-foundation-announces-partnership-with-the-earthshot-prize.

220 **"Next year is the 60th anniversary":** Emma Platoff, "Boston Welcomes Prince and Princess of Wales for Earthshot Awards, in a Showcase for Michelle Wu's Climate Agenda," *Boston Globe*, November 30, 2022, https://www.bostonglobe.com/2022/11/30/metro/boston-welcomes-prince-princess-wales-earthshot-awards-showcase-michelle-wus-climate-agenda.

221 **"It was important to the Earthshot Prize":** Platoff, "Boston Welcomes Prince and Princess of Wales."

221 **"At first, the mayor was surprised":** Tiffany Chu, interview with author, May 2023.

221 **"We undertook a fact-finding mission":** Platoff, "Boston Welcomes Prince and Princess of Wales."

222 **"We thought, 'This is an amazing opportunity'":** Chu, interview with author, May 2023.

222 **"wanted to make sure that they could hear voices":** Chu, interview with author, May 2023.

222 **"There is no more important":** "The Earthshot Prize Is Heading to Boston in December 2022," *The Earthshot Prize*, July 20, 2022, https://earthshotprize.org/news/the-earthshot-prize-is-heading-to-boston-in-december-2022.

222 **"In Boston, we're not just aiming":** "Newly Independent Earthshot Prize Announces Boston, USA, as Host City for 2022 Awards Ceremony," Royal Foundation, July 21, 2022, https://royalfoundation.com

/newly-independent-earthshot-prize-announces-boston-usa-as-host-city
-for-2022-awards-ceremony.

223 **"Our goal is to become a global brand":** Victoria Ward, "Prince and
Princess of Wales 'Won't Be Distracted' by Sussexes During US Visit,"
The Telegraph, November 26, 2022, https://www.telegraph.co.uk/royal
-family/2022/11/26/prince-princess-wales-wont-distracted-sussexes-us
-visit.

224 **"We wanted to make sure the press":** Chu, interview with author,
May 2023.

224 **"As a person of African descent":** Sara Nathan, "Exclusive: Royal
Reverend Denies Aiming Racism Speech at Prince William, Kate amid
Scandal," Page Six, *New York Post*, December 1, 2022, https://pagesix
.com/2022/12/01/royal-reverend-denies-aiming-racism-speech-at-prince
-william-kate-amid-scandal.

225 **"Jesus, Mary, and Joseph?":** Jeff Skversky, "Joe Mazzulla Asked About
Royal Family Attending Celtics Game," Jeff Skversky, YouTube, accessed September 17, 2025, https://www.youtube.com/watch?v=GxG
gDtkh9oY.

229 **"heroic" stand against structural racism:** Janine Henni, "Meghan
Markle and Prince Harry to Be Awarded for Stance Against 'Structural
Racism,' Says Kerry Kennedy," People.com, November 21, 2022, https://
people.com/royals/meghan-markle-prince-harry-receiving-award-for
-heroic-stand-structural-racism-monarchy-kerry-kennedy.

Chapter 17: A Ripple of Hope

231 **"Do you have a message for your family, Harry?":** "Prince Harry
Asked If 'He Has a Message for His Family' After Docuseries Trailer
Release," *Daily Mail*, YouTube, December 7, 2022, https://www.youtube
.com/watch?v=8y7P3nMThic.

231 **"Are you putting money before family?":** "Harry & Meghan: 'Are You
Putting Money Before Family?!,'" Sky News, December 7, 2022, https://
news.sky.com/video/harry-and-meghan-are-you-putting-money-before
-family-12763221.

231 **"so many questions":** "'Are You Putting Money Before Family?!,'"
Sky News.

231 **"In this role and this job":** ITV News (@ITVNews), "'Every single
time I hear a click, every single time I see a flash, it takes me straight

back' Prince Harry tells ITV his grief for Diana is still a 'wound that festers' and being followed by the press is the 'worst reminder of her life' #HarryAndMeghan," X (formerly Twitter), October 17, 2019, https://x.com/itvnews/status/1184884700797702145.

232 **"wave of abuse and harassment":** "Prince Harry Condemns Press 'Abuse' of Girlfriend," BBC News, November 8, 2016, https://www.bbc.com/news/uk-37908096.

232 **"Prince Harry is in a really tough position":** A source close to the Sussexes, interview with author, February 2024.

233 **"No one knows the full truth":** Netflix, *"Harry & Meghan | Official Trailer,"* Netflix, YouTube, December 5, 2022, https://www.youtube.com/watch?v=2rlVhiXlcHU.

233 **"personal and raw and powerful":** Nicole Sperling, "Striving to Make Netflix's Harry and Meghan Series 'Personal and Raw,'" *New York Times*, December 8, 2022, https://www.nytimes.com/2022/12/08/business/media/netflix-harry-meghan-documentary.html.

233 **"hounded by the press to answer questions":** Yetunde Beutler (@YBNParis), "At the RFK Ripple of Hope award ceremony. Enjoyed ourselves despite being hounded by the press to answer questions around Harry and Meghan @sussexroyal and racism within the monarchy family. Heard a great speech from President Zelensky. We also were able to give VIP's a taste of @essenci. #rippleofhopeaward #racism #skynews," Instagram, December 7, 2022, https://www.instagram.com/p/Cl3lI60riBJ.

233 **"Is there another documentary":** Getty Images, "First Three Episodes of Netflix Documentary About Prince Harry and Meghan to Be Released," December 8, 2022, https://www.gettyimages.com/detail/video/first-three-episodes-of-netflix-documentary-about-prince-news-footage/1447736473.

233 **"handles difficult circumstances":** Nina Agrawal, "Prince Harry and Meghan Markle to Attend NYC Gala Hosted by Alec Baldwin," *New York Post*, December 6, 2022, https://nypost.com/2022/12/06/prince-harry-and-meghan-markle-to-attend-nyc-gala-hosted-by-alec-baldwin.

233 **"No I do not":** Jan Moir, "I Wanted to Watch Harry and Meghan's Terrible Betrayal Up Close to See If There Was Even a Flicker of Remorse. I Saw Nothing but Exultation," *Daily Mail*, December 7, 2022, https://www.dailymail.co.uk/debate/article-11513181/JAN-MOIR-wanted-watch-Harry-Meghans-terrible-betrayal-close.html.

234 **"their work on racial justice":** Robert F. Kennedy Human Rights Announces the Duke and Duchess of Sussex as Recipients of the 2022

Ripple of Hope Award," PR Newswire, October 11, 2022, https://www.prnewswire.com/news-releases/robert-f-kennedy-human-rights-announces-the-duke-and-duchess-of-sussex-as-recipients-of-the-2022-ripple-of-hope-award-301646380.html.

234 **"Each time a man stands up for an ideal":** Robert F. Kennedy, "Day of Affirmation Address ('Ripple of Hope')," speech, University of Cape Town, South Africa, June 6, 1966, John F. Kennedy Presidential Library and Museum, Boston, https://www.jfklibrary.org/learn/about-jfk/the-kennedy-family/robert-f-kennedy/robert-f-kennedy-speeches/day-of-affirmation-address-university-of-capetown-capetown-south-africa-june-6-1966.

234 **"When The Duke and Duchess accepted":** "Robert F. Kennedy Human Rights Announces the Duke and Duchess of Sussex as Recipients of the 2022 Ripple of Hope Award," PR Newswire, October 11, 2022, https://www.prnewswire.com/news-releases/robert-f-kennedy-human-rights-announces-the-duke-and-duchess-of-sussex-as-recipients-of-the-2022-ripple-of-hope-award-301646380.html.

235 **"When my father went to South Africa":** Janine Henni, "Kerry Kennedy on Why Meghan Markle, Prince Harry Are Receiving Award," *People*, November 21, 2022, https://www.people.com/royals/meghan-markle-prince-harry-receiving-award-for-heroic-stand-structural-racism-monarchy-kerry-kennedy.

236 **"There's no animosity or feeling":** A source familiar with the Sussexes' perspective, interview with author, February 2024.

237 **"As my brother Douglas":** *Robert F. Kennedy Human Rights Ripple of Hope Awards 2022*, featuring Prince Harry, Duke of Sussex, and Meghan, Duchess of Sussex with Kerry Kennedy, New York City, December 6, 2022.

237 **"We are honored to receive":** "RFK Ripple of Hope Awards," Archewell Foundation, accessed October 18, 2025, https://archewell.org/news/rfk-ripple-of-hope-awards.

238 **"We don't get out much":** *Robert F. Kennedy Human Rights Ripple of Hope Awards 2022*, featuring Prince Harry, Duke of Sussex, and Meghan, Duchess of Sussex with Kerry Kennedy, New York City, December 6, 2022.

238 **"two of the people whose courage":** Michaela Kennedy-Cuomo (@MichaelaKennedyCuomo), "One Tuesday, Two Celebrations, Three Heroes, Infinite Joy . . . ," Instagram, December 8, 2022, https://www.instagram.com/p/Cl7RhuCPJqz/?img_index=1.

238 **"personal heroes":** Michaela Kennedy-Cuomo (@MicLovesMe), "I

was honored to be able to meet two of my personal heroes . . . ," Instagram, December 9, 2022, https://www.instagram.com/p/Cl92ciTvzg4.

239 **"I was in my hometown of Glasgow":** Harry Benson, interview with author, September 2023.

239 **described as "beautiful":** Meghan Markle, "Remarks at the Robert F. Kennedy Human Rights Ripple of Hope Award Gala," speech, New York City, December 6, 2022.

239 **"Hi, Grandma. That's Grandma Diana":** *Harry & Meghan*, Netflix, December 8, 2022, https://www.netflix.com/title/81439256.

239 **"It's the sweetest thing":** *The Me You Can't See*, directed by Dawn Porter and Asif Kapadia, May 21, 2021, Apple TV+.

Chapter 18: Media Moguls

241 **"mutually agreed to part ways":** Sean Seddon and David Willis, "Harry and Meghan: Spotify Podcast Deal with Couple Ends," BBC News, June 15, 2023, https://www.bbc.com/news/uk-65924584.

242 **"For my own self-preservation":** "Meghan, The Duchess of Sussex Warns Against Social Media Addiction," *Fortune*, video interview with Emma Hinchliffe, 2020, https://fortune.com/2020/10/13/meghan-markle-duchess-of-sussex-social-media-addiction-mpw-next-gen-conversation.

242 **"scary place" for the duchess:** A source familiar with Meghan's thinking on social media, interview with author, January 2025.

243 **"Did They Think Twerking":** Sarah Vine, "Did They Think Twerking like Trailer-Trash Teens Would Endear Them to the Masses?," *Daily Mail*, June 4, 2025, https://www.dailymail.co.uk/news/royals/article-14781557/SARAH-VINE-Did-think-twerking-like-trailer-trash-teens-endear-masses.html.

243 **"After the Pregnant Twerking":** Melanie McDonagh, "After the Pregnant Twerking, Can Meghan and Harry Sink Any Lower?," *The Standard*, June 5, 2025, https://www.standard.co.uk/comment/meghan-markle-prince-harry-twerking-b1231385.html.

243 **"Meghan Markle and Prince Harry Channeled MomTok":** Miranda Siwak, "Meghan Markle and Prince Harry Channeled MomTok with Hospital Dance Before She Gave Birth to Lilibet," *Us Weekly*, June 4, 2025, https://www.usmagazine.com/celebrity-moms/news/pregnant-meghan-markle-dances-with-harry-in-hospital-video.

243 **"Tignanello is a full-bodied red wine":** "Actress Meghan Markle on:

The TIG," *Tory Daily* (blog), August 12, 2014, https://www.toryburch
.com/en-us/blog-post/blog-post.html?bpid=108151.

244 **"Well, I loved The Tig"**: Erin Hill, "Meghan Markle's Most Intimate
Interview in Years: Harry, the Kids and Getting Real About Her
'Learning Curve,'" *People*, March 3, 2025, https://people.com/meghan
-markle-intimate-interview-prince-harry-kids-as-ever-brand-netflix-series
-exclusive-11689103.

245 **citing an "editorial issue"**: Mitchell McCluskey and Jessie Yeung,
"News Agencies Recall Image of Catherine, Princess of Wales, Citing
Manipulation Concerns," CNN, March 11, 2024, https://www.cnn
.com/2024/03/10/uk/news-agencies-recall-image-of-catherine-princess
-of-wales.

245 **"Like many amateur photographers"**: The Prince and Princess of
Wales (@KensingtonRoyal), "Like many amateur photographers, I do
occasionally experiment with editing. I wanted to express my apologies for any confusion the family photograph we shared yesterday
caused. I hope everyone celebrating had a very happy Mother's Day.
C," X (formerly Twitter), March 11, 2024, https://x.com/Kensington
Royal/status/1767135566645092616.

246 **"astonishing in its intimacy"**: Victoria Murphy, "Kate Middleton's
Latest Video Is Astonishing in Its Intimacy," *Town & Country*, September 9, 2024, https://www.townandcountrymag.com/society/tradition
/a62120283/kate-middletons-cancer-free-video-intimacy-analysis.

247 **"For the first time since Jack and I"**: Jackie Kennedy, Campaign
Wife, Papers of John F. Kennedy, Pre-Presidential Papers, Presidential
Campaign Files, 1960, John F. Kennedy Presidential Library and Mu-
seum, Boston.

247 **"If you are going to write about politics"**: Kate Storey, "The Inside
Story of John F. Kennedy Jr.'s *George* Magazine," *Esquire*, April 22, 2019,
https://www.esquire.com/news-politics/a27031243/john-kennedy-jr
-george-magazine-true-story.

248 **"I've learned a lot about temptation recently"**: John F. Kennedy Jr.,
"Don't Sit Under the Apple Tree," *George*, September 1997.

249 **"like a tone-deaf defense"**: Storey, "The Inside Story of John F. Kennedy Jr.'s *George* Magazine."

249 **"I intend to do all I can"**: "Investigation of Kennedy Sex Case Is
Halted," *New York Times*, July 9, 1997, https://www.nytimes.com/1997
/07/09/us/investigation-of-kennedy-sex-case-is-halted.html.

249 **"I did that because that was something"**: Abigail Pogrebin, "The
Politics of Personality," *Brill's Content*, March 1999, 98.

249   **"You don't know Jack"**: William Cohan, "You Don't Know Jack!," *Town & Country*, August 20, 2024, https://www.townandcountrymag .com/society/politics/a61098000/jack-schlossberg-jfk-interview -2024.

249   **"Schlossberg is unmistakably a Kennedy"**: Hannah Jackson, "Jack Schlossberg Is Just Being Himself," *Vogue*, July 10, 2024, https://www .vogue.com/article/jack-schlossberg-interview.

250   **"Hey Anna Wintour!"**: Jack Schlossberg (@JackUno), Instagram reel, April 24, 2025, https://www.instagram.com/reel/DI2Dg-ySQvj.

250   **"It's difficult to break through"**: Jen Psaki, "Why Are We So Cautious? with Jack Schlossberg," *The Blueprint with Jen Psaki* (podcast), MSNBC, February 10, 2025, https://podcasts.apple.com/us/podcast /why-are-we-so-cautious-with-jack-schlossberg/id1707410660?i=10006901 37237.

251   **"It's not me"**: Reeves Wiedeman, "Hijacking the Kennedys," *New York Magazine*, August 25, 2025, https://nymag.com/intelligencer/article /kennedy-family-legacy-dynasty-rfk-jr-trump.html.

251   **"I see my grandfather and my uncle"**: "Ryan Murphy's TV Show Gets the Kennedy Family All Wrong," Jack Schlossberg, YouTube, July 26, 2025, https://www.youtube.com/watch?v=vG1KyBNY4bY.

252   **"She was the only person in America"**: Dean Goodman, "Michael Jackson Book a Headache for Jackie O," Reuters, July 4, 2009, https:// www.reuters.com/article/us-jackson-jackieo/michael-jackson -book-a-headache-for-jackie-o-idUSTRE5631S420090704.

252   **"According to her Doubleday colleagues"**: Greg Lawrence, *Jackie as Editor: The Literary Life of Jacqueline Kennedy Onassis* (Thomas Dunne Books, 2011), 74.

252   **"What has been sad for many women"**: Greg Lawrence, "Jackie O, Working Girl," *Vanity Fair*, January 2011, https://www.vanityfair.com /culture/2011/01/jackie-o-working-girl-201101.

Chapter 19: Family Feuds

255   **"Kennedy, Kennedy, Kennedy"**: "Robert Kennedy Jr Super Bowl Ad 2024," MAHA PAC, YouTube, February 11, 2024, https://www.youtube .com/watch?v=nvXJJRjGVT4.

255   **to "Vote Independent"**: "Robert Kennedy Jr Super Bowl Ad 2024," MAHA PAC.

256   **"My cousin's Super Bowl ad"**: Bobby Shriver (@BobbyShriver), "My

cousin's Super Bowl ad used our uncle's faces—and my Mother's. She would be appalled by his deadly health care views. Respect for science, vaccines, & health care equity were in her DNA. She strongly supported my health care work at @ONECampaign & @RED which he opposes," X (formerly Twitter), February 11, 2024, https://x.com/bobbyshriver/status/1756869648044499232.

256 **"I agree with my brother":** Mark K. Shriver (@Mark_Shriver), "I agree with my brother @bobbyshriver simple as that," X (formerly Twitter), February 11, 2024, https://x.com/Mark_Shriver/status/1756885426479005979.

256 **"I'm so sorry":** Robert F. Kennedy Jr. (@RobertKennedyJr), "I'm so sorry if the Super Bowl advertisement caused anyone in my family pain. The ad was created and aired by the American Values Super PAC without any involvement or approval from my campaign. FEC rules prohibit Super PACs from consulting with me or my staff. I love you all. God bless you," X (formerly Twitter), February 11, 2024, https://x.com/RobertKennedyJr/status/1756900265368723562.

257 **"robust intra-family dialogue":** Shia Kapos, "Kennedy Family Feud Cools as RFK Jr.'s Independent Run Rattles Republicans," *Politico*, October 14, 2024, https://www.politico.com/news/2023/10/14/rfk-jr-s-independence-pivot-is-a-relief-for-the-kennedys-00121480.

257 **"I love my brother Bobby":** Trip Gabriel, "Robert F. Kennedy Jr. Makes His White House Run Official," *New York Times*, April 19, 2023, https://www.nytimes.com/2023/04/19/us/politics/robert-kennedy-presidential-run.html.

257 **"This is a difficult situation for me":** Edward-Isaac Dovere, "Robert F. Kennedy Jr. Can't Count on Family Support to Take on Biden," CNN, April 16, 2023, https://www.cnn.com/2023/04/16/politics/robert-f-kennedy-family-biden-2024.

257 **virus was "ethnically targeted":** Jon Levine, "RFK Jr. Says COVID May Have Been 'Ethnically Targeted' to Spare Jews," *New York Post*, July 15, 2023, https://nypost.com/2023/07/15/rfk-jr-says-covid-was-ethnically-targeted-to-spare-jews.

258 **"I strongly condemn my brother's":** Kerry Kennedy, "Statement by Kerry Kennedy on Robert F. Kennedy Jr. Recent Remarks," May 2, 2024, https://rfkhumanrights.org/press/statement-by-kerry-kennedy-on-robert-f-kennedy-jr-recent-remarks.

258 **"Bobby's comments are morally and factually wrong":** Tal Kopan, "Kennedys Denounce Robert F. Kennedy Jr. over 'Deplorable' Antisemitic Comments," *Boston Globe*, July 17, 2023, https://www.bostonglobe

.com/2023/07/17/nation/rfk-jr-antisemetic-comment-condemnation-sister
-kerry-kennedy.

258 **"My uncle's comments":** Joe Kennedy III (@JoeKennedy), "My uncle's comments were hurtful and wrong. I unequivocally condemn what he said," X (formerly Twitter), July 17, 2023, https://x.com/joekennedy/status/1681023900459704321.

258 **"embarrassment" and a "vanity project":** Jack Schlossberg (@JackUno), Instagram, July 21, 2023, https://www.instagram.com/reel/Cu84b32N8VM.

258 **in "tense discussions":** Peter Baker, "Anguish in Camelot: Kennedy Campaign Roils Storied Political Family," *New York Times*, August 6, 2023, https://www.nytimes.com/2023/08/06/us/politics/rfk-campaign-kennedy-family.html.

258 **"I bear them no ill will":** Dovere, "Robert F. Kennedy Jr. Can't Count on Family Support."

258 **"Our family was raised in a milieu":** Mike Memoli, Peter Alexander, and Kelly O'Donnell, "Kennedy Family Set to Step Up Its Efforts to Help Biden's Campaign," NBCNews.com, March 20, 2024, https://www.nbcnews.com/politics/2024-election/kennedy-family-rfk-biden-2024-election-rcna144163.

258 **I love my brother deeply:** Baker, "Anguish in Camelot."

259 **"is unequivocally supportive of her children":** Kapos, "Kennedy Family Feud Cools."

259 **"a betrayal of the values":** Kerry Kennedy (@KerryKennedyRFK), "I am sharing a personal statement that my family and I have made in response to my brother's announcement," X (formerly Twitter), August 23, 2024, https://x.com/KerryKennedyRFK/status/1827061350452887816.

259 **"guru shaman figure":** Jack Schlossberg (@JBKSchlossberg), "But it's like why did you say that? So you could convince people you're this guru shaman figure and get them into your cult," X (formerly Twitter), January 29, 2025, https://x.com/JBKSchlossberg/status/1884634114646503550.

259 **"I'm asking the media to ask my cousins":** Jack Schlossberg (@JackUno), "Wake up," Instagram, January 24, 2025, https://www.instagram.com/reel/DFOB3wZSVjC.

260 **"I hope he gets the help he needs":** Isabel Vincent, "JFK Grandson's Foul Rants Destroying the Image of Dynasty," *New York Post*, February 6, 2025, https://nypost.com/2025/02/06/us-news/jfk-grandsons-foul-rants-destroying-the-image-of-dynasty.

260 **"tarnishing the family reputation"**: "IN FULL: Ambassador Caroline Kennedy's Address to the National Press Club," National Press Club of Australia, YouTube, November 19, 2024, https://www.youtube .com/watch?v=wpvrsc7jOQQ.

260 **"predator" and shared**: Jack Schlossberg (@JBKSchlossberg), "Ambassador Caroline Kennedy's statement to the US Senate on RFKJr's nomination for HHS Secretary This is a reading of a letter she just sent to Senate Committee on Health, Education, Labor and Pensions I'm so proud of my courageous mother, who's lived a life of dignity, integrity and service. she's the kindest funnest smartest you'll ever meet," X (formerly Twitter), January 28, 2025, https://x.com/JBK Schlossberg/status/1884294384474046900.

261 **"We just don't hear from her"**: Rachel Raposas, "Kennedy Family 'in Tatters' amid 'Unprecedented' Public Battle Between Cousins Caroline Kennedy and RFK Jr. (Exclusive Source)," *People*, January 29, 2025, https://people.com/kennedy-family-in-tatters-unprecedented-battle-car oline-rfk-jr-exclusive-source-8782573.

261 **"I did not comment"**: Jack Schlossberg (@JBKSchlossberg), "Ambassador Caroline Kennedy's statement."

261 **"As I spent more and more of my life"**: Tatiana Schlossberg, "A Battle with My Blood," *New Yorker*, November 22, 2025, https://www .newyorker.com/culture/the-weekend-essay/a-battle-with-my-blood.

262 **"One reason the Kennedy family"**: Reeves Wiedeman, "Hijacking the Kennedys," *New York Magazine*, August 25, 2025, https://nymag.com /intelligencer/article/kennedy-family-legacy-dynasty-rfk-jr-trump.html.

263 **"was overcome, I'm frank to say"**: "Ted Kennedy Addresses Chappaquiddick Accident," ABC News, YouTube, April 5, 2018, https://www.youtube.com/watch?v=zmtsnOKEblg.

264 **"Just to state the obvious"**: Wiedeman, "Hijacking the Kennedys."

264 **"There is no 'family'"**: Wiedeman, "Hijacking the Kennedys."

265 **"It's a national soap opera"**: Richard Palmer, interview with author, April 2025.

265 **for the "foreseeable future"**: Mark Landler, "After Disastrous Epstein Interview, Prince Andrew Steps Down from Public Duties," *New York Times*, November 20, 2019, https://www.nytimes.com/2019/11 /20/world/europe/prince-andrew-quits-epstein.html.

266 **"In discussion with The King"**: "A Statement by Prince Andrew," The Royal Family, October 17, 2025, https://www.royal.uk/news-and -activity/2025-10-17/a-statement-by-prince-andrew.

266 **"His Majesty has today initiated"**: "A Statement from Buckingham

Palace," The Royal Family, October 30, 2025, https://www.royal.uk/news-and-activity/2025-10-30/a-statement-from-buckingham-palace.

266 **said, "Oh, yes":** "Royal Foundation Forum—2018," British Movietone Royals, YouTube, April 26, 2018, https://www.youtube.com/watch?v=3MM9SQQrWGg.

267 **"They are both very passionate about":** Kate Mansey and Jane Flanagan, "Revealed: Why Prince Harry and Prince William Fell Out," *The Times*, February 2, 2024, https://www.thetimes.com/uk/royal-family/article/why-prince-william-harry-first-fell-out-reason-relationship-soured-fcl5drv80?region=global.

268 **"Africa and Invictus, these had long been":** Prince Harry, *Spare* (Random House, 2023), 255.

268 **"Why can't you both work on Africa?":** Prince Harry, *Spare*, 255.

268 **"It's too fast, he'd told me":** Prince Harry, *Spare*, 319.

269 **"Harry felt William wasn't rolling out the red carpet":** Katie Nicholl, "Tension Between Harry and William May Have Inspired Harry and Meghan's Move to the Suburbs," *Vanity Fair*, November 16, 2018, https://www.vanityfair.com/style/2018/11/prince-harry-prince-william-tension-move.

269 **"to clear the air":** Prince Harry, *Spare*, 343.

269 **"Was this really happening?":** Prince Harry, *Spare*, 344.

270 **"I was a hugger":** *Harry & Meghan*, Netflix, December 8, 2022, https://www.netflix.com/title/81439256.

270 **"the reverse happened":** Meghan, Duchess of Sussex, and Prince Harry, Duke of Sussex, interview by Oprah Winfrey, *Oprah with Meghan and Harry: A CBS Primetime Special*, CBS, March 7, 2021.

270 **"I can tell you that all the papers":** Stephanie Petit, "Meghan Markle and Kate Middleton Both Cried 'Their Eyes Out' over Bridesmaid Dress Dispute, Bombshell Book Claims," *People*, May 14, 2025, https://people.com/meghan-markle-kate-middleton-both-cried-over-bridesmaid-dress-dispute-11734571.

271 **"difficult," "rude," and "abrasive":** Prince Harry, *Spare*, 358.

271 **"Inevitably, you know, stuff happens":** Melissa Gray and Leona Siaw, "Prince Harry Acknowledges Tensions with His Brother William for the First Time, Says They're on Different Paths," CNN, October 21, 2019, https://www.cnn.com/2019/10/20/uk/prince-harry-prince-william-tensions-trnd.

272 **"bullied" out of the royal family:** *Harry & Meghan*, Netflix.

272 **"I was told about a joint statement":** *Harry & Meghan*, Netflix.

272 **"would love reconciliation with my family":** Nada Tawfik and Sean

Coughlan, "Prince Harry Tells BBC He Wants 'Reconciliation' with Royal Family," *BBC News*, May 3, 2025, https://www.bbc.com/news/articles/c8074n5z597o.

Chapter 20: Man Becomes Myth

275 **"I'm afraid it's serious":** *The Crown*, season 6, episode 8, "Ritz," Left Bank Pictures, 2023.

276 **"It's a very beautiful":** Chris Murphy, *"The Crown* Episode 8: Lesley Manville Says Ta-Ta to Princess Margaret," *Vanity Fair*, December 19, 2023, https://www.vanityfair.com/hollywood/the-crown-episode-8 -lesley-manville-says-ta-ta-to-princess-margaret.

276 **Staunton and Manville were told that they might:** "Imelda Staunton Heard About Queen Elizabeth's Passing on the *Crown* Set," *The Graham Norton Show*, December 15, 2023, https://www.youtube.com/watch ?v=6clAsugoA8k.

276 **"Following further evaluation this morning":** "A Statement from Buckingham Palace," September 8, 2022, Royal Household, https://www.royal.uk/statement-buckingham-palace.

276 **"It was a very strange day":** Charlotte Gallagher and Guy Lambert, "The *Crown*'s Imelda Staunton on the 'Shock' of Playing the Queen When the Queen Died," *BBC News*, December 1, 2023, https://www .bbc.com/news/entertainment-arts-67580268.

276 **"The Queen died peacefully":** Announcement of the Death of the Queen, September 8, 2022, Royal Household, https://www.royal.uk /announcement-death-queen.

277 **'I felt a loss, I really did":** Clark Collins, *"The Crown* Star Imelda Staunton Says She Was 'Devastated' by Queen's Death," *Entertainment Weekly*, October 19, 2022, https://ew.com/tv/the-crown-imelda -staunton-devasted-by-queen-death.

278 **"I got my head around it":** "Imelda Staunton Heard About Queen Elizabeth's Passing," *The Graham Norton Show*.

278 **"We're not pretending this is a chronological record":** Robert Lacey, interview with author, November 2019.

279 **show of "crude sensationalism":** Judi Dench, "Crown Affair," *The Times*, letter to the editor, October 20, 2022, https://www.thetimes.com /comment/article/times-letters-the-pensions-triple-lock-and-stretched -public-finances-9zmsqvxjf.

280 **"It's fictional, but it's loosely based on the truth":** "An Afternoon

with Prince Harry & James Corden," *The Late Late Show with James Corden*, February 26, 2021, https://www.youtube.com/watch?v=7oxl CKMlpZw.

280 **"All history is gossip"**: Steven Stark, "The Cultural Meaning of the Kennedys," *The Atlantic*, January 1994, https://www.theatlantic.com /magazine/archive/1994/01/the-cultural-meaning-of-the-kennedys/30 6664.

281 **"the most-talked-about part of the year"**: "PT 109—Original Trailer," Turner Classic Movies, accessed September 22, 2025, https://www.tcm .com/video/289227/pt-109-original-trailer.

282 **"For one brief shining moment there was Camelot"**: Theodore H. White, "For President Kennedy: An Epilogue," *Life*, December 6, 1963, 159.

Conclusion: The Future Generations

285 **"For over 50 years"**: Joseph R. Biden Jr., "Remarks by President Biden at a Memorial Service for Mrs. Robert F. Kennedy," Cathedral of St. Matthew the Apostle, Washington, DC, October 16, 2024, The White House (archived), https://bidenwhitehouse.archives.gov/briefing-room /speeches-remarks/2024/10/17/remarks-by-president-biden-at-a -memorial-service-for-mrs-robert-f-kennedy.

285 **"vital force in the Kennedy political dynasty"**: Douglas Martin, "Ethel Kennedy, Passionate Supporter of the Family Legacy, Dies at 96," *New York Times*, October 10, 2024, https://www.nytimes.com/2024 /10/10/us/politics/ethel-kennedy-dead.html.

286 **"These things don't happen by themselves"**: R. Couri Hay, interview with author, April 2025.

286 **"They're very adept at staying in the news"**: Hay, interview with author, April 2025.

288 **"We chose to host our wedding weekend events"**: Emily Strohm and Henry Chandonnet, "Robert F. Kennedy's Granddaughter Sarah Marries on the Family Compound—with Kennedy Heirlooms!," *People*, August 23, 2023, https://people.com/robert-f-kennedy-granddaughter -sarah-kennedy-married-jam-sulahry-7644350.

289 **"By the time you get to the fourth generation"**: Sheila Weller, "Bobby's Girls," *Glamour*, April 30, 2008, https://www.glamour.com/story /bobby-kennedy-daughters.

290 **"I hope with all my heart you vote for Joe"**: Peter Canellos, "The Unlikely Kennedy Who Ended the Kennedy Dynasty," *Politico*, September 1, 2020, https://www.politico.com/news/magazine/2020/09/01 /joe-kennedy-end-of-a-dynasty-407474.

290 **"The Kennedy dynasty is dead"**: Canellos, "The Unlikely Kennedy."

290 **"the only Kennedy who could run"**: Reeves Wiedeman, "Hijacking the Kennedys," *New York Magazine*, August 25, 2025, https://nymag .com/intelligencer/article/kennedy-family-legacy-dynasty-rfk-jr-trump .html.

291 **"This district should have a representative"**: Jack Schlossberg (@ JackUno), "250 years after America was founded, . . . ," Instagram, November 11, 2025, https://www.instagram.com/p/DQ8TqPSAK 0J/?hl=en.

291 **"I always shudder when I hear"**: Maureen Dowd, "Jack Schlossberg, Social Media Provocateur, Gives Politics a Try," *New York Times*, November 11, 2025, https://www.nytimes.com/2025/11/11/style/jack -schlossberg-congress-kennedy-family.html.

292 **"was like a family office"**: Jane Mayer, "A Young Kennedy, in Kushner-land, Turned Whistle-Blower," *New Yorker*, September 21, 2020, https:// www.newyorker.com/magazine/2020/09/28/a-young-kennedy-in-kush nerland-turned-whistle-blower.

292 **He says his time in the country**: J. Conor Kennedy, Instagram post, October 14, 2022, https://www.instagram.com/p/CjsK25bO3Gf/?hl=en.

293 **"live in a constant state of fear"**: Craig Brown, *A Voyage Around the Queen* (Farrar, Straus and Giroux, 2024), 306.

293 **"It's all to do with the precarious nature"**: Craig Brown, interview with author, October 2024.

293 **"Fear of the public"**: Prince Harry, *Spare*, 237.

295 **"most beautiful member of the royal family"**: *Tatler*, April 2016.

PHOTO CREDITS

Page 1: (*top*) © Bettman Archive via Getty Images; (*bottom left and right*) © CORBIS/Corbis via Getty Images

Page 2: (*top*) © ullstein bild/ullstein bild via Getty Images; (*bottom*) © Keystone/Hulton Archive/Getty Images

Page 3: (*top*) © Express Newspapers/Getty Images; (*bottom left*) Chris Jackson/Getty Images; (*bottom right*) © Toni Frissell/John F. Kennedy Presidential Library

Page 4: (*top*) © Collection at the John F. Kennedy Presidential Library and Museum, Boston; (*bottom left*) © Tim Graham Photo Library via Getty Images; (*bottom right*) © Cecil Stoughton/White House Photographs/John F. Kennedy Presidential Library and Museum, Boston

Page 5: (*top left*) © Jeff J Mitchell/AFP via Getty Images; (*top right*) © Bettmann Archive via Getty Images; (*bottom left*) © Abbie Rowe/White House Photographs/John F. Kennedy Presidential Library and Museum, Boston; (*bottom right*) © Robert Knudsen/White House Photographs/John F. Kennedy Presidential Library and Museum, Boston

Page 6: (*top*) © Bettmann Archive via Getty Images; (*bottom*) © *Evening Standard*/Hulton Archive/Getty Images

Page 7: (*top*) © Kirsty O'Connor/WPA Pool/Getty Images; (*bottom left*) © Robert Knudsen/White House Photographs/John F. Kennedy Presidential Library and Museum, Boston; (*bottom right*) © Samir Hussein/WireImage via Getty Images

Page 8: (*top*) © Kevin Mazur/Getty Images for 2022 Robert F. Kennedy Human Rights Ripple of Hope Gala; (*bottom left*) © Arnaldo Magnani/Liaison via Getty Images; (*bottom right*) © Karwai Tang/WireImage via Getty Images

INDEX

ABOUT THE AUTHOR

Caroline Hallemann is the digital director of *Town & Country* magazine, where she writes about culture, society, entertainment, and the world of the rich and powerful. Her work has often focused on the British monarchy and the closest thing America has to a royal family: the Kennedys. She lives in Nashville, Tennessee.

VISIT CAROLINE HALLEMANN ONLINE

carolinehallemann.com

X CHallemann